ROUTLEDGE LIBRARY EDITIONS:
EXCHANGE RATE ECONOMICS

Volume 6

SEASONAL MOVEMENTS OF EXCHANGE RATES AND INTEREST RATES UNDER THE PRE-WORLD WAR I GOLD STANDARD

SEASONAL MOVEMENTS OF EXCHANGE RATES AND INTEREST RATES UNDER THE PRE-WORLD WAR I GOLD STANDARD

ELLEN L. FOSTER

Routledge
Taylor & Francis Group
LONDON AND NEW YORK

First published in 1994 by Garland Publishing, Inc.

This edition first published in 2017
by Routledge
4 Park Square, Milton Park, Abingdon, Oxon OX14 4RN

and by Routledge
605 Third Avenue, New York, NY 10017

Routledge is an imprint of the Taylor & Francis Group, an informa business

British Library Cataloguing in Publication Data
A catalogue record for this book is available from the British Library

ISBN: 978-0-415-79325-4 (Set)
ISBN: 978-1-315-21117-6 (Set) (ebk)
ISBN: 978-1-138-74390-8 (Volume 6) (hbk)
ISBN: 978-1-315-17967-4 (Volume 6) (ebk)

Publisher's Note
The publisher has gone to great lengths to ensure the quality of this reprint but points out that some imperfections in the original copies may be apparent.

Disclaimer
The publisher has made every effort to trace copyright holders and would welcome correspondence from those they have been unable to trace.

SEASONAL MOVEMENTS OF EXCHANGE RATES AND INTEREST RATES UNDER THE PRE-WORLD WAR I GOLD STANDARD

ELLEN L. FOSTER

GARLAND PUBLISHING, INC.
NEW YORK & LONDON / 1994

Library of Congress Cataloging-in-Publication Data

Foster, Ellen L., 1957–
Seasonal movements of exchange rates and interest rates under the pre-World War I gold standard / Ellen L. Foster.
p. cm. — (The Financial sector of the American economy)
Includes bibliographical references (p. –) and index.
ISBN 0–8153–1722–0 (alk. paper)
1. Interest rates—United States—Mathematical models—History.
2. Interest rates—Great Britain—Mathematical models—History.
3. Foreign exchange rates—United States—Mathematical models—History. 4. Foreign exchange rates—Great Britain—Mathematical models—History. I. Title. II. Series.
HG1623.U5F67 1994
332.8'2'0973—dc20 94–10896
CIP

Printed on acid-free, 250-year-life paper
Manufactured in the United States of America

To Hamp and Elizabeth

Contents

Seasonal Movements of Exchange Rates and Interest Rates Under the Pre-World War I Gold Standard

I

Introduction

This work investigates seasonal fluctuations of U.S. and British short term nominal interest rates, the dollar-sterling exchange rate and short term interest rate differentials between the United States and Britain during the period 1883–1913. Several recent studies have investigated the strong seasonal fluctuations of short term nominal interest rates in the United States and Britain during this period, but scant attention has been paid to comparing the seasonal patterns of interest rates in the two countries and to investigating the relationships between exchange rate movements and the short term nominal interest rate differentials between the United States and Britain during this period. In this study, significant differences are found in the seasonal patterns of short term nominal interest rate fluctuations in the United States and Britain. According to uncovered interest parity, interest rate differentials between two countries should be offset by expected exchange rate movements. It is found here that during the pre-World War I gold standard, seasonal movements in exchange rates did not tend to offset the seasonal fluctuations in interest rate differentials. The series of *ex post* returns from borrowing in Britain and investing in the United States which takes account of exchange rate movements shows much stronger seasonal fluctuations than the interest rate differentials between U.S. and British short term nominal interest rates.

This result, which suggests that uncovered interest parity may not have held during the gold standard, is consistent with reports in the contemporary literature of predictable profit opportunities caused by seasonal fluctuations of exchange rates between the gold points. The interest of this study is not merely in documenting the existence of seasonal fluctuations in *ex post* returns from borrowing in Britain and investing in the U.S. money market, but also in understanding and explaining the persistence of those apparent profit opportunities throughout the period. Two major questions are addressed here. First, why did seasonal fluctuations of short term nominal interest rates and exchange rates exist during the gold standard period? Second, can the profit opportunities identified in this study be considered unexploited profit opportunities?

In the contemporary literature, seasonal fluctuations in U.S. and British short term nominal interest rates are attributed to seasonal fluctuations in output and the associated demand for credit. According to Kemmerer (1911) and Palgrave (1903), nominal interest rates rose during periods of increased demand for money. These periods of increased demand were associated both with the harvest cycle and with traditional patterns of business and settlements. Seasonal fluctuations of the dollar-sterling exchange rate are attributed in the early literature to seasonal fluctuations in the U.S. balance of trade. The dollar tended to appreciate during the late summer and fall when the U.S. tended to run seasonal balance of trade surpluses associated with the export of crops. The dollar tended to be weakest during the late spring and early summer months when imports were large relative to exports. These early explanations of exchange rate seasonality clearly maintain that seasonal movements in the balance of trade caused movements in exchange rates. It was acknowledged that capital flows could also affect exchange rates and that short term capital flows could offset movements in the balance of trade, but the effect of those capital flows did not overwhelm the effects of the balance of trade on the supply and demand for foreign exchange.

A review of the literature reveals that a satisfactory model which can explain both the seasonal fluctuations of short term nominal interest rates and the seasonal fluctuations of the dollar-sterling exchange rate has yet to be developed. Officer (1989) argues that exchange rate movements under the gold standard are most appropriately modeled using an asset approach. He maintains that the actions of speculators will tend to keep exchange rates at the equilibrium level, which is the midpoint of the gold point spread. Officer's model of exchange rate movements during the gold standard is at odds both with the conventional story told in the early literature to explain exchange rate movements and with findings of predictable seasonal fluctuations of exchange rates. Seasonal fluctuations in short term nominal interest rates in one country can be generated in a closed economy model with a fixed money stock and seasonal demands for credit associated with seasonal output fluctuations. Miron (1986) uses such a model to show that the establishment of the Federal Reserve, which had the power to adjust the stock of high powered money to meet seasonal fluctuations in money demand, could explain the disappearance of strong seasonal fluctuations in short term nominal interest rates after World War I. Clark (1986) points out that the strong seasonal fluctuations of short term nominal interest rates prior to World War I and the disappearance of those strong seasonal fluctuations after World War I is a worldwide phenomenon. A closed economy model is clearly not capable either of explaining the seasonal fluctuations of interest rates worldwide or of distinguishing among alternative explanations of the disappearance of seasonal fluctuations. Such alternative explanations include the establishment of the Federal Reserve, the outbreak of World War I and the breakdown of the international gold standard.

Barsky et al. (1988) develop a two country model of the gold standard in which seasonal fluctuations of interest rates can occur if only one of those countries has a central bank, and that single central bank has the dual objectives of minimizing gold flows and smoothing interest rates. If a second central bank is established, the two central banks can cooperate and achieve both objectives: gold flows can be eliminated and the interest rate can be kept at its target level. Barsky et al. claim that this model supports the argument that the establishment of the Federal Reserve caused the disappearance of strong seasonal fluctuations of short term interest rates. Their model can not, however, explain all the stylized facts concerning seasonal fluctuations of interest rates and exchange rates during the gold standard. The real interest rate process in their model is assumed to be exogenous, short term nominal interest rates in the two countries are identical and the exchange rate is assumed to be fixed at mint par.

This study explores whether seasonal fluctuations of interest rates and exchange rates can be explained in a simple two country, cash-in-advance, optimizing model with flexible exchange rates. This model is used to derive the path of interest rates and exchange rates when one country experiences seasonal fluctuations in endowments. The time path of exchange rates and interest rates in this model depends upon how international trade is financed. If all international trade is conducted using the seller's currency, the exchange rate, the interest rate and the domestic currency price of goods fluctuate seasonally. If all international trade is financed using the buyer's currency, prices of goods denominated in both currencies fluctuate seasonally, but the exchange rate and the nominal interest rate are constant. If all international trade is conducted in the currency of the country with constant output (foreign currency in this model), the results are similar to the buyer's currency model: prices in both countries fluctuate seasonally, but exchange rates and interest rates are constant. In this model, however, prices in both countries and the exchange rate are indeterminate.

During the pre-World War I gold standard period, most international trade was financed using sterling bills of exchange. The dollar was rarely used in international transactions before World War I. In this case, the relevant model is the version in which all international trade is financed using foreign currency. This version of the model predicts that interest rates and exchange rates should be constant. This implication is contradicted by the empirical evidence of seasonal fluctuations of both interest rates and exchange rates for this period. The explanation of the constant path of exchange rates and interest rates in the model is that seasonal fluctuations of domestic and foreign currency prices are able to bear the full burden of adjustment to seasonal fluctuations in endowment. In the case where all international trade is conducted using foreign currency, the exchange rate must be constant because both the buyer's goods market arbitrage condition and the seller's goods market arbitrage condition must be satisfied simultaneously. The buyer's goods market arbitrage condition says that a buyer must be indifferent between purchasing in the two goods markets. This implies that $p_t = e_t p_t^*$, where p_t (p_t^*) is the domestic (foreign) currency price of goods at time t and e_t is the domestic currency price of foreign currency at time t. The seller's goods market arbitrage condition says that the seller must be indifferent between selling in the two markets: $p_t = e_{t+1} p_t^*$. The seller uses next period's exchange rate to calculate relative returns from selling in the two markets because income from the sale of goods is not received until the end of the period, and receipts in one currency can not be converted to the other currency until the next asset market.

The exchange rate must be constant in order to satisfy both goods market arbitrage conditions.

Further research is clearly needed to develop a model which can explain both seasonal fluctuations of nominal interest rates and seasonal fluctuations of exchange rates within the gold points. These fluctuations can not be satisfactorily explained by a closed economy model, by the Barsky et al. model or by a simple optimizing cash-in-advance constraint model. The disappearance of strong seasonal fluctuations of short term nominal interest rates after World War I can not be satisfactorily explained until the reasons for the seasonal fluctuations of short term nominal interest rates and the dollar-sterling exchange rate during the gold standard are well understood.

According to reports in the contemporary literature, the seasonal fluctuations in the dollar-sterling exchange rate created opportunities for profit by borrowing short term in Britain during the late spring and early summer months, investing in U.S. money markets and repaying the loan in the fall of the year after the dollar had appreciated. Using data on U.S. and British short term nominal interest rates and the prices of sight and sixty day bills of exchange, this study finds that there were significant differences in the seasonal patterns of U.S. and British short term nominal interest rates. It also finds that seasonal fluctuations of the dollar-sterling exchange rate did tend to increase the apparent profit opportunities from borrowing in Britain during the late spring and early summer months. Seasonal fluctuations of the dollar-sterling exchange rate did not offset the differentials between U.S. and British rates, as would be expected if uncovered interest parity held.

Deviations from uncovered interest parity do not necessarily imply that unexploited profit opportunities existed. These deviations from uncovered interest parity can be attributed to several factors other than unexploited profit opportunities. These factors include transactions costs, exchange risk premia, the peso problem, risk premia associated with assets which are not strictly comparable, liquidity constraints and unexploited profit opportunities. It is shown here that transactions costs can explain some, but by no means all of the seasonal profit opportunities identified in this study. Liquidity constraints imposed on arbitrageurs by a risk averse London discount market stand out as a potentially important explanation for the persistence of seasonal profit opportunities during this period. There are several reports in the contemporary literature that the London discount market limited the amount of loans made to the American market. Discount rates charged to arbitrageurs who drew "too many" finance bills would increase above published market rates. The existence of these liquidity constraints means that exchange rates and interest rates might not have been able to move such that all seasonal profit opportunities would be eliminated. In this scenario, all profit opportunities would be exploited at the margin, but arbitrageurs would make profits on the inframarginal units of finance bills drawn.

Two other potential explanations for deviations from uncovered interest parity deserve further consideration: the "peso problem" and the existence of an exchange risk premium. During periods of uncertainty concerning whether the United States would remain on the gold standard, agents may have expected the dollar to depreciate past the gold export point. Given that the United States was able to remain on the gold standard throughout the period, it may appear *ex post* as if agents made systematic exchange rate forecast errors. In this case the calculated *ex post* returns from borrowing sterling and investing in the United States overstate the *ex ante* returns. In studies of uncovered interest parity for more recent historical periods, exchange risk premia have been identified as the most probable explanation of deviations from uncovered interest parity. It is possible that an exchange risk premium existed during the gold standard as well. In order for an exchange risk premium to explain seasonal fluctuations in deviations from uncovered interest parity, however, that exchange risk premium must fluctuate seasonally. Developing models of a seasonal exchange risk premium and of the "peso problem" during the gold standard are identified in this study as areas of future research.

The plan of this book is as follows. The next chapter presents a review of the literature on seasonal fluctuations of interest rates and exchange rates during the gold standard. Contemporary accounts of interest rate and exchange rate seasonality, empirical studies of seasonal fluctuations of interest rates and exchange rates as well as models of interest rate seasonality and exchange rate behavior are all discussed. An overview of the foreign exchange market and a discussion of international short term capital flows during this period are also included. A two country cash-in-advance model which is designed to investigate the behavior of prices, interest rates and exchange rates in a world with seasonal fluctuations in endowments is developed in Chapter 3. The results indicate that when all international trade is financed using foreign currency, as was the case for the United States during the gold standard, seasonal fluctuations of interest rates and exchange rates can not be generated in a simple, equilibrium, optimizing, cash-in-advance model with no transactions costs.

The following two chapters constitute the empirical part of this work. Chapter 4 explains the univariate time series methodology used here for modeling seasonal fluctuations of interest rates, exchange rates, and interest rate differentials. This chapter also presents the results of the time series models for U.S. and British short term nominal interest rates and the dollar-sterling sight and sixty day bill of exchange rates. The results reported here are in accordance with the findings of earlier studies. Interest rates and exchange rates both show significant seasonal fluctuations. Chapter 5 investigates the behavior of interest rate differentials between the United States and Britain. It is found here that there were significant differences in the patterns of seasonal fluctuations of U.S. and British interest rates. Seasonal movements in exchange rates between the gold points do not offset seasonal differences in U.S. and British interest rates during this period, as would be expected according to uncovered interest parity. These results indicate that seasonal exchange rate movements may have increased the profit opportunities associated with borrowing in London and investing in the United States during the late spring and summer months. Studies of uncovered interest parity during more recent historical periods are reviewed and explanations for deviations from uncovered interest parity in this literature are discussed.

This work concludes with a summary of results and a discussion of directions for further work. Significant seasonal fluctuations were found in U.S. and British short term nominal interest rates and the dollar-sterling exchange rate. Significant differences were also found in the seasonal patterns of interest rates in the two countries. Seasonal exchange rate movements tended to increase, rather than offset, the differentials between interest rates in the two countries. One important conclusion drawn from these findings is that a satisfactory model of seasonal fluctuations of short term nominal interest rates and the dollar-sterling exchange rate has yet to be developed. The role of an exchange risk premium and the "peso problem" in explaining deviations from uncovered interest parity also deserve careful consideration in future work.

II

The Seasonal Behavior of Interest Rates and Exchange Rates During the Gold Standard–A Review of the Literature

INTRODUCTION

This chapter presents a review of the literature concerning seasonal fluctuations in interest rates and exchange rates in the United States and Britain during the pre-World War I period. Both contemporary accounts and more recent studies of seasonal behavior are discussed here. There is clear evidence of strong seasonality of short term interest rates and exchange rates before World War I and of a weakening of seasonal patterns after World War I. The change in the seasonal behavior of short term interest rates has received more attention in recent years than the seasonal behavior of exchange rates because of a debate concerning the role played by the Federal Reserve in eliminating seasonality of short term interest rates in the United States after its establishment in 1914. Several key observations can be drawn from this literature review. First, the findings of strong short term interest rate seasonality before 1914 and its disappearance after 1914 are consistent across studies and do not appear to be sensitive to the choice of interest rate or method of statistical analysis. Second, several studies have found exchange rate seasonality during the period 1880–1914, but there are indications that the pattern of seasonal fluctuations was not stable over the time period. Seasonal fluctuations appear to have diminished in amplitude, but not to have disappeared completely by the outbreak of World War I. Third, most recent work concerning the behavior of exchange rates during the gold standard is concerned with the issue of the efficiency of the gold standard. One approach in this literature focuses on the determination of the gold points and whether or not exchange rates moved outside the gold points. In a more recent work, Officer (1989) develops a model of gold standard efficiency in which the actual loss due to deviations of the dollar-sterling exchange rate from its theoretical asset market equilibrium level is compared with the expected loss under "neutral speculation." Neutral speculation refers to the case where speculators expect that every level of exchange rates within the gold points has an equal probability of occurring. Officer characterizes foreign exchange market efficiency during the gold standard as "remarkable." While this efficiency literature is concerned with the behavior of exchange rates during the gold standard, it ignores seasonal fluctuations of exchange rates and does not explore the issue of whether or not predictable profit opportunities existed because of predictable seasonal fluctuations of exchange rates.

Finally, it is clear that the interrelationships of exchange rate movements and interest rate movements in the United States and Britain have not received sufficient study in recent years. There have been very few studies of seasonal movements of interest rate differentials between the United States and Britain. The results seem to be sensitive to the choice of series and technique. Morgenstern (1959) finds a different pattern of seasonal fluctuations in the differential between the U.S. commercial paper rate and the British discount rate than does Goodhart (1969) for the differential between U.S. time loan rates and British discount rates or the differential for U.S call loan rates and British rates. Clark (1982) does not find any seasonality in the differential he constructs between U.S. call loan rates and British call loan rates. Clearly, if one wishes to study arbitrage opportunities between the London and New York financial markets, exchange rate movements as well as interest rates in New York and London must be taken into account. Goodhart (1969) tries to take both seasonal exchange rate movements and seasonal interest rate movements into account in his study of the New York money market and short term international capital movements. The oldest approach in the literature, dating back to work of Goschen, is the international solidarity of money markets hypothesis, which views the gold points as setting limits on expected exchange rate movements.[1] These expected exchange rate movements set limits on "permissible" interest rate differentials. Morgenstern (1959) and Officer (1986) have both examined interest rate differentials between the United States and Britain in this spirit and found that interest rate differentials between the two countries often exceed the maximum possible expected depreciation given the gold points. Calomiris and Hubbard (1987) allow for transactions costs in their test of interest parity between the United States and Britain during this period. Based upon their estimates of transactions costs in financial markets, they argue that gold interest parity held during the period from 1897 to 1909.

This chapter first examines the literature concerning interest rate seasonality in both the United States and Britain. Contemporary views of interest rate seasonality, the results of empirical studies of seasonal fluctuations of interest rates and explanations for interest rate seasonality during the gold standard are all reviewed. The next section focuses on the behavior of exchange rates during the gold standard. An overview of the foreign exchange market during the gold standard is followed by a review of both earlier work on developing seasonal indices of exchange rate movements and more recent work concerning the behavior of exchange rates and the efficiency of the gold standard. The literature concerning the behavior of interest rate differentials and exchange rate movements is reviewed in the final section.

INTEREST RATE SEASONALITY

Seasonal fluctuations of interest rates were a well known feature of both the U.S. and British economies during the period 1880 to 1914. These seasonal fluctuations are generally attributed to fluctuations in money demand caused by seasonal fluctuations of output and economic activity due to the agricultural cycle and customary patterns of business activity and settlements. Both contemporary accounts of interest rate seasonality in the United States and Britain and recent empirical investigations of interest rate seasonality are reviewed in this section. Much of the recent empirical work on short term interest rate seasonality has focused on the issue of what role the establishment of the Federal Reserve played in eliminating seasonality in U.S. short term interest rates after its establishment in 1914. The early work on the role of the Federal Reserve in eliminating interest rate seasonality relies on a purely domestic explanation of interest rate seasonality. Barsky et al. (1988) have developed a model in which the establishment of a second central bank in a two country gold standard world enabled both central banks to cooperate and smooth interest rate fluctuations.

Contemporary Accounts of Interest Rate Seasonality

In a study of seasonal variations in the demand for currency and capital in the United States for the National Monetary Commission, Kemmerer (1911) found that interest rates tended to be high in early January, decrease through the end of February, rise to a spring peak in April, and then decline to a midsummer slump. This slump was briefly interrupted by a peak in interest rates at the end of June/early July associated with semi-annual settlements (which included such things as interest and dividend payments). At the end of July, rates began to climb to their peak in late September. Rates might decline somewhat, but typically remained high until they reached their highest levels of the year in late December. His explanations of this pattern focused on the high demand for money during the harvest and crop moving period of fall and early winter together with the demands of the Christmas season and customary patterns of business settlements.

Palgrave (1903: 107–108) discusses the role of both internal and external factors in explaining the seasonal pattern of British interest rates, which were highest in the fall and winter and lowest in the spring and summer months, except for a brief rise in interest rates during the month of May. He says that business activity in Britain during this period is highest during the fall and early winter months and notes that there is an increase in money demand during the harvest season. An additional source of pressure on British interest rates comes from seasonal gold drains to Scotland and Ireland due to the requirements of the Bank Act of 1844. Palgrave also explicitly mentions pressure resulting from seasonal fluctuations in the balance of trade, in particular the large agricultural imports from the United States during the fall of the year.

Empirical Investigations of Interest Rate Seasonality

Many empirical studies have confirmed the existence of short term nominal interest rate seasonality in the United States and Britain during the pre-World War I period. In his classic study of international financial transactions, Morgenstern (1959) found that short term interest rates fluctuated seasonally in the four countries he investigated: Britain, the United States, France and Germany. Interest rates in all countries tended to be highest in November and December and lowest in June and July. Seasonal fluctuations of short term U.S. interest rates were also found to be significant in more recent studies by Clark (1982, 1986), Miron (1986), Sharp (1988), and Barsky et al. (1988). Clark (1982, 1986) also found significant seasonal fluctuations in British, German and French interest rates. Barsky et al. (1988) confirmed the short term interest rate seasonality in Britain during this period. These studies all compare the seasonal behavior of short term interest rates before and after 1914, but differ according to the exact interest rates investigated and statistical techniques used.

Miron (1986) examines seasonality of call loan rates by testing for the significance of a set of seasonal dummy variables. Barsky et al. (1988) investigate the seasonality of U.S. three month time loan rates and the rate on three month bankers' bills in London based on the significance of seasonal dummy variables and autocorrelation functions. Clark examines a whole set of U.S. interest rates: monthly average call money rates, monthly average 60–90 day U.S. commercial paper rates and the 90 day time money rate as well as monthly averages of British, German and French open market discount rates. He finds significant autocorrelations at seasonal lags of the first differences of the interest rate series and a significant seasonal pattern in the estimated monthly means of the first differences of interest rates. He also compares the forecasting performance of seasonal and nonseasonal interest rate models in predicting interest rates from January 1913 to June 1916. Clark finds weak evidence in support of seasonality of interest rates in the first part of this period: mean absolute errors (MAE) and root mean squared errors (RMSE) were lower for the seasonal models, but the difference in forecast performance is not significant at the 5% level. He finds that the nonseasonal models significantly outperform the seasonal models in the later part of this test period, indicating a disappearance of significant seasonal behavior.

Sharp (1988) uses nonparametric techniques which are not sensitive to trends in interest rates or changes in interest rate volatility to identify significant seasonal patterns. He ranks the monthly first differences of 90 day time loan rates within each year and compares the pattern of ranks to that expected under the null hypothesis of no seasonality. He strongly rejects the hypothesis of no seasonality based upon the large sum of third quarter ranks. He does find evidence of seasonality in the period 1916–1933, but also finds evidence of a significant weakening in seasonal behavior when this period is compared with the earlier period. Sharp also finds significant short term interest rate seasonality during the years 1952–1985.

Objectives of Recent Research and Explanations of Interest Rate Seasonality

One of the main objectives of recent studies of interest rate seasonality before and after World War I is to determine the role played by the establishment of the Federal Reserve in 1914 in changing the time series behavior of interest rates.[2] As one of its primary responsibilities, the Federal Reserve was charged with smoothing seasonal fluctuations of interest rates by providing a more 'elastic' currency. A substantial literature has addressed the question of whether the Federal Reserve can be credited with smoothing seasonal fluctuations of interest rates after 1914. Part of this debate naturally centers on what explanations of interest rate seasonality during this period are. Two explanations have emerged in the literature. The first is a purely domestic explanation which focuses on the demand for and supply of money in the United States. The second is an explanation which tries to explain interest rate seasonality within the context of the international gold standard.

Miron (1986) argues that the sharp reduction in interest rate seasonality is clearly due to the founding of the Federal Reserve and its role in smoothing interest rates by seasonally adjusting the money supply to offset seasonal fluctuations in money demand. He traces the desire of monetary authorities to smooth seasonal fluctuations of interest rates to the close association of financial panics and periods of seasonal strain in money markets. He explains seasonality of short term interest rates in the United States using a closed economy model of the banking system which assumes that the level of high-powered money is fixed and independent of the behavior of the economy and in which the nominal interest rate depends positively on output, which he uses as a proxy for a measure of the real demand for credit in the economy. In his model, seasonal fluctuations in output generate seasonal fluctuations in nominal interest rates and the loan reserve ratio of banks. Miron justifies his assumption of a fixed stock of high-powered money by arguing that gold flows were "sluggish" under the pre-World War I gold standard.[3] Miron finds the evidence from the years 1890–1908 to be consistent with the implications of his model: call loan interest rates and the loan reserve ratio of banks are both highest in the fall of the year and lowest in the summer months. He credits the establishment of the Federal Reserve with causing the sharp reduction of short term interest rate seasonals in the United States. He supports this by showing that the seasonal pattern of nominal interest rates and the loan reserve ratio both decline appreciably after 1914, and by showing that there is a strong increase in federal reserve credit outstanding in the fall of the year which can account for both the decline in nominal interest rate seasonality and in the seasonality of the loan reserve ratio.

Clark (1986) finds a significant seasonal pattern of U.S. short term nominal interest rates before 1914 and a disappearance of seasonality after World War I. He also finds that both currency in circulation and high powered money showed only limited seasonal movements before 1914, but strong seasonal movements after World War I. The patterns of interest rate fluctuations, currency in circulation and high powered money before 1914 are consistent with the traditional story that seasonal fluctuations of money demand given a relatively inelastic supply of money are the cause of seasonality in short term interest rates. Clark differs from Miron, however, in that he questions the role of the Federal Reserve in eliminating short term interest rate seasonality in the United States. Based on evaluations of model forecast performance and switching regression models, Clark finds that short term interest rate seasonality in the United States disappeared in 1914, well before the currency in circulation and high powered money became more strongly seasonal in 1917. He also finds that seasonal fluctuations in short term interest rates were a world wide phenomenon before 1914: there were significant seasonal fluctuations in German, French and British short term interest rates as well as in U.S. interest rates during this period. Seasonality in all the rates disappeared after World War I. Clark points out that a satisfactory explanation for the disappearance of interest rate seasonals must be able to explain the change of interest rate behavior in the United States as early as 1914 and the disappearance of interest rate seasonals in all countries after World War I. Clark does not find the evidence that the Federal Reserve played the key role in changing the seasonal behavior of interest rates completely convincing.

Two special factors are noted which could explain the disappearance of interest rate seasonality during the 1914–1916 period: the lowering of bank reserve requirements in November 1914 and the massive gold imports during 1915–1916 resulting from the effects of war in Europe. Both of these factors could have worked to eliminate the seasonal upward movements of interest rates during the fall of the year. The decrease in reserve requirements occurred at a time when there was seasonal pressure on interest rates, and the gold imports served to increase the reserves of the banking system throughout the period. The existence of these "special factors" during the 1914–1916 period does allow a role for the Federal Reserve in eliminating interest rate seasonality in later years. Clark argues, however, that a satisfactory explanation of the existence of worldwide seasonality of interest rates before 1914 and the disappearance after World War I has yet to be developed. He points to a need for more attention on international connections of financial markets and a greater understanding of the role played by the breakdown of the international gold standard.

Seasonality of British interest rates before World War I underscores the need for a closer examination of the causes of interest rate seasonality during this period. Certainly, the British experience indicates that having a central bank is not enough to eliminate interest rate seasonality. Britain had a central bank, the Bank of England, that was capable of moderating interest rate movements by rediscounting bills of exchange or by making advances to the discount market against bills of exchange held as collateral. The Bank of England was, however, limited in its ability to eliminate seasonal fluctuations of interest rates by its obligation to protect Britain's gold reserves and ensure that Britain remained on the gold standard. In fact, the Bank sometimes took actions to tighten British money markets during the fall of the year when there was a threat of loss of gold reserves to foreign countries, especially the United States, due to balance of trade pressures.[4] Sayers (1936: 132–133) argues that the failure of the Bank of England to take actions to prevent the "seasonal drain" from increasing interest rates every autumn to be the "most serious blot on its record."

Barsky et al. (1988) develop a model of the international gold standard that could account for the worldwide change in the behavior of interest rate seasonality. They argue that the Federal Reserve could have been the critical factor needed for interest rate stabilization even if World War I and the downfall of the gold standard had not occurred. They develop a model in which one central bank acting in a two country gold standard world could not completely eliminate fluctuations of interest rates if it also tried to eliminate gold flows. If both countries have a central bank, however, it is possible for them to cooperate and achieve the dual objectives of smoothing interest rates and of minimizing gold flows. The major shortcoming of this model is that it does not explain the seasonality of short term interest rates. The money demand function in this model is a very simple form of the quantity equation which says that the money supply in each country is equal to the price level; output is assumed to be fixed. The exchange rate is assumed to be fixed at mint parity; there are no fluctuations of exchange rates between gold points in this transactions costless world. Given this fixed exchange rate, the assumption of purchasing power parity insures that price levels, and therefore inflation rates, are identical in the two countries. The real rate of interest is determined exogenously and the rate of inflation is equal to the rate of growth of the world money supply. The nominal interest rate is the sum of the real rate and the rate of inflation and is the same in both countries.

In the case where there is only one central bank in the world, it is impossible for that central bank to both eliminate gold flows and smooth interest rates. It can only affect interest rates by changing the money supply. Since the rates of growth of the money supply have to be equal in the two countries in order to satisfy purchasing power parity, an increase in the money supply of the country with the central bank immediately causes a gold flow. There is thus a tradeoff between gold flows and interest rate smoothing, and the central bank will not smooth interest rates at all if it has a strong aversion to gold flows.

In the case with two central banks under a gold standard, there is no conflict between the objectives of stabilizing interest rates and minimizing gold flows. The two central banks can eliminate gold flows by setting the rate of growth of each country's money supply (x_t, x_t^*) equal to the difference between the nominal interest rate target $(\bar{i})_t$ and the real interest rate (r_t):

$$x_t = x_t^* = \bar{i}_t - r_t.$$

Thus, whenever real interest rates tend to be high, central banks should smooth nominal interest rates by decreasing the money supply and causing deflation of prices. Whenever real interest rates are low, the central bank should increase the rate of growth of the money supply and thereby have inflation of prices offset the low real interest rates.

Barsky et al. do not discuss the seasonal pattern of changes in the money supply which would have been required to smooth interest rates according to their model. However, it is clear that the central banks would have to decrease the rate of growth of the money supply in periods of high real interest rates and to increase the rate of growth of the money supply in times of low real interest rates. If the seasonality in interest rates during the gold standard was a seasonality in real rates of interest, then this model predicts that in order to smooth interest rates the Federal Reserve and the Bank of England should have decreased the money supply, not increased the money supply during the fall of the year when interest rates were high. If high nominal interest rates during the fall of the year in both countries were not due to high real rates, this model would attribute the high nominal rates to high inflation, and therefore to an excessive rate of growth of the money supply. Once again, the policy prescription would be to decrease the money supply in periods when interest rates are high and increase the money supply in periods when interest rates are low.

The policy for smoothing interest rates during the gold standard prescribed by this model is at odds with the conventional explanation that provision of a "more elastic" currency was successful in smoothing interest rates in the United States. According to the work of both Clark and Miron discussed earlier, the conventional explanation of the disappearance of interest rate seasonality is that the Federal Reserve smoothed interest rates by increasing high powered money in periods when the demand for money, and therefore interest rates, were high. One explanation for the opposite policy actions implied by this model is the specification of the nominal interest rate in the model:

$$i_t = r_t + \pi_t$$

where i_t is the nominal interest rate, r_t is the real interest rate and π_t is the rate of inflation. The simple quantity equation assumed in the model states that the money supply (M_t, M_t^*) equals the price level (P_t, P_t^*) in each country. Given the fixed exchange rate, the assumption of purchasing power parity implies that the price levels in the two countries must be equal ($P_t = P_t^*$). The simple quantity equation, the fixed exchange rate and purchasing power parity together imply that the rates of inflation in the two countries are equal. This inflation rate is determined by the rate of growth of the money supply in each country:

$$\Pi_t = \frac{M_t - M_{t-1}}{M_{t-1}} = \frac{M_t^* - M_{t-1}^*}{M_{t-1}^*}$$

The nominal interest rate in this model depends not on expected inflation, but rather on current inflation (that is, inflation realized this period). If nominal interest rates depended upon expected inflation, then nominal interest rates would be smoothed in periods of high real interest rates by expected deflation. This would imply that a central bank should increase the current period's money supply or decrease next period's money supply in order to have seasonal fluctuations of the inflation rate offset seasonal fluctuations of the real interest rate.

Barsky et al.'s work raises the important issue of whether the seasonal fluctuations of interest rates during the gold standard were real interest rate fluctuations as well as nominal interest rate fluctuations. Unlike previous work on inflation rates during the gold standard, this study finds that inflation rates were seasonal during the gold standard.[5] In the United States, the one month inflation rate tended to be highest in the summer months and lowest in the late fall, winter and early spring. In Britain, seasonal fluctuations of the inflation rate during the gold standard were much milder. Inflation rates tended to be high during the summer months and during the first two months of the year, and lowest during the late fall. Barsky et al. also find that seasonal fluctuations in real rates of interest were significant at the 10%, but not the 5% level during the gold standard years 1890–1910. There was not a significant seasonal in the real rate in the post World War I period 1920–1933. In this study Barsky et al. were unable to reject a hypothesis of no change in the seasonal behavior of interest rates in the two periods and therefore conclude that there was not a significant change in the behavior of real rates of interest caused by the founding of the Federal Reserve.

EXCHANGE RATE SEASONALITY

Seasonal fluctuations of dollar-sterling exchange rates are also a well known feature of the pre-1914 gold standard. Conventional explanations of the phenomenon point to the importance of agriculture in the United States economy and the pronounced seasonal fluctuations in U.S. exports which resulted. The U.S. residual balance of trade, defined as the net balance of merchandise trade adjusted for gold flows, was highest during the autumn harvest and lowest during the summer months.[6] Most international trade during this period was financed using commercial sterling bills of exchange. Seasonal fluctuations in the balance of trade caused seasonal fluctuations in the supply of and demand for commercial sterling bills of exchange in the New York market which in turn caused seasonal fluctuations in exchange rates. These seasonal fluctuations in exchange rates reportedly created arbitrage opportunities in international short term capital markets. Although drawings of loan and finance bills were very sensitive to movements in interest rates and expected exchange rate changes, the effects of asset market influences on exchange rates were not, according to contemporary accounts, sufficient to completely overwhelm the effects of balance of trade fluctuations on exchange rates.

This section begins with an overview of the foreign exchange market during the gold standard and a discussion of bill of exchange and short term international capital flows. This is followed by a review of contemporary accounts of exchange rate seasonality and empirical investigations of exchange rate seasonality. The section concludes with a review of recent studies of exchange rate behavior and the efficiency of the gold standard.

The Foreign Exchange Market During the Gold Standard

A basic understanding of the structure and operations of the foreign exchange market as it existed prior to World War I is a necessary prerequisite for any study of the pattern of British-American exchange rate fluctuations and arbitrage activities during the period. Since both the United States and Britain were on the gold standard, a "mint par" exchange rate, equal to $4.8665 per pound sterling, was established by the gold content of the dollar and the pound.[7] Exchange rates were not fixed precisely at this level, but could fluctuate within a band determined by the costs of shipping gold. These costs were not fixed, but varied with changes in direct costs (costs of shipping, insuring, packing, etc.) or in indirect costs of interest lost on funds tied up in gold shipment. As long as the exchange rate remained within the gold points, it was cheaper to make international payments using bills of exchange rather than shipping gold. The foreign exchange market in the United States during this period was essentially the market for bills of exchange of different maturities and cables drawn on foreign countries and denominated in foreign currencies. As discussed more fully below, most bills were sterling bills drawn on London. Gold arbitrage, carried out principally by a few large banks, served to keep exchange rates within the gold points.

Structure of the Foreign Exchange Market

As the financial center of the nation during this period, New York was also the center of the foreign exchange market.[8] Large banks and foreign exchange dealers which had established "correspondent" relationships with banks overseas provided the framework of the system.[9] The number and strength of the relationships between U.S. banks and European banks increased throughout the period, spurred by the growth of foreign trade and the associated increased importance of international finance.[10] The bulk of the banks' foreign exchange business involved buying commercial bills of exchange from exporters and selling bills of exchange to importers or others needing to make payments abroad. Commissions earned from these activities were an important source of revenue. The relationships between New York banks and their overseas correspondents also provided channels permitting free flow of short term capital as well as providing important services in the finance of international trade.

There was an important asymmetry in the foreign exchange market before World War I: most bills of exchange were sterling bills drawn on London. Although theoretically it is possible for exporters of either country to draw bills on importers in the other country, the common practice was for exporters in the United States to draw sterling bills on importers abroad and for importers in the United States to pay debts abroad by remitting a sterling bill of exchange. Trade with third countries was often financed by means of sterling exchange. As trade with continental Europe grew, however, German bills of exchange and French bills of exchange became increasingly important.

The reasons for the overwhelming importance of sterling in international finance during the period are not completely clear, but three factors seem to be important.[11] The first is the long history of stability of the British pound . Britain's ties to gold were very strong. The pound had been convertible into gold at its mint price since the redeemability of the paper pound into gold after the Napoleonic wars in 1821. This was not true in the United States, which had suspended specie payments during the Civil War and had resumed specie payments only in 1879. Adherence to the gold standard in the United States was a source of political controversy, especially at times in the 1880's and during the early 1890's. A second factor is Britain's dominance of international trade during the period. The third, and perhaps most important factor, was the existence of a large discount market for bills of exchange in Britain which had no counterpart in the United States. Clean bills of exchange could easily be discounted in London after acceptance, and so were highly liquid assets. Bills of exchange drawn on the United States were usually held until maturity because of the lack of discounting facilities.[12] The relative insignificance of dollar exchange and the importance of sterling exchange indicate that it is reasonable to study the development of international short term capital flows and arbitrage activities during this period by focusing on the market for sterling exchange in New York.

Bills of Exchange and Short Term International Capital Flows

Most foreign exchange market transactions during the nineteenth and early twentieth centuries were carried out using bills of exchange. A bill of exchange is defined in the United States by the Uniform Negotiable Instruments Law and in Britain by the Bills of Exchange Act as:

> *an unconditional order in writing addressed by one person to another, signed by the person giving it, requiring the person to whom it is addressed to pay on demand or at a fixed or determinable future time a sum certain in money to order or to bearer.*[13]

There are three parties to a bill of exchange: the drawer, the drawee and the payee.[14] The drawer is the person or institution which draws the bill of exchange, i.e. orders the drawee to make a specified payment of money. The drawee is the person or institution on which the bill of exchange is drawn. The drawee is not legally bound to make payment until he (she, it) "accepts" the bill. Acceptance is the act of acknowledging one's obligation to make payment, which is usually done by writing "accepted" with the date and one's signature across the face of the bill. The payee is the person or institution who receives payment from the drawee at maturity. Negotiability is an important characteristic of a bill of exchange: the payee can be, but need not be the same as the drawer. A simple example of a case when the drawer and the payee are not the same would be a case where an exporter draws a bill on an importer and then sells that bill to an exchange dealer or bank dealing in foreign exchange. The bank or exchange dealer sends the bill abroad for acceptance. If the bill is sold on the London discount market, the buyer of the bill in London would then become the payee of the bill.

There are many types of bills of exchange.[15] Bills differ both in time to maturity and in the nature of the transactions which gave rise to the bill. Sight bills are payable at sight, that is at the time of presentation of the bill.[16] A sight bill drawn in New York would be due when it reached London. The sight exchange rate, or the dollar price of a sterling sight bill of exchange, is thus not equivalent to a spot rate because it reflects the interest cost while the bill is in transit. The seller of the bill in New York gets control of dollars immediately, while the buyer is entitled to pounds only when the bill reaches London. Long bills are due a specified number of days (often 60 or 90) after sight or after date.[17] Prices of long sterling bills (in dollars per pound) are lower than sight bills because the allowance for interest is greater. "Cables" or international transfers of funds using the transatlantic cable, are not strictly speaking bills of exchange because they are nonnegotiable. The rate on cables could, under certain circumstances, be thought of as a spot rate of exchange because it contains no interest component. The cable rate was not, however, equivalent to a spot rate throughout the entire period because, especially in the early years, the cable rate was too high to be accounted for simply by an interest component. Sight bills dominated cables as a means of payment throughout the period, although the use of cables was becoming more widespread in later years.[18]

Trade or commercial bills arise out of commercial transactions. In this case documents which constitute the title to the goods shipped are attached to the bill and act as security for the bill. This kind of bill was often drawn by exporters on importers. The importer would gain possession of the documents either upon acceptance of the bill (i.e. upon acknowledgment of indebtedness) or upon payment for the goods, depending upon the nature of the arrangements made. A bill was known as a "clean" bill if it had no documents attached and as a documentary bill if it had documents attached. Documentary bills would become clean bills if documents were surrendered upon acceptance. Clean bills could be discounted in the London discount market but documentary bills could not.

Bills of exchange could also arise out of purely financial transactions. International short term loans and arbitrage operations were carried out primarily through the use of bankers' long bills, which were drafts issued by a U.S. bank on a foreign bank. The term of the bill was usually 90 days but sometimes 60 or 30 days (Cross 1923: 200, Margraff 1903: 35). The initiative for lending or arbitrage operations could be taken by either foreign or domestic banks. Depending on the nature of the agreement between domestic and foreign institutions, the exchange risk could be born by different parties. Three different types of arbitrage operations are discussed below: finance bills, dollar loans and sterling loans.[19]

Finance Bills

The distinguishing feature of finance bills is that they are undertaken at the initiative of the domestic (New York) bank, and that the New York bank bears the exchange risk. Finance bills are often, but not always, backed by collateral security deposited by the New York bank in a local trust company. The New York bank draws a 90 day draft on its London correspondent. The London correspondent agrees to accept the draft for a set commission. The New York bank then sells the draft for dollars at the prevailing rate for 90 day drafts and invests those dollars. At the end of 90 days the New York bank must buy a sight draft to cover the 90 day draft maturing in London plus the acceptance commission. The New York bank's profit depends crucially upon the sight rate prevailing at the end of 90 days. The London bank's role in this transaction is merely to guarantee payment of 90 day draft: it advances none of its own funds. The New York bank, likewise, advances none of its own funds, but merely lends funds it had borrowed.

An alternative way in which dollars could be obtained by drawing finance bills has been described by Cross (1923: 211) and Whitaker (1919: 364). Rather than selling the 90 day draft on the New York market, the New York bank could send the draft to another of its correspondents in London and have the draft accepted and discounted immediately in the London market. The sterling thereby attained would be credited to the New York bank's account with its "other" correspondent in London. The New York bank could then sell sterling sight drafts in New York against this balance built up in London. According to Cross, the New York bank would follow this procedure in order to take advantage of a favorable discount rate in London and a high rate for demand drafts in New York.

Whitaker notes that if discount rates in London were low and the dollar was expected to appreciate so that conditions were favorable for drawing finance bills, then it would be highly unlikely that a finance bill drawn by a New York bank would be held to maturity by the original purchaser. The original purchaser was likely to be an exchange dealer or a bank which purchased the bill for immediate discount upon acceptance. This purchaser used the bill to build up accounts abroad against which bills could be sold in the United States and not as a short term investment. Clare (1907: 95) notes that it was relatively rare for sterling bills to be held for investment by American bankers, but much more common for such bills to be held as investments by continental European bankers. The short run effects of the sale of finance bills were therefore to increase the supply of loanable funds in the United States and to build up sterling reserves of American banks and exchange dealers in London.

There were two transactions costs involved in drawing finance bills: the acceptance commission which is the London bank's return for guaranteeing payment of the bill and the British stamp tax. The British stamp tax was 1/20% of the sterling value of the bill and allowance for the stamp tax was included in the price of a long bill of exchange. It is more difficult to get reliable estimates of the standard acceptance commission throughout the period. Whitaker (1919: 367–370) and Cross (1923: 209) both give a figure of 3/8% for a typical acceptance commission on a 90 day finance bill, which is 1 and 1/2% on an annual basis. Margraff (1903: 36–38) gives a range of 1/16–1/4% as standard for the acceptance commission on finance bills. The exact commission was a function of the length and quality of the bill. His range of rates is not expressed in annual percentage terms. The example in his text uses a 1/8% commission on a 90 day bill, which would translate to a 1/2% annual rate of commission. Furniss (1922: 156) gives an example of a 3/8% annual commission rate. Based upon this range of rates available in the literature, a range of 1/2 to 1 and 1/2% is a reasonable range for estimates of total transactions costs on finance bills.

It is not clear from the sources reviewed above exactly how acceptance commissions changed during the period 1880–1914. All the quotes cited above are from the early 20th century. The highest quote of 1 and 1/2% per annum is cited in both Cross (1923) and Whitaker (1919). This is much higher than the 1/2% annual commission rate found in Margraff's 1903 text and than the 3/8% annual commission rate cited by Furniss (1922). Other indications in the literature suggest that the terms of a New York bank's correspondent account with a London bank improved over the course of the period 1880–1914. A decrease in commissions on items cleared through a correspondent's account is noted by both Margraff (1903: 109–111) and Whitaker (1919: 202–207). These decreases may have applied only to commissions on bills drawn under letters of credit and not to commissions on finance bills.[20] Whitaker (1919: 206) discusses an arrangement for compensation of a correspondent whereby the U.S. bank would pay a fixed amount per annum and would not be required to pay commissions on individual items passed through the account. It is not clear whether finance bills could be drawn under such an arrangement.

Dollar Loans

In the case of a dollar loan, also known as a currency loan or a loan bill, a foreign bank loans money in the U.S. market with the help of an American bank which acts as its intermediary. The foreign bank assumes all exchange risk. The American bank draws a 90 day draft on the London bank and then immediately sells the bill on the open market at the going rate for 90 day bills. The proceeds of the sale are then lent to an American borrower at the interest rate previously agreed upon by the American and London banks. The London bank accepts the bill (draft) which was sold on the open market, but need not advance any of its own funds directly. At the end of 90 days the American borrower repays the principal (which was equal to the proceeds of the sale of the draft) plus the accrued interest. This sum is then converted into sterling at the current rate for demand (sight) bills and remitted back to the London bank to cover the maturing 90 day draft. The American bank is paid a small commission for its role as intermediary in arranging the loan.

Sterling Loans

If the borrowing American firm accepts the exchange risk inherent in the international loan and the foreign bank accepts a commission on the loan negotiated using bankers' long bills, then the loan is known as a "sterling loan" (or other foreign currency denominated loan). In this case the American bank which acts as intermediary turns the foreign draft itself, and not the dollar proceeds of the sale of the draft, over to an American firm for appropriate security. The American firm then sells the draft on the open market and uses the dollars so obtained to finance its activities. At the end of the 90 days, the American firm must supply a demand draft to cover the maturing 90 day draft plus the commission, usually 3/8%. The dollar value of the remittance naturally depends upon the demand rate at the end of 90 days. The firm's benefits (in terms of the "lower cost" of the loan) are greater the lower the demand rate at the end of the 90 day period.

According to contemporary accounts, drawings of finance bills and loan bills were sensitive to movements in interest rates and exchange rates. They were drawn mainly in three sets of circumstances: to take advantage of seasonal fluctuations of exchange rates, to help finance new bond and stock issues, and to take advantage of relatively high interest rates in New York. Large quantities were drawn in the summer months, especially in the later years of the period, in order to exploit the profit opportunities afforded by the expected appreciation of the exchange rate in the fall. This is perhaps the most widely noted use of finance bills and loan bills. Finance bills also helped finance new bond and stock issues. In this case long bills were drawn with securities deposited as collateral. Sometimes a renewal of these finance bills was necessary before the entire issue was sold (Escher 1918a: 38). Finance bills also figured prominently in episodes of stock market speculation in New York. In this case they would be drawn to take advantage of the relatively high interest rates in New York during periods of stock market speculation.

The risks, as well as the profit potential, from dealing in finance bills are discussed in the literature. Escher (1918a: 94) pointed out that "finance bills make money, but they make trouble, too." He notes that many finance bills were drawn in 1909 in anticipation of large exports from the United States due to predictions of unusually large harvests. The large harvests and large exports did not materialize. The dollar did not appreciate as expected, and many sellers of finance bills "had administered to them a lesson which they will be a good while in forgetting" (Escher 1918a: 98).

Even though there are many reports of sellers of finance bills speculating on movements of exchange rates, it was possible to buy sterling futures to cover the sale of finance bills. No published data on futures or forward rates are available. However, there are many reports of the existence of a futures market. Margraff (1903: 57–58), Escher (1918b: 90), and Whitaker (1919: 90) all note that sellers of finance bills could eliminate exchange risk by purchasing futures. Einzig

(1962: 180–183) describes the development of the forward market. He notes that in the United States an important source of the supply of futures came from exporters who had sold goods abroad for future delivery and wanted to eliminate their exchange risk.

Contemporary Accounts of Exchange Rate Seasonality

The typical scenario painted by contemporaries is that the dollar tended to appreciate in the fall when U.S. exports were high relative to imports given the large export of fall harvested crops.[21] The dollar-sterling exchange rate was highest during the summer months when exports tended to be low relative to imports. This pattern of expected appreciation of the dollar during the late summer and early fall made it profitable for bankers and others involved in international exchange to borrow money abroad during the late spring and summer months by drawing finance bills on correspondent banks in London. The proceeds from the sale of these bills in the New York market would be invested in the United States for the term of the bill (usually 2–3 months). At the end of the period, the loan (finance bill) could either be paid off by buying sight exchange and remitting to London to cover the maturing bill and commission charges, or could be rolled over by drawing another finance bill to provide the funds necessary to pay off the first. The use of finance bills and loan bills served to dampen seasonal fluctuations in exchange rates by increasing the supply of sterling exchange (and hence lowering the rate) in the summer when rates were typically high and increasing demand for exchange in the fall when the supply of bills was typically high and the price of exchange low. By serving as a channel for the free flow of international short term capital which offset movements in the balance of trade, finance bills also served to decrease seasonal gold flows.

Clearly, the conventional explanation of exchange rate seasonality maintains that movements of the balance of trade caused movements in exchange rates, even though short term capital flows could offset movements in the balance of trade.[22] Two important empirical issues are determining whether increased use of finance bills over the course of the period weakened seasonal fluctuations in exchange rates and determining whether profit opportunities created by seasonal fluctuations in exchange rates were completely arbitraged away. There was definitely a perception in the early 20th century that increased use of finance bills and loan bills weakened seasonal fluctuations in exchange rates. Kemmerer (1911: 141) provides the following quote from a banker who claimed that the well known seasonal fluctuations described by Kemmerer in his study had disappeared:

> *Your exchange charts are extremely interesting and show how in the past foreign exchange rates have followed the price of money, but apart from showing what has already happened their usefulness is at an end owing to the entire change which has come over the exchange market during recent years. The raising of capital in Europe by means of London credits has completely revolutionized exchange, which is affected now-a-days much more by the drawings under these credits than by commercial conditions, and hence we frequently find in the Fall very high rates ruling instead of the absolute reverse to which we have been accustomed.*

It does not appear, however, that seasonal fluctuations of exchange rates completely disappeared by 1914. In his discussion of the crisis in international financial markets caused by the outbreak of World War I in the summer of 1914, Sprague (1915: 500–501) comments that there was a large amount of bankers' long bills outstanding in the market, drawn in anticipation of appreciation of the exchange rates in the fall. Given the state of the exchange rate in July 1914, Sprague notes that money borrowed in London by means of finance bills in New York would probably "cost the borrower little or nothing." Purchasers of the bills in New York would most probably have immediately discounted the bills in London and sold sight exchange in New York against the proceeds:

> *No other course would have been reasonable because of the practical certainty of a further decline in rates with the approach of autumn. To hold the bills for investment or to build up foreign balances from the discounted proceeds of the bills would have involved an inevitable loss provided*

> *events should take the usual course during the remainder of the year.*

Sprague's account certainly indicates that seasonal movements of exchange rates had not completely disappeared by the outbreak of World War I and points to the existence of profit opportunities from drawing finance bills during the summer months.

Empirical Investigations of Exchange Rate Seasonality

Kemmerer (1911) and Cole (1929) both develop seasonal indices of dollar-sterling sight exchange rates. Cole (1929) studies changes in seasonal patterns of exchange rates from 1825–1913. He finds that a distinctive seasonal pattern emerges about 1850 and distinguishes three periods when a "stable" seasonal pattern existed: 1850–1860, 1880–1886, and 1897–1913. Cole attributes the change in the seasonal pattern from the 1850's to the 1880's to a change in the timing of exports. In the earlier decade exchange rates tended to be lowest from January to April when most cotton was exported. In later years, with improvements in transportation, exports tended to be highest during the fall. He attributes the change in pattern between 1880–1886 and 1897–1913 to the "increasing intimacy of the relations between the London and American money markets". The increase in short term capital flows in the later period caused a decrease in seasonal fluctuations of exchange rates. His results are consistent both with the earlier work of Kemmerer (1911) and with the later work of Morgenstern (1959). Morgenstern (1959: 211–218) found significant seasonal fluctuations in exchange rates between the United States and London, France and Germany before World War I. These seasonal patterns of exchange rates confirm the traditional story: the dollar tended to be highest in the late spring and early summer months and lowest in the fall and early winter months. Morgenstern also notes a decline in the amplitude of the seasonal fluctuations of exchange rates between 1880 and 1914, which he too attributes to increased integration of financial markets, and to a disappearance of seasonal fluctuations in exchange rates in the post World War I period.[23]

Exchange Rate Behavior and the Efficiency of the Gold Standard

Although seasonal fluctuations of exchange rates have not been investigated empirically in recent years, several papers have considered the implications of exchange rate movements for the efficiency of the gold standard. There are two strands in this efficiency literature. The first considers the issue of whether or not exchange rates "violated", or went beyond, the gold points. The second considers the movement of exchange rates within the gold point spread.

Gold import and export points, determined by the costs of shipping gold, placed limits on the actual and expected fluctuations of exchange rates during the gold standard.[24] Changes in costs of shipping gold affect the gold points and thereby affect fluctuations in exchange rates. The ties between the foreign exchange market and gold arbitrage activities were quite direct. Almost all gold shipments were undertaken by bankers, not merchants, as transactions costs of specie shipments were lower for bankers (Whitaker 1919: 518). If the exchange rate rose to the point where it became profitable to buy gold in the United States, ship the gold to London and exchange the pound proceeds back into dollars, gold would flow from the United States to Britain. If the exchange rate fell to the point where it became profitable to buy gold from the Bank of England, ship the gold to the United States and convert the gold into dollars, gold would flow from Britain to the United States.

These gold movements had an immediate impact on the exchange market. In the case of a gold export, bankers would sell sight bills of exchange against a shipment of gold, rather than against accounts already built up in London. This increased the supply of sight bills of exchange and thus put downward pressure on the dollar-sterling sight rate, keeping it from rising above the gold export point. There was no exchange risk involved in this transaction because the exchange transaction (the conversion of pounds back to dollars by the sale of the sight bill) took place at the time of the gold shipment. In the case of a gold import, dollars would be converted to pounds using sight bills, or sometimes cables, for the purchase of gold. This would increase the demand for sight bills and thus put upward pressure on the exchange rate, keeping it within the gold points. Gold imports entailed an additional cost in terms of interest foregone because funds were tied up in gold purchase and shipment from the time the sight bill (or cable) was purchased until the gold arrived in the United States and could be converted back into dollars. There was no interest lost, except a possible account overdraft charge in the case of gold export, because the sale of the sight bill returned dollar balances to the arbitrageur at the beginning, and not the end of the operation.

Violations of the gold points during this period have been investigated by Morgenstern (1959: 241–279), Clark (1984) and Officer (1986).[25] Morgenstern and Clark both found movements of exchange rates beyond the gold point spread and concluded that the gold standard did not function efficiently in the sense of rapidly eliminating profit opportunities. Officer, using more precise estimates of the gold points, finds only 3 months of profitable gold shipment during the 1890–1908 period and no further occurrences of profitable shipment. He concludes that the gold standard did function efficiently because gold point violations were infrequent and were rapidly eliminated when they did occur.

All three of these studies are flawed in that they use cable rates of exchange rather than sight exchange rates in their investigations.[26] Morgenstern uses the median gold points reported in contemporary newspapers and journals to represent the gold points for the entire period. Clark, who tries to overcome some of the shortcomings of Morgenstern's study by allowing for variable interest costs in estimating the gold points, also finds frequent violations of the gold points. Officer points out that Clark's estimates of direct costs of shipping gold simply assumed that this component was either fixed throughout the period at 0.3125% of parity or decreased from 0.5% of parity (1890–1904) to 0.3125% of parity in 1905. Officer carefully develops a set of gold point estimates which accounts for interest rate changes, changes in the direct costs of shipping gold and deviations of the transactions price of gold from the mint price of gold. Because of these modifications in the estimation of the gold points, he finds that violations of the gold points were infrequent, not frequent, phenomena and concludes that the gold standard operated efficiently in the sense of rapidly eliminating profit opportunities from gold arbitrage.[27]

In his work, Officer (1985, 1986, 1989) has clearly recognized that consideration of exchange rate movements within the gold points as well as exchange rate movements which violate the gold points are necessary for an evaluation of foreign exchange market efficiency during the gold standard. In his 1989 paper, Officer develops a model of gold standard efficiency in which deviations of exchange rates from their theoretical asset market equilibrium level are compared with deviations of exchange rates which would prevail under "neutral speculation." His analysis of dollar-sterling exchange rate speculation during the dollar-sterling gold standard assumes absolute confidence in the maintenance of the gold standard and perfect arbitrage. According to Officer, perfect arbitrage implies that exchange rates always lie within the gold point spread. Speculators are assumed to have exchange rate expectations which give all exchange rates within the spread equal probabilities of being realized within the speculators' time horizon and which give a zero probability of an exchange rate occurring outside the spread. The implication of these assumptions about exchange rate expectations is that speculators will expect positive average profits from buying pounds and/or selling dollars when the dollar-sterling exchange rate is below the spread midpoint and from buying dollars and/or selling pounds when the dollar-sterling exchange rate is above the spread midpoint. The amount of funds committed will be proportional to the profit potential, and will therefore be a positive function of the distance of the current exchange rate from the midpoint of the spread.

Officer (1989: 14–15) concludes that the midpoint of the gold point spread is the equilibrium exchange rate in this model of foreign exchange market efficiency because it is the exchange rate at which there is no speculative demand or supply of foreign exchange. The midpoint of the spread is not mint parity under the dollar-sterling gold standard because of the greater interest costs associated with a gold import than a gold export. As explained above, because sight bills of exchange could be sold against a shipment of gold from New York to London, the gold arbitrageur had control of dollars at the beginning of the arbitrage operation and so did not lose interest during a gold export. There was an interest cost associated with a gold import into the United States because dollars were tied up from the time of the purchase of the sight bill (or cable) until the gold shipped from London could be converted back to dollars. Given the assumption of perfect arbitrage, which keeps the exchange rate within the gold point spread, perfect speculation should keep the exchange rate at its equilibrium level. Because the profit potential from speculation increases the further the exchange rate is from its equilibrium level, speculative pressures forcing the exchange rate back to its spread midpoint should increase the further the exchange rate is from its midpoint.

Officer measures the loss due to inefficiency in the case of perfect arbitrage and perfect speculation as a function of the absolute distance of the exchange rate from the midpoint of the spread.[28] The experienced average loss under the assumption of perfect market efficiency is compared to the hypothetical loss under the assumptions of perfect arbitrage and "neutral" speculation. Officer (1989: 17) defines neutrality of speculation as the case where "the realized pattern of the exchange rate corresponds precisely to speculators' expectations" – the exchange rate takes on a uniform distribution within the gold point spread. Officer finds that the ratio of experienced, or actual, average loss to the hypothetical average loss is less than one for all three loss functions he calculates. He finds that the efficiency ratios calculated for the gold standard period 1890–1906 are very similar to, though slightly lower than, efficiency ratios calculated for the Bretton Woods period 1950–1966. He therefore concludes that the exchange-market efficiency of the gold standard period was "remarkable":

> *Speculators and arbitrageurs acting quickly and thoroughly made the gold-standard foreign exchange market more efficient than if gold arbitrage were perfect and exchange-rate speculation neutral and almost as efficient as under the actual experience of Bretton Woods, when the equivalent of perfect arbitrage (absence of "parity-point violations") reigned. (p. 35)*

Officer has carefully developed and tested a well defined model of foreign exchange market efficiency under the conditions of a gold standard, and his conclusions concerning the efficiency of exchange rate speculation during the gold standard concur with his conclusions concerning the efficiency of gold arbitrage in earlier work. However, it is not clear that his model is entirely appropriate for conditions of the gold standard and may leave unanswered the most interesting questions concerning the behavior of exchange rates and the role of exchange rate speculators during the gold standard. Although Officer carefully documents the ways in which gold arbitrage took place, he is not as careful about documenting the way in which exchange rate speculation was carried out during the gold standard. No attention is paid to the fact that exchange rate speculation was carried out using loan bills and finance bills, and that much speculation was based upon expected seasonal movements of exchange rates.[29] Officer's assumption that speculators have exchange rate expectations which give all exchange rates within the spread equal probabilities of being realized within the speculator's time horizon is not in accord with accounts of expected seasonal exchange rate movements in the literature or with empirical findings of seasonal movements of exchange rates. Officer (1989:18) claims that his analysis of efficiency does not critically depend upon the assumption of neutrality of speculation. It is not clear, however, that his conclusion concerning the efficiency of exchange rate speculation under the gold standard would be sustained if expectations of seasonal exchange rate movements and methods of conducting exchange rate speculation were taken into account.

INTEREST RATE DIFFERENTIALS BETWEEN THE UNITED STATES AND BRITAIN

There are very few studies which attempt to look at the implications of seasonality of interest rates and exchange rates for international short term capital movements between the United States and Britain. The results for interest rate differential series appear to be sensitive to the choice of interest rates for comparison.[30] Morgenstern (1959) and Clark (1982) both examine the seasonal pattern of interest rate differentials between the United States and Britain under the gold standard. Morgenstern (1959:137–141) found significant seasonal fluctuations in the differential between the New York commercial paper rate and the London discount rate. He found that the seasonal in this differential was positive in the summer and early fall (highest in September) and negative in the late fall and winter months (lowest in November). Clark (1982) found no significant seasonal pattern in the differential between New York and British mid-month call loan rates. Calomiris and Hubbard (1987) did not investigate the seasonality of interest rate differentials, but they do develop a set of arbitrage conditions which take account of transactions costs in financial markets. Based upon their estimates of transactions costs, they conclude that gold interest parity between the United States and Britain held before World War I.

Goodhart (1969: 47–53) calculates monthly averages of differences between U.S. time loan rates and British open market discount rates and differences between U.S. call loan rates and British rates for the period 1900–1913. On the basis of this evidence, he finds that interest rate differentials between the United States and Britain were highest during the months July through January, with a peak in the differential series occurring in September or October. The interest rate differentials were lowest from February through June. Goodhart argues that this pattern of interest rate movements is at odds with the pattern of international short term capital flows. On the basis of movements in the balance of trade, gold flows, tourist receipts and other remittances, it is clear that there must have been a seasonal movement of short term capital out of Britain during the late spring and summer months and from the United States to Britain during the fall and early winter when the United States ran large balance of trade surpluses. Goodhart correctly notes that the return to investment between countries must take account not only of the interest rates in the two countries but also of exchange rate movements. Based on monthly averages of exchange rates during the period 1900–1913, Goodhart (1969: 60–73) finds that the returns from dollar appreciation in the late spring and summer and the effect of exchange rate depreciation during the fall and winter tend to offset the pattern of interest rate differentials. When both exchange rate movements and interest rate differentials are taken into account, it appears to be profitable to transfer capital from Britain to the United States during the late spring and summer months and from the United States to Britain in the late autumn and early winter. His results are, however, sensitive to his choice of sight exchange rates. He had to use extreme movements of the sight exchange rate over a three month period in order to have movements in exchange rates offset the behavior of interest rate differentials.

Goodhart's work suffers from two important shortcomings. First, he bases his analysis on the pattern of simple monthly averages and so does not control for cyclical effects or the effects of periods of financial panic in New York money markets. High rates in New York money markets during the panic of the fall of 1907, for example, may have skewed the differential between the New York and London money markets towards the New York market during the fall of the year. Secondly, he does not look at the arbitrage opportunities measured at a particular point in time, but rather tries to get an indication of the pattern of "average" arbitrage profit by comparing the average monthly interest rate differential and the average actual three month appreciation of the exchange rate each month. A more accurate picture of the pattern of arbitrage opportunities could be obtained by examining the pattern of arbitrage profits over time

Another approach to looking at the interrelationship between exchange rates and interest rates under the gold standard is based on the international solidarity of money markets hypothesis. According to Morgenstern (1959: 166–168) this hypothesis was first articulated by Goschen in the 1860's. This approach recognizes that if there is confidence in the gold standard, then the gold points set limits on the maximum possible expected exchange rate movements. These expected exchange rate movements set limits on "permissible" interest rate differentials. Both Morgenstern (1959:326–327) and Officer (1986:1072) find that interest rate differentials between the United States and Britain often exceed the maximum possible expected depreciation of the exchange rate given the gold points.

Calomiris and Hubbard (1987) use an approach to testing interest parity which attempts to account for transactions costs in financial markets. Based upon their estimates of transactions costs, Calomiris and Hubbard (1987: 6–12) argue that British open market discount rates, U.S. commercial paper rates and the discount rate on sterling bills of exchange in New York all satisfy gold interest parity. They develop a set of allowable bounds on differentials between British and U.S. rates from arbitrage conditions in currency and short term money markets. They find that the differential between New York and London short term rates always lies within the bounds they derive.

Calomiris and Hubbard provide an innovative test of gold interest parity. However, their results must be interpreted cautiously. In their empirical work, they acknowledge that data on transactions costs in the various markets are not available, and proceed to estimate these transactions costs. In developing these estimates, Calomiris and Hubbard assume that no profit opportunities were afforded at any time by borrowing sterling in the London discount market and investing in sterling bills in the New York market (or *vice versa*). If this assumption is wrong, then Calomiris and Hubbard overestimate transactions costs. Calomiris and Hubbard also overestimate the bounds for the allowable interest rate differential between New York and London interest rates by including an allowance for gold transport costs. The existence of an extensive correspondent network between New York banks and London banks during this period means that it was not necessary to ship gold in order to arbitrage away differences in the sight rates in the two locations. The transactions costs associated with buying exchange in one location and selling exchange in another using the correspondent network would be much smaller than the transactions costs associated with buying, insuring and shipping gold between the two centers. Because most foreign exchange transactions took place within the gold points, there may have been profitable arbitrage opportunities within the bounds determined by Calomiris and Hubbard. These bounds are a weak test of interest parity in the sense that if the interest rates fall outside the estimated bounds, interest parity is clearly violated. However, some profit opportunities may exist within the bounds as well. These profit opportunities will not be identified using the test developed by Calomiris and Hubbard.

CONCLUSION

Seasonality of interest rates in both the United States and Britain during the pre-World War I gold standard is well established. A completely satisfactory explanation for the strong seasonal fluctuations of both U.S. and British interest rates during the gold standard and the disappearance of interest rate seasonality after 1914 has, however, not yet been developed. Most conventional explanations of interest rate seasonality focus on seasonal fluctuations in the demand for money and credit caused by seasonal fluctuations in output, given a relatively inelastic money supply. The Federal Reserve was able to eliminate short term interest rate seasonality in the United States by accommodating these seasonal fluctuations in the demand for money and credit. These closed economy explanations do not, however, take into account the international linkages among countries under the gold standard and can not explain the disappearance of interest rate seasonality in most countries following World War I.

Barsky et al. (1988) develop a model of the gold standard in which interest rates can be smoothed only if all key countries in the system have central banks. Fluctuations in interest rates can be smoothed if central banks cooperate to adjust money supply growth rates in ways which will smooth interest rates and minimize gold flows. There are several drawbacks of this open economy model. First, seasonal fluctuations of interest rates are not explained within the model. Second, the policy prescriptions for smoothing interest rates implied by the model is at odds with seasonal changes in the behavior of high powered money by the Federal Reserve which are generally credited with smoothing interest rates. Finally, the explanation for interest rate smoothing relies on the cooperation of central banks and coordinated monetary policies for the successful elimination of interest rate seasonals. The breakdown of the gold standard may have eased, or contributed to, the "worldwide" smoothing of interest rate seasonals by enabling central banks of individual countries to target interest rates within their countries without concern for international gold flows.

Exchange rate seasonality during the gold standard is generally attributed to seasonal fluctuations in the balance of trade. United States balance of trade surpluses during the fall and early winter months caused an appreciation of the dollar in the late summer and early fall. These expected movements of exchange rates were believed to have caused predictable profit opportunities from drawing finance bills during the late spring and early summer months. These short term international capital flows served to dampen, but not completely eliminate the seasonal fluctuations in exchange rates. Officer (1989) has developed an asset market approach to the determination of exchange rates during the gold standard. In his approach, the equilibrium exchange rate is the midpoint of the gold point spread, and actions of speculators will tend to move the exchange rate towards this equilibrium level. He finds that the foreign exchange market during the gold standard was very efficient in the sense that the average loss due to deviations of the exchange rate from the midpoint of the gold point spread was smaller than the average loss which would have resulted if the exchange rate had a uniform distribution within the gold point spread.

The comparison of Officer's work with earlier accounts of seasonal fluctuations of exchange rates raises the issue of what the most appropriate model of exchange rate determination during this period is. Clearly, Officer believes that exchange rate speculation was so pervasive that movements of the dollar-sterling exchange rate are best modeled using an asset approach. This is very different than the approach found in earlier work which maintained that seasonal fluctuations of exchange rates were due to seasonal fluctuations in the balance of trade. In this literature—even though drawings of loan bills and finance bills were acknowledged to be very sensitive to interest rate and expected exchange rate movements—balance of trade influences, and not the actions of speculators, were considered the cause of seasonal exchange rate movements.

The behavior of interest rate differentials between the United States and Britain has not received sufficient attention in the literature. The results concerning seasonal fluctuations of interest rate differentials are mixed. Morgenstern (1959) and Goodhart (1969) found significant seasonal fluctuations of interest rate differentials between the U.S. and Britain. Clark (1982) did not. Goodhart found that profit opportunities from drawing finance bills during the late spring and summer months were greater when exchange rate movements are taken into account. Based on their estimates of transactions costs, Calomiris and Hubbard (1987) find that gold interest parity was always satisfied during the period 1897–1909, and argue that it probably held in earlier years as well. Their estimates of transactions costs are, however, subject to measurement error and are constructed in a way which tends to overestimate total transactions costs associated with borrowing in one financial center and investing in the other center.

The next chapter of this study develops a cash-in-advance optimizing model in order to investigate the behavior of prices, interest rates and exchange rates in a world with seasonal endowment fluctuations, fixed money stocks, flexible exchange rates and no transactions costs. The following two chapters are empirical. Chapter 4 discusses the methodology used in this study and identifies the seasonal patterns of short term interest rates and exchange rates during the gold standard using this methodology. Chapter 5 investigates the time series behavior of interest rate differentials between the two countries.

NOTES

1. Morgenstern (1959: 166–168) attributes this international solidarity of money markets hypothesis to Goschen and discusses early investigations of the relationship between exchange rates and interest rate differentials.

2. In closely related work, other studies have examined the effect of the founding of the Federal Reserve on the term structure of interest rates. These studies include: Mankiw and Miron (1986), Mankiw, Miron and Weil (1987, 1990), and Fishe and Wohar (1990).

3. Calomiris and Hubbard (1987) dispute the "stylized fact" that the U.S. gold supply was inelastic during this period. They find that gold flows can be modeled as either an AR(1) or an MA(2) process with full adjustment to disturbances occurring within 3 months. It is not clear, however, that their findings are necessarily inconsistent with the position taken by Goodhart (1969: 25–44), Miron (1986) and Clark (1982, 1986) that gold flows were not "sufficiently large" or "sufficiently elastic" to cause movements in high powered money that could eliminate interest rate seasonality in the face of seasonal fluctuations of money demand. Calomiris and Hubbard do not find significant seasonal movements in gold flows: their time series model of gold flows is nonseasonal. This lack of seasonality in gold flows would tend to support the position of Goodhart, Miron and Clark that seasonal movements in high powered money were not "large enough" during the gold standard period. Full adjustment of gold flows to disturbances within 3 months may not be rapid enough to satisfy seasonal fluctuations in the demand for money.

4. The best accounts of the operations of the Bank of England during this period are found in Sayers (1936, 1976).

5. Barsky (1987) models inflation during the period 1870–1913 as "essentially white noise." No mention of this result is made in Barsky, Mankiw, Miron and Weil (1988), where inflation is found to have significant seasonal fluctuations.

6. See Bullock, Williams and Tucker (1919) for a discussion of movements in the balance of trade during this period.

7. One pound sterling contained 123.27447 grains of gold 11/12 fine (Coinage Act of 1816). A $10 American gold eagle coin contained 258 grains of gold 9/10 fine (Coinage Act of 1837). This meant that there were 113 grains of pure (or fine) gold in one pound and 232.2 grains of pure gold in ten dollars, establishing a mint par of 113/23.22 or $4.8665/pound sterling. The mint price of gold in the U.S. was $18.60565/ounce of gold 9/10 fine. There are 480 grains of gold per ounce. See Officer (1986) or Whitaker (1919).

8. See Officer (1985) for a discussion of integration of foreign exchange markets within the United States. Some banks outside of New York did establish correspondent relationships directly with foreign banks and did not use New York banks as intermediaries in their foreign exchange business. Margraff, a Chicago banker, wrote his 1903 text as a guide for American bankers entering the international banking field. However, the foreign exchange market was concentrated in New York throughout the period. For the purposes of this study it is not necessary to examine the development of the foreign exchange market within the United States in detail. The term "New York banks" is used loosely to refer to banks in the United States engaged in foreign exchange operations.

9. According to Escher (1918a: 59–63), there were three main classes of participants in the New York foreign exchange market: large banks with foreign departments, foreign exchange dealers and bill brokers. The bill brokers brought together buyers and sellers of bills of exchange for a commission. They played a prominent role in early years, but were being supplanted by larger dealers and bankers in later years. Increased competition in the bill market had driven commissions down to a level where small brokers could no longer remain in business. Large foreign exchange dealers were specialists in bills who invested for their own account as well as bought and sold to bankers.

10. Perkins (1975) describes the establishment of several correspondent relationships prior to 1880. Margraff (1903) and Escher (1918: 40–41) discuss the growth of the "foreign department" for U.S. banks. The terms of the account between the U.S. banks and London correspondents were subject to negotiation and not constant over the period (Margraff 1903: 109–11, Whitaker 1919: 202–207).

11. The overwhelming importance of sterling in international finance is noted by all authors on the subject. Many references are made to "custom and tradition" but customs and traditions have historical origins. The factors cited in the text seem to provide a reasonable explanation. See Clare (1907: 13–15) for a British view, or Brown (1914), Whitaker (1919) or Cross (1923) for an American interpretation. Bloomfield (1963: 37) and Yeager (1966: 255–258) review this subject.

12. The lack of a discount market in the United States may have been due in part to the fact that under the National Banking Act, U.S. national banks were prohibited from accepting any bills arising out of a foreign trade transaction. In Britain, banks often accepted bills for their customers under commercial letter of credit agreements. Such bank acceptances were much more marketable than bills accepted by individual merchants and constituted a large part of the discount market in Britain.

The National Banking Act did not prohibit non national banks from accepting trade bills and so can not be the sole explanation for the lack of a discount market. Withers (1918: 111–112) argues that it was not the National Banking Act but the reputation of American firms which stood in the way of the growth of the acceptance business in New York:

> *If drafts on America were wanted, there are plenty of private firms which could accept, but in New York both the private firms and the banks are believed by the outside world, rightly or wrongly, to be often much more deeply involved in stock-market operations than would be thought safe and proper by the English accepting houses and banks.*

Another factor is that banks looked upon discounting commercial paper (and bills of exchange) as a sign of weakness. This explanation also is insufficient as British banks did not usually discount commercial paper and bills of exchange, but held such short term assets until maturity. Another class of financial institutions, the discount houses, did freely discount and rediscount bills. British banks lent money at call to the discount houses to keep a certain portion of their assets in a very liquid form. This is similar to the American banking practice during this period of lending money at call to the stock market.

There are many indications in the literature that American bankers wanted to capture part of the lucrative international finance business. According to Brown (1914: 73), the Federal Reserve Act of 1913 was designed in part to encourage the growth of a discount market in the United States which would facilitate the growth of New York as an international financial center.

13. See Cross (1923: 22) and Spalding (1919: 12) for the definition of a bill of exchange according to U.S. and British laws.

14. This section is based on Whitaker (1919: 12–17). See Whitaker for a more complete discussion.

15. This discussion is by no means comprehensive. More extensive coverage of types of bills and technicalities associated in dealing with bills can be found in Whitaker (1919), Cross (1923) and Escher (1918a, 1918b), which are the principal sources on which this discussion is based.

16. Sight bills are not accepted by the drawee as payment on sight both acknowledges and pays off the debt.

17. A three day grace period was allowed on long, but not on sight bills, in London.

18. The consensus of recent literature is that sight exchange rates should be used as representative exchange rates in studies of the period. Morgenstern (1959), in his classic study of international financial transactions, used cable rates. Officer (1985: 559–560) argues that cables remained relatively unimportant in exchange transactions until 1900 and that sight drafts remained important throughout the period. Perkins (1978: 406–407) found that the price of cables in 1880 was too high to be accounted for simply by an interest component. He found evidence that fees on cables were much higher than those on sight bills, an occurrence which he attributed to high costs of portfolio adjustment in London at the time. It is not clear exactly how the fee structure changed over the period. Margraff (1903: 49–50) says that the higher price of cables relative to sight bills could be attributed to the interest cost associated with sight bills. He notes, however, that cables could command an additional premium during times when there was an unusual demand in New York for immediate payment in sterling.

19. There is some dispute in the literature concerning appropriate terminology. This section follows the usage of Cross (1923: 206–207) and Escher (1918a: 95). Whitaker (1919: 378–81) uses the term finance bill to refer to loans made in the United States using bills of exchange drawn on a foreign money market, regardless of which party bears the exchange risk.

20. The acceptance commissions for trade bills or bills drawn under letter of credit agreements seem to have been much lower 1/40%–1/4% than acceptance commissions on finance bills (Margraff 1903: 110, Cross 1923: 492, Whitaker 1919: 206).

21. See, for example, Brown (1914: 82), Withers (1918: 76–77), Kemmerer (1911: 136–141), Escher (1918a: 35) or Cross (1923: 213).

22. Clare (1907: 77–87, 135–136) details both trade influences and banking and stock exchange influences that can effect the supply and demand for exchange and thereby affect exchange rates. He explains that in the case of exchange rates between London and the Continent, it is very hard to separate out the influences on exchange rates. However, in the case of London and New York, the large volume of agricultural exports from the U.S. to Britain in the fall clearly have an impact on the exchange rates.

23. Myers (1931) also discusses a decline in seasonal fluctuations of exchange rates before W.W.I, which she attributes to a narrowing of the gold points and increased international integration of financial markets.

24. Most early texts discuss the determination of gold import and export points. See, for example, Whitaker (1919) or Cross (1923).

25. Spiller and Wood (1988) also investigate gold arbitrage opportunities during the years 1899–1908. They assume that arbitrage costs are unobservable and vary stochastically. They use a two limit stochastic Tobit model to estimate the transactions costs of gold arbitrage econometrically.

Like Officer, this study finds that gold point violations did not occur frequently.

26. As discussed above, sight bills of exchange, and not cables, were the standard means of remittance for international short term transmission of funds. Officer (1986, 1989) and Clark (1984) both acknowledge the problem with using cable rates in studying gold point violations, and Officer does use sight exchange rates in his 1989 study. This study is not, however, a study of gold point violations.

27. Most of the gold point violations identified by Morgenstern in the London-New York market occurred in the 1880's, a period not covered in either Clark's or Officer's investigations. Morgenstern identified 31 violations before 1890, 13 violations during 1891–1896, and only one other violation in September 1906 (see Table 53: pp. 246–7). He bases his conclusion that the gold standard did not function efficiently in the sense of rapidly eliminating profit opportunities from gold arbitrage more on evidence of violations involving the Berlin and Paris markets rather than markets involving New York. Officer's work can not be construed as a complete rebuttal of Morgenstern's findings because it does not deal with the entire period or with all the markets that Morgenstern investigated.

28. Officer (1989: 16) investigates three loss functions: the identity loss function, which treats the disutility of the inefficiency as the deviation itself, the square loss function, which measures the disutility as the square of the deviation, and the exponential loss function, which assumes that the disutility of the inefficiency varies exponentially with the size of the deviation.

29. Officer (1989: 21) dismisses earlier work which had tied increases in foreign exchange market efficiency with a decrease in seasonal variation of exchange rates on the grounds that those studies do not take the "unique arbitrage and speculative operations of the gold standard" into account because they disregard the implications of the gold point spread and the existence of an equilibrium exchange rate, or "norm value" under a gold standard.

30. In the discussion in this section, interest rate differentials are always defined as the U.S. rate minus the British rate.

III

The Effect of Seasonal Endowment Fluctuations in a Cash-in-Advance, Optimizing Model

INTRODUCTION

The purpose of the model developed in this chapter is to investigate the behavior of prices, interest rates and exchange rates in a world with seasonal fluctuations in output, fixed money stocks and flexible exchange rates. As discussed in the review of the literature in the last chapter, seasonal fluctuations of short term nominal interest rates and seasonal fluctuations of exchange rates within the gold points were features of the pre-World War I gold standard. The model developed here is designed to address the issue of whether or not seasonal fluctuations of output can generate seasonal fluctuations of interest rates and exchange rates in an equilibrium, optimizing world with no transactions costs. The model is a two country, flexible exchange rate, cash-in-advance, optimizing model with foreign bonds and two currencies as the only tradable assets. Exchange rates were not, of course, completely flexible during the gold standard because exchange rate fluctuations were limited by the gold points. Given that the interest of this study is on fluctuations of exchange rates within the gold points, a flexible exchange rate model is more appropriate than a fixed rate model for deriving implications for the time series behavior of exchange rates.

The model developed here is well suited to investigating the implications of changing conventions regarding which currency is used to conduct international trade. Kimbrough (1986) points out the importance of these conventions for goods market arbitrage conditions. During the heyday of the gold standard, most international trade was conducted using sterling exchange. In other historical periods, other invoicing conventions have been widely practiced.[1] This study does not investigate why a particular invoicing convention is adopted, but rather explores the time series behavior of the exchange rate, interest rates and prices under different specifications for the finance of international trade. The objective here is to determine whether the way in which trade is financed matters for the time series behavior of interest rates and exchange rates in a two country world with seasonal endowment fluctuations, fixed money stocks and flexible exchange rates.

It is shown here that the time series behavior of prices, interest rates and exchange rates depends upon which currency is used for international trade. If all international trade is conducted using the seller's currency, exchange rates, interest rates and the domestic currency price of goods fluctuate seasonally. If all international trade is conducted in the buyer's currency, prices of goods in both countries fluctuate seasonally, but the exchange rate between the two currencies and the nominal interest rate on foreign bonds are constant. If all international trade is conducted in the currency of the country with constant output (foreign currency in this model), prices in both countries fluctuate seasonally, and exchange rates and interest rates are constant. The level of prices and exchange rates is indeterminate.

The next section of this chapter presents a general description of the model. The following three sections derive and discuss the results for each version of the model: the seller's currency version (in which all international trade is financed using the seller's currency), the buyer's currency version (in which all international trade is financed using the buyer's currency), and the foreign currency finance version (in which all international trade is financed using foreign currency). The chapter concludes with a summary and interpretation of the results derived in these three versions of the model.

DESCRIPTION OF MODEL[2]

The model developed here is a two country, representative agent, utility maximizing model with cash-in-advance constraints. It draws upon the framework used by Kimbrough (1986). There is no uncertainty in this model. The world consists of two countries, the domestic (or home) country and the foreign country, each represented by a single agent. Each country receives a fixed endowment of the single perishable world good every period. The endowment stream is owned by the agent who lives in the country.[3] The endowment stream of the domestic country fluctuates seasonally, but the endowment stream of the foreign country is constant. Seasonal fluctuations of world endowment are thus caused by the seasonal fluctuations of endowment in the home country. Domestic currency, foreign currency and a foreign-currency-denominated bond are the only assets in this model. The infinite time horizon consists of the repetition of harvest periods, defined as periods when world endowment is high, and off periods, defined as periods when world endowment is low. Each period consists of an asset market, when agents adjust holdings of money and bonds, followed by a goods market, where agents purchase goods with money. All goods must be purchased with money before they can be consumed.

The trading sequence is summarized in Figure 3-1. At the beginning of each period, agents make (receive) payments of interest and principal on bonds sold (purchased) last period. During the asset market, agents choose how to divide up their wealth among domestic

- agents make(receive) payments of interest and principle on last period's bonds	- agents trade assets to achieve desired portfolio composition - interest rates and exchange rates adjust to clear money and bond markets	-all endowments must be purchased with money held when goods market opens - prices of goods adjust to clear the goods markets	- agents receive payments for goods sold
beginning of period	ASSET MARKET	GOODS MARKET	end of period

Figure 3-1: SUMMARY OF TRADING SEQUENCE

currency, foreign currency and bonds. Each agent's wealth consists of receipts from the sale of goods last period, payments of interest and principal on bonds purchased last period, and any excess money balances carried over from the previous asset market. Interest rates and exchange rates adjust to clear the bond and money markets. Agents are allowed to borrow and lend freely using one period foreign bonds. These bonds do not represent an increase in world wealth since the bonds purchased by one agent are a liability to the other agent. They do, however, allow agents to smooth their consumption streams given seasonal fluctuations in world endowment.

The foreign bond will always dominate foreign currency as a form of holding wealth if it pays a positive nominal interest rate. As discussed more fully below, the foreign bond will dominate domestic currency as long as the nominal return on foreign bonds is greater than the rate of depreciation of the exchange rate. This condition insures that the domestic currency proceeds from converting domestic money to foreign currency, buying foreign bonds, and then converting the proceeds back to domestic currency will be greater than the initial amount of domestic currency invested. If the foreign bond always dominates both currencies as a form of holding wealth, agents will carry no excess money balances over from one period to another. In this case, an agent's demand for money balances is determined by her demand for goods and by the conventions concerning which currency can be used to purchase endowments.

After the asset market closes, the goods market opens. Goods must be purchased with money before they can be consumed. Agents receive cash payments from the sale of goods at the end of the period, after the goods market has closed. This insures that all goods must be sold for money which is held before the goods market opens. Three different specifications for the sale of internationally traded goods are compared. In the first version of the model, international trade is conducted using the seller's currency. The home country sells all its goods for domestic currency, but uses two currencies to purchase goods: domestic currency is used to purchase home endowment and foreign currency is used to purchase foreign endowment. The foreign country sells all its endowment for foreign currency, but must use foreign currency to purchase foreign endowment and domestic currency to purchase goods from the home country. In the second version of the model, all international trade is conducted using the buyer's currency. The domestic agent purchases all goods using domestic currency, but receives foreign currency for the goods it exports. In a similar fashion, the foreign agent purchases all goods using foreign currency, but sells her goods to the home country for domestic currency . In the third version of the model, all international trade is conducted using foreign currency. The domestic agent purchases home endowment using domestic currency and exports goods in exchange for foreign currency. The foreign agent buys and sells all goods for foreign currency.

In all versions of the model, each representative agent maximizes lifetime utility subject to budget and cash-in-advance constraints. Since goods are nonstorable, agents must consume all endowment in the period in which it is received. Agents have identical utility functions of the form:

$$U = \sum_{t=0}^{\infty} \beta^t [U(c_t)],$$

where c denotes consumption, β is a discount factor equal to $1/(1+\rho)$, and ρ is the agent's marginal rate of time preference. For ease in solving the model, it is assumed that the utility function is the simple one good logarithmic utility function shown below:

$$U = \sum_{t=0}^{\infty} \beta^t [\ln(c_t)], \quad (1)$$ [4]

Agents maximize utility subject to two sets of constraints. The first set of constraints is a set of budget constraints. At the end of the asset market prior to the opening of the goods market in any period, the sum of receipts from the sale of goods last period plus interest and principal payments for bonds purchased last period must equal the sum of current period money balances plus current period bond holdings. The bonds in this model are one period foreign-currency-denominated bonds which pay a nominal interest rate of r_t. This specification of the budget constraints assumes that the cash-in-advance constraints are binding. As explained above, agents will not carry over any money balances from the previous period if bonds dominate money as a store of value.

The second set of constraints is a set of cash-in-advance constraints which dictate that all goods must be purchased with money. The exact form of these constraints depends upon which currency is used to purchase internationally traded goods.[5] In the seller's currency version of the model, the domestic agent's purchases of home endowment must be less than or equal to the stock of domestic currency which the agent holds when the goods market opens. The domestic agent's purchases of foreign goods must be less than or equal to foreign money balances. For the foreign agent, these constraints say that her consumption of foreign endowment must be less than or equal to her foreign money balances and that her consumption of home endowment must be less than or equal to her domestic money balances. In the buyer's currency version of the model, each agent uses her own country's currency to purchase all goods. In the version where all international trade is conducted using foreign currency, the domestic agent's cash-in-advance constraints are the same as for the seller's currency model and the foreign agent's cash-in-advance constraints are the same as for the buyer's currency model.

Conditions for equilibrium in the goods, money and bond markets complete the model. Equilibrium in the home and foreign money markets requires that the sum of the stocks of each currency held by each agent is equal to the world stock of each currency. These money market equilibrium conditions are shown below:

(2)
$$M_{ht} + \tilde{M}_{ht} = M_H$$
$$M_{ft} + \tilde{M}_{ft} = M_F$$

where M_H is the stock of home country currency, M_F is the stock of foreign country currency, M_{ht} is the domestic agent's demand for home currency, $\tilde{M}_{ht}$ is the foreign agent's demand for home currency, M_{ft} is the domestic agent's demand for foreign currency and $\tilde{M}_{ft}$ is the foreign agent's demand for foreign currency. The stocks of money, M_H and M_F, are fixed. Goods market equilibrium requires that prices adjust so that the world endowment (y_t) equals the sum of domestic consumption (c_t) and foreign consumption ($\tilde{c}_t$) every period:

(3)
$$c_t + \tilde{c}_t = \bar{y}_t$$

World endowment is equal to the sum of domestic endowment (y_t) plus foreign endowment ($\tilde{y}_t$) every period: $y_t = y_t + \tilde{y}_t$. Bond market equilibrium requires that the sum of domestic bond holdings (b_t) and foreign bond holdings ($\tilde{b}_t$) must be zero each period:

(4) $$b_t + \tilde{b}_t = 0.$$

Endowment streams are the only source of net world wealth in this model.

In the next section, the steady state solutions to all three version of the model are derived. The solutions to the utility maximization problems of the two representative agents give consumption, money and bond demands in terms of endowment streams, prices, exchange rates and interest rates. These demands, together with market equilibrium conditions and goods market arbitrage conditions, imply solutions for levels of consumption, bond holdings, prices, exchange rates and interest rates in terms of endowment streams and the marginal rate of time preference.

SELLER'S CURRENCY MODEL

In the seller's currency version of the model, all goods must be sold using the currency of the country of origin. All home country endowment must be sold for domestic currency and all foreign country endowment must be sold for foreign currency. Given this convention for transactions and assuming the logarithmic utility function specified in (1), it can be shown that domestic currency prices, interest rates and exchange rates will fluctuate seasonally, but that foreign currency prices are constant. For both agents, the ratio of consumption in the two periods is equal to the ratio of world endowment. The pattern of price and exchange rate fluctuations follows directly from the conditions for goods market and money market equilibrium. Since all domestic endowment must be sold for domestic currency and all foreign endowment must be sold for foreign currency, the price level is simply equal to the money stock of the country divided by its endowment. Seasonal fluctuations of domestic endowments cause seasonal fluctuations in domestic prices. Foreign prices are constant because the foreign endowment stream is constant. In order for goods market equilibrium to be satisfied, agents must be indifferent between consuming the goods of either country. This implies the goods market arbitrage condition $p_t = e_t \tilde{p}_t$. Since foreign prices are constant, fluctuations in the domestic price level cause fluctuations in the exchange rate. The nominal interest rate on foreign bonds is low during harvest periods and high during off periods in this version of the model. Given the constant foreign price level, these fluctuations in the interest rate reflect fluctuations in the opportunity cost of saving. During the harvest period when output is high, consumption is high and the marginal utility of consumption is lower than it is during the off period. Given a constant rate of time preference, the opportunity cost of saving (consumption foregone) is lower during the harvest period, and a lower level of the interest rate is consistent with market equilibrium.

The solution to this model is derived below. First, the maximization problems of the two agents are presented and discussed, and the agents' consumption and bond demands are derived. This is a perfect foresight model: it is assumed that individual agents know and take as given the time path of prices, exchange rates and interest rates. Next, conditions for money and goods market equilibrium are used to solve explicitly for the level of prices, exchange rates and interest rates in terms of endowment streams and the marginal rate of time preference. A stationary solution to this model is assumed and shown to be consistent with individual agent utility maximization and market equilibrium. Since endowment streams fluctuate seasonally in a stable pattern over time, it is assumed that prices, exchange rates, interest rates, consumption and bond holdings will fluctuate seasonally as well.

The domestic and foreign agent problems and first order conditions for the case where all international trade is conducted using the seller's currency are shown in Table 3-1.[6] Both agents maximize utility subject to budget constraints and cash-in-advance constraints. There is only one good in this model, and it is assumed that the two agents have the same logarithmic utility function and the same rate of time preference shown above in equation (1).

Each agent sells all her endowment for her own country currency. Each agent is free to buy the endowment of either country but must pay for the goods using the seller's currency. The budget constraints implied by these conditions are shown for the home agent in (5) and for the foreign agent in (5*) below:

(5) $$M_{ht} + e_t M_{ft} + e_t b_t = p_{t-1} y_{t-1} + e_t (1 + r_{t-1}) b_{t-1}$$

(5*) $$\tilde{M}_{ht} + e_t \tilde{M}_{ft} + e_t \tilde{b}_t = e_t \tilde{p}_{t-1} \tilde{y}_{t-1} + e_t \left(1 + \tilde{r}_{t-1}\right) \tilde{b}_{t-1}$$

where $M_h(\tilde{M}_h)$ is the stock of home country currency held by the home (foreign) country agent, $M_f(\tilde{M}_f)$ is the stock of foreign country currency held by the home (foreign) country agent, e is the domestic currency price of a unit foreign currency, $p(\tilde{p})$ is the home (foreign) currency price of goods, $b(\tilde{b})$ is the domestic (foreign) agent's stock of foreign-currency-denominated bonds, and r is the nominal interest rate on one period foreign-currency-denominated bonds. These budget constraints say that the current domestic currency value of income from the sale of goods last period plus the current period value of bonds purchased (or sold) last period must equal the sum of domestic and foreign money balances and bonds. The specification of the budget constraint shown in (5) and (5*) assumes that cash-in-advance constraints are binding: no money balances in excess of goods purchased are carried over from one period to the next.

In this version of the model, agents may purchase goods from either country and may therefore need stocks of both currencies in order to buy those goods. This gives rise to the following set of cash-in-advance constraints. For the domestic agent, we have:

(6) $$M_{ht} \geq p_t c_{ht}$$ $$M_{ft} \geq \tilde{p}_t c_{ft}.$$

For the foreign agent, we have:

(6*) $$\tilde{M}_{ht} \geq p_t \tilde{c}_{ht}$$ $$\tilde{M}_{ft} \geq \tilde{p}_t \tilde{c}_{ft}.$$

In a world with no transactions costs where a consumer can buy the same good using two different currencies, the following "buyer's" goods market arbitrage condition must be satisfied in order to insure equilibrium in the good's market:

(7) $$p_t = e_t \tilde{p}_t.$$ [7]

This condition says that buyers must be indifferent between purchasing goods in the two markets. If this condition did not hold, buyers would demand goods only from the country with the lower price. This would cause excess demand for goods in the lower price country and excess supply of goods in the higher price country, and would trigger an adjustment of prices such that (7) held. This goods market arbitrage condition is assumed to hold in the specification of the cash-in-advance constraints in the two problems shown in Table 3-1. In any period, the domestic agent can consume goods from either country. Using the goods market arbitrage condition (7), the total value of consumption purchases in any period can easily be shown to equal total consumption times the domestic price level:

$$p_t c_{ht} + e_t \tilde{p}_t c_{ft} = p_t c_t .$$

Similarly, the total value of consumption by the foreign agent is equal to total consumption times the domestic price level:

$$p_t \tilde{c}_{ht} + e_t \tilde{p}_{ft} \tilde{c}_{ft} = p_t \tilde{c}_t .$$

The consumption demands of each agent are thus for consumption of the one available good, but not for the good of a specific country. The two cash-in-advance constraints shown above for each agent can be combined into one condition which says that the domestic currency value of total money balances must be greater than or equal to the domestic currency value of consumption for each agent:

(8) $$M_{ht} + e_t M_{ft} \geq p_t c_t$$

(8*) $$\tilde{M}_{ht} + e_t \tilde{M}_{ft} \geq p_t \tilde{c}_t$$

The first order conditions on money holdings (2^h, 3^h, 2^f, 3^f) indicate that the marginal utility of wealth (λ_t) is equal to the marginal utility of money (μ_t) every period.[8] The remaining four first order conditions provide four equations to solve for four unknowns each period: the demand for consumption, the demand for bonds, the demand for money and the marginal utility of wealth/money, μ_t ($=\lambda_t$). Individual agents take prices, exchange rates, interest rates and endowments as given.

The bond market first order conditions (4^h, 4^f) are Euler equations: first order difference equations which describe how the marginal utility of wealth evolves over time. The solution for the domestic agent is shown below. The solution for the foreign agent is analogous. Both agents face the same exchange rates and interest rates but their initial conditions will be different because their endowment streams differ. Although the ratio of marginal utilities in two adjacent periods is equal for the two agents, the levels of marginal utilities could (and will) differ.

The solution to each difference equation is by iteration, where it is assumed that exchange rates and interest rates fluctuate in a recurring pattern over time. Consider the following version of (4^h):

$$\mu_{t+1} = \frac{e_t}{e_{t+1}(1+r_t)}\mu_t.$$

Let $e_t = e$ and $r_t = r$ for even periods ($t = 0, 2, 4, \ldots$). Let $e_t = e'$ and $r_t = r'$ for odd periods (t = 1, 3, 5, . . .). This implies the following values of μ for the first four periods of the world:

when t = 0,

$$\mu_1 = \frac{e}{e'(1+r)}\mu_0;$$

when t = 1,

$$\mu_2 = \frac{e'}{e(1+r')}\mu_1$$

$$\mu_2 = \frac{e'}{e(1+r')}\frac{e}{e'(1+r)}\mu_0$$

$$\mu_2 = \frac{1}{(1+r')(1+r)}\mu_0$$

when t = 2,

$$\mu_3 = \frac{e}{e'(1+r)}\mu_2;$$
$$\mu_3 = \frac{e}{e'(1+r)}\frac{1}{(1+r')(1+r)}\mu_0$$
$$\mu_3 = \frac{e}{e'}\frac{1}{(1+r')(1+r)^2}\mu_0$$

when t = 3,

$$\mu_4 = \frac{e'}{e(1+r')}\mu_3;$$
$$\mu_4 = \frac{e'}{e(1+r')}\frac{e}{e'}\frac{1}{(1+r')(1+r)^2}\mu_0$$
$$\mu_4 = \frac{1}{(1+r')^2(1+r)^2}\mu_0$$

By observation, the marginal utility of wealth during even periods is:

$$\mu_t = \left(\frac{1}{(1+r')^{\frac{t}{2}}(1+r)^{\frac{t}{2}}}\right)\mu_0 \text{ for } t=2,4,\ldots$$

The marginal utility of wealth during odd periods is:

$$\mu_t = \frac{e}{e'}\left(\frac{1}{(1+r')^{\frac{t-1}{2}}(1+r)^{\frac{t+1}{2}}}\right)\mu_0 \text{ for } t=1,3,\ldots$$

Let $p_t = p$ and $c_t = c$ for even periods ($t = 0, 2, 4, \ldots$). Let $p_t = p'$ and $c_t = c'$ for odd periods ($t = 1, 3, 5, \ldots$). We can now use the first order condition on consumption (1^h) to solve for μ_0:

$$\mu_0 = \frac{\beta^0}{p_0 c_0} = \frac{1}{pc}.$$

Using the results for μ_t (for $t = 2, 4, \ldots$) and μ_0 together with (1^h), we have the result that during even periods:

$$\beta^t = \left(\frac{1}{(1+r')^{\frac{t}{2}} (1+r)^{\frac{t}{2}}} \right).$$

When $t = 2$, the value of β can be found by substituting into the above equation:

(9) $$\beta = \left(\frac{1}{(1+r')^{\frac{1}{2}} (1+r)^{\frac{1}{2}}} \right).$$

Now let t continue to be even, such that $t+1$ is odd. Using the same conditions during odd periods, we have the result that:

$$\beta^{t+1} = \frac{e}{e'} \left(\frac{1}{(1+r')^{\frac{t}{2}} (1+r)^{\frac{t}{2}+1}} \right) \frac{p'c'}{pc}.$$

Using these results for β, β^t and β^{t+1}, we can show that:

$$\beta = \left(\frac{1}{(1+r')^{\frac{1}{2}} (1+r)^{\frac{1}{2}}} \right) = \frac{1}{(1+r)} \frac{ep'c'}{e'pc}.$$

This implies the following ratio of consumption levels for domestic agents in the harvest and off periods:

(10) $$\frac{c'}{c}=\left(\frac{1+r}{1+r'}\right)^{\frac{1}{2}}\frac{e'p}{ep'}.$$

Using the same procedure for the foreign agent problem, we find that the ratio of consumption levels for the foreign agent is the same as for the domestic agent:

$$\frac{\tilde{c}'}{\tilde{c}}=\left(\frac{1+r}{1+r'}\right)^{\frac{1}{2}}\frac{e'p}{ep'}.$$

Using the goods market arbitrage condition, we can rewrite the condition for the foreign agent using foreign prices:

(10*) $$\frac{\tilde{c}'}{\tilde{c}}=\left(\frac{1+r}{1+r'}\right)^{\frac{1}{2}}\frac{\tilde{p}}{\tilde{p}'}.$$

The additional information needed to solve for the levels of consumption comes from the agent's budget constraint and stationarity conditions.

If cash-in-advance constraints are binding, as will be shown below, the cash-in-advance constraint can be substituted into the budget constraint each period:

$$p_{t-1}y_{t-1}+e_t\left(\left(1+r_{t-1}\right)b_{t-1}-b_t\right)-p_tc_t=0$$

This budget constraint says that in any period the value of income from goods sold last period plus the current period value of bonds purchased (or sold) last period must be equal to current period bond holdings plus the value of current period consumption. A stationary solution to this model implies that an agent's consumption can fluctuate seasonally, but can not increase or decrease without bound over time.[9] No agent in this world can continually accumulate debt to finance consumption. Bonds are short term debt instruments used to reallocate consumption between agents in the two countries during harvest and off periods. The sum total of bonds in the world at any point in time is zero. The implication of stationarity is that over any 2 period cycle, the present discounted value of endowments must equal the present discounted value of consumption. Using no primes to denote even periods and primes to denote odd periods, the two period budget constraint is:

$$pc + \frac{1}{1+r}p'c' = p'y' + \frac{1}{1+r}py. \tag{11}$$

The form of this two period budget constraint takes account of the trading sequence specified in the model. Endowments during the off period are used as income for the purchase of goods in the harvest period. Endowments during the harvest period are used as income for the purchase of goods during the off period. Equations (10) and (11) enable us to solve for the levels of consumption in the harvest and off periods in terms of prices, exchange rates and interest rates:

$$\begin{aligned} c &= \frac{e}{p}\left(\frac{1+r}{1+r'}\right)^{\frac{1}{2}}\left(\frac{(1+r)p'y' + py}{e(1+r)^{\frac{1}{2}}(1+r')^{\frac{1}{2}} + e'}\right) \\ c' &= \frac{e'}{p'}\left(\frac{(1+r)p'y' + py}{e(1+r)^{\frac{1}{2}}(1+r')^{\frac{1}{2}} + e'}\right) \end{aligned} \tag{12}$$

The home agent's bond demands during the harvest and off periods can be found by substituting the consumption demands back into the one period budget constraint.

Foreign agent consumption demands can be derived using exactly the same procedure as was used to derive home agent consumption demands. The form of the consumption demands is very similar, as can be seen by comparing (12) with (12*):

(12*)
$$\tilde{c} = \frac{e}{p}\left(\frac{1+r'}{1+r}\right)^{\frac{1}{2}}\left(\frac{(1+r)e\tilde{p}'\tilde{y}' + e'\tilde{p}\tilde{y}}{e(1+r)^{\frac{1}{2}}(1+r')^{\frac{1}{2}} + e'}\right)$$
$$\tilde{c}' = \frac{e'}{p'}\left(\frac{(1+r)e\tilde{p}'\tilde{y}' + e'\tilde{p}\tilde{y}}{e(1+r)^{\frac{1}{2}}(1+r')^{\frac{1}{2}} + e'}\right)$$

Foreign consumption depends upon foreign endowments. Foreign currency prices, rather than domestic currency prices appear in the numerators because in the seller's currency model foreign goods are sold for foreign currency.

The binding cash-in-advance constraints and money market equilibrium conditions can be used to solve for home and foreign currency prices in the two periods. Since all home endowment is sold for home currency and agents hold no excess money balances, home country prices depend only on the stock of home currency, M_H, and the level of endowment in the home country:

(13)
$$p = \frac{M_H}{y}$$
$$p' = \frac{M_H}{y'}.$$

The ratio of domestic currency prices in the two periods depends only on the ratio of endowments in the two periods because the stock of currency is assumed to be fixed:

(14)
$$\frac{p}{p'} = \frac{y'}{y}.$$

Domestic currency prices will be lower during harvest season and higher during the off season.

The foreign currency price of goods is constant. All foreign endowment must be sold for foreign currency. Since the stock of foreign currency is fixed and the foreign country endowment is fixed, the price of foreign goods is constant:

(15) $$\tilde{p} = \tilde{p}' = \frac{M_F}{\tilde{y}}.$$

The exchange rate is the domestic price of foreign currency. In this version of the model, the "buyer's" goods market arbitrage condition explained above determines the exchange rate:

$$e_t = \frac{p_t}{\tilde{p}_t}.$$

Using the results for p_t and $\tilde{p}_t$ found above we have:

(16) $$e = \frac{M_H}{M_F}\frac{\tilde{y}}{y} \text{ and } e' = \frac{M_H}{M_F}\frac{\tilde{y}}{\tilde{y}'}.$$

As long as the foreign endowment is constant, the ratio of exchange rates in the two periods will be equal to the inverse of ratio of endowments:

(17) $$\frac{e}{e'} = \frac{y'}{y}.$$

The ratio of exchange rates is shown by equations (14) and (17) to be equal to the ratio of domestic prices in this model.

Goods market equilibrium requires that the sum of domestic and foreign consumption equals world endowment each period:

(18) $$c + \tilde{c} = \bar{y} = y + \tilde{y}$$
$$c' + \tilde{c}' = \bar{y}' = y' + \tilde{y}'.$$

Substitution of consumption demands (12, 12*), prices (13, 15) and exchange rates (16) into the goods market equilibrium conditions (18) gives us the following result linking interest rate fluctuations and fluctuations in world endowment:

(19) $$\left(\frac{1+r'}{1+r}\right)^{\frac{1}{2}} = \frac{\bar{y}}{\bar{y}'}.$$

This says that interest rates will be high during off (odd) periods and low during harvest (even) periods. Condition (19) can be used with condition (9) linking β and interest rates to solve explicitly for the level of the interest rate each period:

(20)
$$r = \frac{\bar{y}' - \beta\bar{y}}{\beta\bar{y}}$$
$$r' = \frac{\bar{y} - \beta\bar{y}'}{\beta\bar{y}'}.$$

Interest rates will be positive as long as $\bar{y} > \beta\bar{y}'$ and $\bar{y}' > \beta\bar{y}$. Since $\beta = (1/(1+\rho))$ where ρ is the marginal rate of time preference, interest rates will be positive as long as seasonal fluctuations in endowment expressed in percentage terms are less than the marginal rate of time preference:

$$\rho > \frac{\bar{y}' - \bar{y}}{\bar{y}} \text{ and } \rho > \frac{\bar{y} - \bar{y}'}{\bar{y}'}$$

When foreign endowment is constant, the above expression is equivalent to:

$$\rho > \frac{y' - y}{y} \text{ and } \rho > \frac{y - y'}{y'}.$$

The results of this model will be valid as long as seasonal fluctuations in output are not "too large", where "too large" is defined with respect to the marginal rate of time preference.

Positive nominal interest rates on foreign bonds insure that foreign bonds will always dominate foreign currency as a form of holding wealth. This means that foreign currency cash-in-advance constraints will always be binding. An additional condition is necessary to insure that foreign bonds will always dominate domestic currency as a form of holding wealth. Agents deciding whether to hold domestic currency or foreign bonds must compare the return from holding domestic currency to the return from converting domestic currency to foreign currency, buying foreign denominated bonds, and then converting the proceeds back to domestic currency. If the domestic currency proceeds from buying foreign bonds are greater than the initial investment of domestic currency, then foreign bonds dominate domestic currency as a form of holding wealth. In order for foreign bonds to dominate domestic currency, the following conditions must hold:

$$\frac{e'}{e}(1+r)>1, \text{ or } r>\frac{e-e'}{e'} \text{ during the harvest period}$$

and $$\frac{e}{e'}(1+r')>1, \text{ or } r'>\frac{e'-e}{e} \text{ during the off period}$$

The nominal interest rate on foreign bonds must be greater than the rate of depreciation of the exchange rate when the exchange rate next period is used as the base for calculating the expected (actual) rate of depreciation this period. After substitution for exchange rates and interest rates, we can rewrite the above condition as a condition on endowment streams and the marginal rate of time preference:

$$\rho>\frac{\tilde{y}}{y}\frac{y'-y}{\bar{y}'} \text{ and } \rho>\frac{\tilde{y}}{y'}\frac{y-y'}{\bar{y}}.$$

These conditions say that not only must seasonal fluctuations in endowment not be too large relative to world endowment, but also that foreign endowment must not be too large relative to domestic country endowment. This additional constraint derives from the fact that domestic currency price fluctuations (and hence exchange rate fluctuations) will be larger relative to interest rates when domestic output is small relative to world output.[10]

Assuming that the pattern of endowments over time is such that cash-in-advance constraints are always binding and that interest rates are always positive, we can solve explicitly for the level of consumption and bonds each period by substituting results for prices (13, 15), exchange rates (16) and interest rates (20) back into consumption and bond demand functions. The results for consumption are summarized below:

(21)
$$c = \left(\frac{\bar{y}' + \beta\bar{y}}{y' + \beta y} \right) \frac{yy'}{\bar{y}'}$$
$$c' = \left(\frac{\bar{y}' + \beta\bar{y}}{y' + \beta y} \right) \frac{yy'}{\bar{y}}$$

(21*)
$$\tilde{c} = \left(\frac{y'\bar{y}' + \beta y\bar{y}}{y' + \beta y} \right) \frac{\tilde{y}}{\bar{y}'}$$
$$\tilde{c}' = \left(\frac{y'\bar{y}' + \beta y\bar{y}}{y' + \beta y} \right) \frac{\tilde{y}}{\bar{y}}$$

The ratio of consumption in the two periods is equal to the ratio of world endowments for both agents:

$$\frac{c}{c'} = \frac{\tilde{c}}{\tilde{c}'} = \frac{\bar{y}}{\bar{y}'}.$$

Although the final distribution of world endowment between the two agents depends upon the relative size and the timing of their endowment streams, both agents are able to smooth consumption such that the fluctuations in their consumption paths reflect the fluctuations in world endowments.

Domestic and foreign agent equilibrium bond holdings are shown below:

(22)
$$b = \frac{M_F}{\bar{y}'} \frac{\beta}{\beta^2 - 1} \frac{(y' - y)(y' - \beta^2 y)}{y' + \beta y}$$
$$b' = \frac{M_F}{\bar{y}} \frac{\beta^2}{\beta^2 - 1} \frac{(y' - y)^2}{y' + \beta y}$$

$$\tilde{b} = \frac{M_F}{\bar{y}'}\frac{\beta}{\beta^2 - 1}\frac{(y'-y)(\beta^2 y - y')}{y' + \beta y}$$

(22*)

$$\tilde{b}' = \frac{M_F}{\bar{y}}\frac{\beta^2}{\beta^2 - 1}\frac{(y'-y)(y - y')}{y' + \beta y}$$

The role of bonds in this model is to provide agents with a short term debt instrument which enables them to smooth their consumption over time. It is easily seen from the solutions given above that the sum total of domestic and foreign bonds in any period is zero. The level of bond holdings of each agent depends upon endowment streams and the marginal rate of time preference. The solution requires that b', the bond holdings of the domestic agent during odd periods, be negative regardless of the nature of the endowment stream. Domestic agents always borrow money by selling bonds during the odd periods and foreign agents always lend money by buying bonds during the odd periods.

What matters for consumption smoothing, however, is not the level of bond holdings, but rather the change in the net value of bond holdings. Insights into whether agents save or dissave in a particular period can be gained by examining the budget constraints. The budget constraint says that the difference between the income from the sale of goods last period and the value of consumption this period must be equal to the value of the change in bond holdings:

$$p'y' - pc = e(b - (1+r')b') = \beta M_H \frac{\bar{y}(y - y')}{\bar{y}'(y' + \beta y)}$$

$$py - p'c' = e'(b' - (1+r)b) = M_H \frac{\bar{y}(y' - y)}{\bar{y}(y' + \beta y)}$$

If y is a harvest period and y' is an off period, it can easily be seen that the domestic agent's net asset position improves during the harvest season and worsens during the off season. The conditions above can thus be interpreted as indicating that if y is a harvest period and y' is an off period, the domestic agent saves during the harvest period and dissaves during the off period. The opposite is true for the foreign agent.

Summary of Results for the Seller's Currency Model

In the seller's currency version of the model, exchange rates, interest rates and domestic currency prices all fluctuate seasonally. Foreign currency prices are constant. Price levels in each currency are determined by the ratio of the stock of money to the size of endowment because all home endowment is sold for domestic currency, all foreign endowment is sold for foreign currency, and the velocity of circulation in a simple cash-in-advance constraint model is unitary, . Foreign prices are constant because foreign endowment is constant. Domestic prices fluctuate inversely with endowment: prices are low during the harvest season and high during the off season. The buyer's goods market arbitrage condition, which says that buyers must be indifferent between buying in the two markets, determines exchange rates as the ratio of the domestic currency price to the foreign currency price each period. Exchange rates follow the same pattern as domestic prices: the domestic currency price of foreign currency is lowest during the harvest season and highest during the off season. The nominal interest rate on foreign bonds also fluctuates seasonally and is lowest during the harvest season and highest during the off season.

BUYER'S CURRENCY MODEL

In the buyer's currency model, all goods must be sold using the currency of the agent who purchases the good. This means that domestic agents hold only domestic currency to purchase goods and foreign agents hold only foreign money to purchase goods. Agents may sell goods in both markets, however, and therefore might receive both currencies in receipt for goods sold. In order for goods market equilibrium to be satisfied, agents must be indifferent between selling goods in either market. The trading sequence dictates that sellers can not convert one currency into another until the next asset market. This implies a slightly different goods market arbitrage condition in the buyer's currency model:

$$p_t = e_{t+1}\tilde{p}_t \,.$$

In a world with this transactions technology and goods market arbitrage condition, both foreign and domestic currency prices fluctuate inversely with the consumption of the foreign and the domestic agent. Given a simple one good logarithmic utility function, it is possible to show that the ratio of harvest to off period consumption for both agents is equal to the ratio of world endowment in the harvest period to world endowment in the off period. Thus, price levels in both countries fluctuate inversely with world endowment. The exchange rate is constant over time, and the nominal interest rate on foreign bonds is constant and equal to the marginal rate of time preference.

The solution to the buyer's currency version of the model is similar to the solution to the seller's currency version of the model described in the last section. Agents' consumption and bond demands are derived from their utility maximization problems. Goods and money market equilibrium conditions can then be used to solve for the level of prices, exchange rates and interest rates. The solutions to the two models differ because of the difference in transactions technology and goods market arbitrage conditions.

The domestic and foreign agent problems and first order conditions for the case where all international trade is conducted using the buyer's currency are shown in Table 3-2.[11] The utility function is the same simple one good logarithmic utility function used in the seller's currency version of the model, but the budget constraints and cash-in-advance constraints differ because all purchases are made using the buyer's currency.

The domestic agent will never hold foreign currency to purchase goods in this version of the model: M_{ft} = 0 all periods. The domestic agent does, however, sell goods for both currencies in this version of the model. This has implications for the budget constraint, which can be written as:

(23) $$p_{t-1}c_{ht-1} + e_t\tilde{p}_{t-1}\tilde{c}_{ht-1} + e_t\big((1+r_{t-1})b_{t-1} - b_t\big) - M_{ht} = 0$$

Kimbrough (1986: 12-13) argues that if seller's are profit maximizers and internationally traded goods are invoiced in the buyer's currency, a seller will sell goods in the two countries only if the returns from selling in the two markets are equal. The seller must be indifferent between selling a good for domestic currency and selling the good for foreign currency. Since the currency obtained from selling goods this period can not be used to purchase goods until next period, the seller will be indifferent only if the domestic currency price of the good is equal to the foreign currency price of the good times next period's exchange rate:

$$p_t = e_{t+1}\tilde{p}_t.$$

If this did not hold, both sellers would sell all endowment to only one agent. The other agent would starve, which is inconsistent with goods market equilibrium. Using this goods market arbitrage condition, the budget constraint shown in (23) can be rewritten as:

$$p_{t-1}y_{t-1} + e_t\left((1+r_{t-1})b_{t-1} - b_t\right) - M_{ht} = 0 \tag{24}$$

This is the form of the budget constraint shown in Table 3-2.

Because the domestic agent never uses foreign currency to purchase goods, the cash-in-advance constraint is :

$$M_{ht} \geq p_t c_t. \tag{25}$$

In the seller's currency version of the model, the total value of the domestic agent's money holdings was determined, but not the individual domestic and foreign currency components. In this version of the model, the domestic agent holds only domestic currency. In this case, domestic currency holdings are determined by consumption of the domestic agent.

Once the binding cash-in-advance constraints are substituted into the budget constraint, the domestic agent problem in the buyer's currency version of the model is identical to the domestic agent problem in the seller's currency version of the model. The domestic agent's bond and consumption demands are therefore the same as in the previous version and are shown by the equations in (12) above.

The foreign agent buys all goods for foreign currency and has no incentive to hold domestic currency, but sells goods for both domestic and foreign currencies. In this problem, the foreign agent budget constraint is:

$$p_{t-1}c_{ft-1} + e_t\tilde{p}_{t-1}\tilde{c}_{t-1} + e_t\left((1+r_{t-1})\tilde{b}_{t-1} - \tilde{b}_t - \tilde{M}_{ft}\right) = 0. \tag{26}$$

Given the buyer's currency goods market arbitrage condition explained above, the budget constraint becomes:

$$(27) \qquad p_{t-1}\tilde{y}_{t-1} + e_t\left((1+r_{t-1})\tilde{b}_{t-1} - \tilde{b}_t - \tilde{M}_{ft}\right) = 0.$$

This is the form shown in Table 3-2.

Because the foreign agent never uses domestic currency to purchase goods, the cash-in-advance constraint is:

$$(28) \qquad \tilde{M}_{ft} \geq \tilde{p}_t\tilde{c}_t.$$

The foreign agent only holds foreign currency in this version of the model; domestic currency holding always equal zero. If the cash-in-advance constraint is binding, the foreign currency holdings of the foreign agent are determined by consumption of the foreign agent. Foreign agent consumption demands as a function of prices, interest rates and exchange rates become:

$$(29) \qquad \begin{aligned} \tilde{c} &= \frac{1}{\tilde{p}}\left(\frac{1+r'}{1+r}\right)^{\frac{1}{2}}\left(\frac{(1+r)p'\tilde{y}' + p\tilde{y}}{e(1+r)^{\frac{1}{2}}(1+r')^{\frac{1}{2}} + e'}\right) \\ \tilde{c}' &= \frac{1}{\tilde{p}'}\left(\frac{(1+r)p'\tilde{y}' + p\tilde{y}}{e(1+r)^{\frac{1}{2}}(1+r')^{\frac{1}{2}} + e'}\right) \end{aligned}$$

These demands are identical to the foreign agent consumption demands shown for the seller's currency model in (12*) above when they are expressed solely in terms of foreign currency prices. The form differs when they are expressed in terms of domestic currency prices because of the different goods market arbitrage condition.

Money market equilibrium requires that money demand equals money supply for both currencies every period. As shown below, this means that price level is determined by the money stock and the level of consumption. For the domestic country, we have:

$$M_H = M_{ht} = p_t c_t.$$

The domestic price level in the even and odd periods are therefore:

(30)
$$p=\frac{M_H}{c} \text{ and } p'=\frac{M_H}{c'}.$$

The ratio of prices in the two periods is simply the inverse of the ratio of the levels of consumption by domestic agents:

$$\frac{p}{p'}=\frac{c'}{c}..$$

In a similar fashion, foreign prices are determined by the foreign money stock and the levels of foreign consumption:

(31)
$$\tilde{p}=\frac{M_F}{\tilde{c}} \text{ and } \tilde{p}'=\frac{M_F}{\tilde{c}'}.$$

The ratio of foreign prices in even and odd periods is equal to the inverse of the ratio of foreign consumption:

$$\frac{\tilde{p}}{\tilde{p}'}=\frac{\tilde{c}'}{\tilde{c}}.$$

These conditions from the money market can be combined with conditions derived from the first order conditions of the individual agents' problems to show that exchange rates and interest rates are constant. From the Euler equation and the first order condition on consumption, we know that:

$$\frac{\tilde{c}'}{\tilde{c}}=\left(\frac{1+r}{1+r'}\right)^{\frac{1}{2}}\frac{\tilde{p}}{\tilde{p}'}.$$ [12]

Since the foreign consumption ratio equals the inverse of the foreign price ratio, the above condition shows that interest rates must be constant. The ratio of consumption levels for the domestic agent shows that exchange rates must also be constant if interest rates are constant:

$$\frac{c'}{c}=\left(\frac{1+r}{1+r'}\right)^{\frac{1}{2}}\frac{e'p}{ep'}.$$

Constant exchange rates and interest rates imply that the ratio of prices in the two periods must be the same in the two countries. This in turn means that the ratio of consumption levels in the two periods is the same for the two agents:

$$\frac{\tilde{p}}{\tilde{p}'} = \frac{\tilde{c}'}{\tilde{c}} = \frac{p}{p'} = \frac{c'}{c}.$$

Since nominal interest rates are constant in the buyer's currency version of the model, $\beta = 1/(1+\rho)$. The nominal interest rate on foreign bonds is equal to the marginal rate of time preference, ρ. The real rate of return depends both on the nominal interest rate and the rate of inflation. This real rate is shown below to be low during harvest periods and high during off periods.

Goods market equilibrium conditions require that domestic and foreign currency prices fluctuate inversely with world endowment:

$$\frac{\tilde{p}}{\tilde{p}'} = \frac{p}{p'} = \frac{\bar{y}'}{\bar{y}}.$$

This additional piece of information allows us to solve for levels of consumption, bonds, prices and exchange rates explicitly in terms of endowment streams, money stocks and the marginal rate of time preference. These results are summarized below:

(32) $$c = \frac{y'\bar{y} + \beta y\bar{y}'}{(1+\beta)\bar{y}'} \text{ and } c' = \frac{y'\bar{y} + \beta y\bar{y}'}{(1+\beta)\bar{y}}$$

(32*) $$\tilde{c} = \frac{\tilde{y}(\bar{y} + \beta\bar{y}')}{(1+\beta)\bar{y}'} \text{ and } \tilde{c}' = \frac{\tilde{y}(\bar{y} + \beta\bar{y}')}{(1+\beta)\bar{y}}$$

(33) $$p = M_H\left(\frac{(1+\beta)\bar{y}'}{y'\bar{y} + \beta y\bar{y}'}\right) \text{ and } p' = M_H\left(\frac{(1+\beta)\bar{y}}{y'\bar{y} + \beta y\bar{y}'}\right)$$

(33*) $$\tilde{p} = M_F\left(\frac{(1+\beta)\bar{y}'}{\tilde{y}(\bar{y} + \beta\bar{y}')}\right) \text{ and } \tilde{p}' = M_F\left(\frac{(1+\beta)\bar{y}}{\tilde{y}(\bar{y} + \beta\bar{y}')}\right)$$

(34) $$e = e' = \frac{M_H}{M_F}\left(\frac{\tilde{y}(\bar{y} + \beta\bar{y}')}{y'\bar{y} + \beta y\bar{y}'}\right)$$

(35) $$b = \beta M_F \frac{y' - y}{\bar{y} + \beta \bar{y}'} \text{ and } b' = 0$$

(35*) $$\tilde{b} = \beta M_F \frac{y - y'}{\bar{y} + \beta \bar{y}'} \text{ and } \tilde{b}' = 0.$$

The solution for consumption levels given in (32) and (32*) show that the ratio of consumption levels is equal to the ratio of world endowment for both agents:

$$\frac{c}{c'} = \frac{\tilde{c}}{\tilde{c}'} = \frac{\bar{y}}{\bar{y}'}.$$

The solutions for bonds, given in (35) and (35*) show that in this version of the model bonds are drawn only during even periods. This result differs from the seller's currency version of the model. In that version, bonds were drawn every period. There is not a simple intuitive explanation of this difference. In this buyer's currency version of the model, the foreign country is a short term lender during even periods if even periods are harvest periods ($y > y'$). If odd periods are harvest periods ($y < y'$), then the domestic country is a short term lender during even periods. More insight concerning savings behavior can be gained by looking at the budget constraint each period. The budget constraint says that the difference between the income from the sale of goods last period and the value of consumption this period must be equal to the value of the change in bond holdings. During even periods we have:

$$p'y' - pc = e\left(b - (1+r')b'\right) = \beta M_H \frac{y(y' - y)}{y'\bar{y} + \beta y \bar{y}'}.$$

During odd periods we have:

$$py - p'c' = e'\left(b' - (1+r)b\right) = M_H \frac{y(y - y')}{y'\bar{y} + \beta y \bar{y}'}.$$

We see that if even periods are harvest periods ($y > y'$), then domestic agents dissave during harvest periods and save during the off periods. This means that income measured in terms of domestic currency from the sale of goods in the off periods is less than the domestic currency value of consumption purchases during the harvest period. The domestic agent repays the debt during the off period. During the off period income from the sale of goods during the harvest period is high.

This result is exactly the opposite of what happens in the seller's currency model. In that model the domestic agent is a net saver during the harvest period and a dissaver during the off period. The difference in results can be traced to the effects of greater seasonal fluctuations of domestic prices in the seller's currency model. In the seller's currency model, the nominal income of the domestic agent is constant because the domestic agent receives the entire stock of domestic currency for the sale of her endowment each period. Because the domestic currency price is lower during the harvest period than during the off period, her real income from the sale of goods last period is higher during the harvest period. In the buyer's currency model, domestic price fluctuations are less extreme than in the seller's model because prices fluctuate in proportion to world endowments rather than in proportion to domestic country endowments. In the buyer's currency model, the domestic currency value of income from the sale of goods last period is greater than the domestic currency value of consumption this period during off periods, not harvest periods.

In the buyer's currency model, cash-in-advance constraints are always binding for both currencies. The exchange rate is constant and the interest rate is equal to the marginal rate of time preference, which is assumed to be positive. Under these conditions, foreign bonds will always dominate both domestic and foreign money as a way of storing wealth. Although the nominal interest rate is constant, the real interest rate is lower during the harvest period and higher during the off periods. This is because the price level is low during harvest periods (expected inflation) and high during off periods (expected deflation). Thus, in the buyer's currency version of the model, we find that the real return from saving is lower during the harvest period when the marginal utility of consumption is lower and higher during the off period when the marginal utility of consumption is higher. This is the same result as in the seller's currency version of the model.

Summary of Results from Buyer's Currency Version

In this version of the model, prices in both currencies fluctuate inversely with world endowments. Prices are low during the harvest season and high during the off season. Domestic currency price fluctuations are milder than in the seller's currency version of the model, but foreign currency price fluctuations are greater. The exchange rate, determined by the seller's goods market arbitrage condition, is constant. The nominal interest rate on foreign-currency-denominated bonds is constant and equal to the marginal rate of time preference. The real rate of interest is low during harvest periods and high during off periods.

FOREIGN CURRENCY FINANCE

In the case where all international trade is conducted using foreign currency, the foreign agent uses only foreign currency for all purchases and sales, while the domestic agent uses both domestic and foreign currency if she buys and/or sells goods in both markets. An interior solution to this version of the model requires that both buyer's and seller's goods market arbitrage conditions be satisfied simultaneously. This implies that exchange rates are constant. Given constant exchange rates, the ratios of domestic and foreign currency prices in the two periods are equal to each other and inversely related to the ratio of world endowments. Nominal interest rates are constant and equal to the marginal rate of time preference. Consumption levels are the same in this version of the model as in the buyer's currency version of the model. The ratio of harvest to off period consumption is equal to the ratio of world endowment in the harvest and off periods for both agents. Although it is possible to show that foreign and domestic currency prices fluctuate seasonally, price levels and the level of the exchange rate are indeterminate. This is because agents are indifferent between consuming home and foreign goods. A whole range of price levels is consistent with equilibrium.

The solution to the model described here assumes that both buyer's and seller's goods market arbitrage conditions hold each period.[13] The foreign agent buys and sells all goods in foreign currency and is not concerned with any exchange transactions. The domestic agent, however, buys and sells in both markets. If the domestic agent is indifferent between buying goods in domestic and foreign markets and is also indifferent between selling goods in the domestic and foreign markets, then:

$$e_t = \frac{p_t}{\tilde{p}_t}, \text{ and } e_t = \frac{p_t'}{\tilde{p}_t'}.$$

This means that the ratios of domestic to foreign prices are equal in the two periods. Exchange rates must therefore be constant.

Given these goods market arbitrage conditions, the domestic agent's utility maximization problem in the foreign currency finance version of the model is identical to the domestic agent's problem in the seller's currency version of the model shown in Table 3-1. The foreign agent's problem in this version is identical to her problem in the buyer's currency version of the model shown in Table 3-2. Consumption demands for the domestic agent are given by (12) above. Consumption demands for the foreign agent are given by (29) above. These demands can be simplified by noting that e = e′.

In this model, cash-in-advance constraints for the domestic agent are the same as those in the seller's currency model, shown in (6) above. Cash-in-advance constraints for the foreign agent are the same as those for the buyer's currency model, shown in (28) above. Binding cash-in-advance constraints give rise to the following money market equilibrium conditions:

$$M_H = M_{ht} = p_t c_{ht}$$

$$M_F = M_{ft} + \tilde{M}_{ft} = \tilde{p}_t\left(c_{ft} + \tilde{c}_{ft} + \tilde{c}_{ht}\right).$$

Domestic currency prices are determined by the stock of domestic currency and domestic consumption of home endowment:

(36) $$p = \frac{M_H}{c_h} \text{ and } p' = \frac{M_H}{c_h'}.$$

Domestic currency prices fluctuate with fluctuations in domestic consumption of home endowment:

$$\frac{p}{p'} = \frac{c_h'}{c_h}.$$

Foreign currency prices are determined by the stock of foreign money, foreign endowment and foreign consumption of domestic endowment:

(37) $$\tilde{p} = \frac{M_F}{\tilde{y} + \tilde{c}_h} \text{ and } \tilde{p}' = \frac{M_F}{\tilde{y} + \tilde{c}_h'}.$$

Foreign currency prices fluctuate because of fluctuations in the foreign consumption of domestic endowment:

$$\frac{\tilde{p}}{\tilde{p}'} = \frac{\tilde{y} + \tilde{c}_h'}{\tilde{y} + \tilde{c}_h}.$$

Since exchange rates are constant, the ratio of prices in odd and even periods is the same for both currencies:

$$\frac{\tilde{p}}{\tilde{p}'} = \frac{p}{p'}.$$

This implies that:

$$\frac{c_h'}{c_h} = \frac{\tilde{y} + \tilde{c}_h'}{\tilde{y} + \tilde{c}_h}.$$

Since the sum of domestic and foreign consumption of the home endowment must be equal to home endowment each period, the ratio of domestic consumption of home endowment in the even and odd periods must be equal to the ratio of world endowments:

$$\frac{c_h'}{c_h} = \frac{\overline{y}'}{\overline{y}}.$$

This means that both domestic and foreign currency prices fluctuate inversely with world endowment:

(38) $$\frac{\tilde{p}}{\tilde{p}'} = \frac{p}{p'} = \frac{\overline{y}'}{\overline{y}}.$$

Given constant exchange rates and the relationship between prices and world endowment, goods market equilibrium requires that interest rates are constant. Interest rates are equal to the marginal rate of time preference in this version of the model, just as they were in the buyer's currency version of the model. If interest rates are constant, the ratio of consumption levels in the two periods for both agents is equal to the ratio of world endowments:

$$\frac{c}{c'} = \frac{\tilde{c}}{\tilde{c}'} = \frac{\bar{y}}{\bar{y}'}.$$

Consumption levels in this model are identical to those in the buyer's currency model and are shown by equations (32) and (32*) above.

The price level and the level of the exchange rate are indeterminate in this model.[14] Equilibrium conditions are satisfied as long as:

$$\frac{c_h}{c_h'} = \frac{c}{c'} = \frac{\tilde{c}}{\tilde{c}'} = \frac{\tilde{p}'}{\tilde{p}} = \frac{p'}{p} = \frac{\bar{y}}{\bar{y}'}$$

Given that home endowment and foreign endowment are perfect substitutes and there are no transactions costs involved with international trade, there is no unique decomposition of domestic consumption into its home endowment and foreign endowment components. Domestic prices will be high if the level of domestic consumption of home endowment is low, and will be lower if the agent consumes higher levels of home endowment. Price levels are bounded, however, by the conditions of the model. A lower limit to domestic currency prices is imposed by the size of home endowment:

$$p_t \geq \frac{M_H}{y_t}.$$

Domestic currency prices will go to infinity if domestic consumption of home endowment falls to zero, but equilibrium in the domestic money market would rule out this case. An upper limit to foreign currency prices is imposed by the size of foreign endowment. All foreign endowment must be purchased with foreign currency. If all world endowment is purchased using foreign currency (as would be the case if $c_{ht} = 0$), then foreign prices are at their lowest possible level given a fixed money stock. However, in order to have equilibrium in the domestic money market, at least some home endowment must be purchased by the domestic agent. These bounds on foreign prices are shown below:

$$\frac{M_F}{\bar{y}_t} < \tilde{p}_t \leq \frac{M_F}{\tilde{y}_t}.$$

Price level fluctuations must satisfy the conditions shown in (38), but can vary within the acceptable ranges discussed above.

Summary of Results from Foreign Currency Finance Model

In this version of the model, both domestic and foreign currency prices fluctuate inversely with world endowment. As in the buyer's currency version of the model, prices are low during the harvest season and high during the off season. Exchange rates are constant in this model. Both buyer's and seller's goods market arbitrage conditions must be satisfied simultaneously. This implies that exchange rates must remain constant. The level of prices and the exchange rate are indeterminate because agents are indifferent between consuming home endowment and foreign endowment. This yields a range of price levels that is consistent with equilibrium in the goods and money markets. The nominal interest rate is constant and equal to the marginal rate of time preference each period. The real interest rate is low during the harvest season and high during the off season.

CONCLUSION

This model clearly indicates that conventions concerning the finance of international trade matter for the paths of exchange rates, interest rates and prices given seasonal fluctuations of endowment in one country. In all versions of the model, agents smoothed their consumption paths such that their ratio of consumption in harvest to off periods was equal to the ratio of world endowments, not own country endowments.[15] However, the paths of prices, interest rates and exchange rates are sensitive to which currency is used to finance international trade.

In the seller's currency version of the model, seasonal fluctuations in domestic endowment cause seasonal fluctuations in domestic prices, exchange rates and nominal interest rates on foreign bonds. These results follow from the fact that domestic prices bear the burden of adjustment when cash-in-advance constraints dictate that goods must be sold using seller's currency. Constant foreign endowment means constant foreign prices. In this world, the exchange rate must fluctuate with domestic currency prices in order to satisfy goods market arbitrage conditions. Interest rate fluctuations reflect fluctuations in the opportunity cost of saving in terms of consumption foregone. Since foreign prices are constant, the nominal interest rate on foreign bonds is the foreign real interest rate. This interest rate is low during harvest periods and high during off periods. This makes intuitive sense because the marginal utility of consumption is lower during harvest periods than off periods.

In the buyer's currency model, both domestic and foreign prices share the burden of adjustment to seasonal fluctuations in domestic endowment. Prices fluctuate inversely to consumption levels in the two periods. Since consumption for both agents fluctuates proportionately with world endowment, prices in both country fluctuate inversely with world endowment. The exchange rate is constant because the ratio of domestic to foreign prices is the same both periods. The nominal interest rate on foreign bonds is constant and equal to the marginal rate of time preference. The real interest rate fluctuates because of price level fluctuations and is lower in the harvest period than in the off period.

The pattern of prices, exchange rates and interest rates in the foreign currency finance version of the model is the same as in the buyer's currency version of the model. Domestic and foreign currency prices fluctuate inversely with world endowment in this model, as they did in the buyer's currency version. The level of prices and exchange rates is, however, indeterminate because agents are indifferent between consuming home endowment and foreign endowment. This yields a range of price levels that is consistent with equilibrium in the goods and money markets.

The general conclusion to be drawn from these results is that whether or not exchange rates fluctuate seasonally in an equilibrium optimizing model with fixed money stocks, no transactions costs and seasonal fluctuations in endowments depends upon how prices in the two countries react to seasonal fluctuations in endowment. If there are the same proportionate changes in prices in the two countries, then the exchange rate will be constant. In all the models, the exchange rate is tied to price levels through the assumption of a purchasing power parity relationship which is derived from the consideration of arbitrage conditions in a competitive goods market. In the seller's currency model, the conventional specification of the law of one price is assumed:

$$p_t = e_t \tilde{p}_t.$$

Buyers will purchase goods in both markets only when this condition holds. In the buyer's currency model, absolute purchasing power parity is modified to reflect the fact that sellers will only sell in both markets if the returns from selling in both markets are the same:

$$p_t = e_{t+1} \tilde{p}_t.$$

This condition arises from the trading sequence specified in the cash-in-advance constraint model. Receipts from the sale of goods in period t can not be converted into another currency until period $t+1$. In the foreign currency finance model, an interior solution requires that both buyer's and seller's goods market arbitrage conditions be satisfied simultaneously. The only possible solution in this case is that exchange rates are constant.

The behavior of the interest rate in this model is problematic. One country models which have been developed to investigate the effect of seasonal fluctuations of output on nominal interest rates have found that nominal interest rates increase during harvest periods.[16] The results of this model indicate that nominal interest rates either decrease during harvest periods or remain constant. This striking difference in results is due to the insensitivity of money demand to interest rates in simple cash-in-advance constraint models. Models where nominal interest rates increase during harvest periods have money demand functions which depend positively upon output and prices and inversely upon interest rates. Given a fixed money supply, an increase in money demand due to an increase in output causes interest rates to rise in order to bring the money market into equilibrium. Here, money demand is not directly linked to interest rates. The velocity of money is unitary and independent of interest rates.[17] Prices bear the full burden of adjustment in this model.

The next two chapters present the results of an empirical investigation into the time series behavior of U.S. and British short term nominal interest rates, the dollar-sterling exchange rate and interest rate differentials between the U.S. and Britain. Given that most international trade was conducted using sterling, the foreign currency finance model suggests that both the exchange rate and nominal interest rates in the two countries should be constant. Like other studies reviewed in the last chapter, this investigation finds seasonal fluctuations of short term nominal interest rates in the two countries and the dollar-sterling exchange rate. These results are not consistent with the implications of the simple two country cash-in-advance, optimizing model which was developed in this chapter. One objective of future research is to develop a model of the gold standard period which can generate seasonal fluctuations of nominal interest rates and exchange rates within the gold points.

NOTES

1. Kimbrough (1986: 13) cites a study by Grossman (1973) which finds that the seller's currency is used to invoice most international trade in manufactured goods between developed countries. Page (1977, 1981) summarizes results of surveys of exporters in several European countries on currency invoicing practices. Pozo (1989) tries to develop a model to explain why different currencies are adopted to invoice international trade.

2. All symbols used in this chapter are defined in Appendix 3-1 at the end of this chapter.

3. This means that the two agents need not have equal wealth. The model solution is sensitive to initial conditions, including the level and fluctuations of endowment streams. It makes a difference in this model whether the world begins with a harvest period or an off period because this specification will affect the discounted present value of the endowment stream and the relative wealth of the two agents. The domestic agent will be relatively wealthier when the world begins with a harvest period. This has implications for the distribution of consumption between the two agents. This sensitivity of the solution to when the world begins could perhaps be eliminated by allowing a market for shares in endowment streams and starting the world with a given distribution of shares in endowment streams. This would be in the spirit of Lucas's "tree model" and the two country cash-in-advance constraint model described by Sargent (1987: 182-192).

4. This utility function, which has the coefficient of relative risk aversion fixed at unity, is commonly used in macroeconomic models. See Blanchard and Fisher (1989: 43-44).

5. The equations for these constraints are presented and discussed in the appropriate sections below.

6. Table 3-1 is found in Appendix 3-2 at the end of this chapter.

7. This is the conventional specification of the law of one price. Kimbrough (1986: 10-11) shows that when internationally traded goods are purchased with seller's currency, this specification of the law of one price emerges as a necessary condition for goods market equilibrium.

8. All first order conditions are shown in Table 3-1, which is found in Appendix 3-2.

9. This is a no Ponzi game condition.

10. When foreign endowment increases, fluctuations in world endowment will become smaller relative to the level of world endowment, as can be seen in the solutions for interest rate levels shown in (20). Thus, interest rates tend to converge towards the marginal rate of time preference.

Fluctuations in domestic prices, which determine exchange rate depreciation will, however, remain the same.

11. Table 3-2 is found in Appendix 3-2 at the end of this chapter.

12. This consumption ratio for the foreign agent is identical to the one derived for the foreign agent in the seller's currency model when foreign prices are used. See equation (10*) above. The condition is different, however, when domestic prices are used because of the different goods market arbitrage condition:

$$\frac{\bar{c}'}{\bar{c}} = \left(\frac{1+r}{1+r'}\right)^{\frac{1}{2}} \frac{ep}{e'p'}.$$

13. The possibility of a corner solution where both goods market arbitrage conditions are not satisfied has not been ruled out and must be analyzed in more detail.

14. This finding of indeterminacy of price levels and exchange rate levels is not unique to this cash-in-advance constraint model. Sargent (1987: 188-190) finds indeterminacy in his two country cash-in-advance constraint model when agents can use either currency to purchase goods in either country. As long as the ratio of prices in the two countries is constant over time, the exchange rate will be constant. Sargent shows that a whole continuum of levels of exchange rates and prices is consistent with equilibrium.

15. The levels of consumption are not exactly the same in buyer's and seller's currency versions. [Compare (19) and (19*) with (30) and (30*).] Presumably this is because differences in interest rate paths in the two models cause changes in the discounted present value of endowment streams and therefore cause differences in the relative real wealth of the two agents.

16. See Miron (1986) for an example of a closed economy model of seasonal interest rate fluctuations caused by seasonal output fluctuations.

17. This shortcoming of simple cash-in-advance constraint models has been widely noted. See, for example, Blanchard and Fisher (1989: 166). They advocate introducing uncertainty as a way of motivating a precautionary demand for money.

APPENDIX 3-1: LIST OF SYMBOLS

b - foreign-currency-denominated bonds held by domestic agent
$\tilde{b}$ - foreign-currency-denominated bonds held by foreign agent
c - total consumption of domestic agent
$\tilde{c}$ - total consumption of foreign agent
c_h - consumption of home endowment by domestic agent
$\tilde{c}_h$ - consumption of home endowment by foreign agent
c_f - consumption of foreign endowment by domestic agent
$\tilde{c}_f$ - consumption of foreign endowment by foreign agent
e - the exchange rate defined as the domestic currency price of foreign currency
p - domestic currency price of goods
$\tilde{p}$ - foreign currency price of goods
M_H - total stock of domestic currency
M_F - total stock of foreign currency
M_h - domestic agent's demand for domestic currency
$\tilde{M}_h$ - foreign agent's demand for domestic currency
M_f - domestic agent's demand for foreign currency
$\tilde{M}_f$ - foreign agent's demand for foreign currency
$\bar{y}$ - world endowment
y - endowment of domestic agent
$\tilde{y}$ - endowment of foreign agent

Primes (′) are used to designate odd periods. No primes indicate even periods. A 't' subscript is used to designate time period.

APPENDIX 3-2: TABLES FOR CHAPTER 3

TABLE 3-1: SELLER'S CURRENCY PROBLEM

Domestic Agent Problem

$$L=\sum_{t=0}^{\infty}\left[\beta^t\left(\ln(c_t)\right)+\lambda_t\left(p_{t-1}y_{t-1}+e_t\left((1+r_{t-1})b_{t-1}-b_t\right)-M_{ht}-e_tM_{ft}\right)+\mu_t\left(M_{ht}+e_tM_{ft}-p_tc_t\right)\right]$$

First Order Conditions

1h) $\dfrac{\partial L}{\partial c_t}=\dfrac{\beta^t}{c_t}-\mu_t p_t=0$

2h) $\dfrac{\partial L}{\partial M_{ht}}=-\lambda_t+\mu_t=0$

3h) $\dfrac{\partial L}{\partial M_{ft}}=-\lambda_t e_t+\mu_t e_t=0$

4h) $\dfrac{\partial L}{\partial b_t}=-\lambda_t e_t+\lambda_{t+1}e_{t+1}(1+r_t)=0$

5h) $\dfrac{\partial L}{\partial \lambda_t}=p_{t-1}y_{t-1}+e_t\left((1+r_{t-1})b_{t-1}-b_t\right)-M_{ht}-e_tM_{ft}=0$

6h) $\dfrac{\partial L}{\partial \mu_t}=M_{ht}+e_tM_{ft}-p_tc_t=0$

TABLE 3-1: SELLER'S CURRENCY PROBLEM (continued)

Foreign Agent Problem

$$\tilde{L} = \sum_{t=0}^{\infty}\left[\beta^{t}\left(\ln(\tilde{c}_t)\right) + \tilde{\lambda}_t\left(e_t\tilde{p}_{t-1}\tilde{y}_{t-1} + e_t\left((1+r_{t-1})\tilde{b}_{t-1} - \tilde{b}_t\right) - \tilde{M}_{ht} - e_t\tilde{M}_{ft}\right) + \tilde{\mu}_t\left(\tilde{M}_{ht} + e_t\tilde{M}_{ft} - p_t\tilde{c}_t\right)\right]$$

First Order Conditions

1f) $$\frac{\partial\tilde{L}}{\partial\tilde{c}_t} = \frac{\beta^t}{\tilde{c}_t} - \tilde{\mu}_t\tilde{p}_t = 0$$

2f) $$\frac{\partial\tilde{L}}{\partial\tilde{M}_{ht}} = -\tilde{\lambda}_t + \tilde{\mu}_t = 0$$

3f) $$\frac{\partial\tilde{L}}{\partial\tilde{M}_{ft}} = -\tilde{\lambda}_t e_t + \tilde{\mu}_t e_t = 0$$

4f) $$\frac{\partial\tilde{L}}{\partial\tilde{b}_t} = -\tilde{\lambda}_t e_t + \tilde{\lambda}_{t+1}e_{t+1}\left(1+r_t\right) = 0$$

5f) $$\frac{\partial\tilde{L}}{\partial\tilde{\lambda}_t} = e_t\tilde{p}_{t-1}\tilde{y}_{t-1} + e_t\left((1+r_{t-1})\tilde{b}_{t-1} - \tilde{b}_t\right) - \tilde{M}_{ht} - e_t\tilde{M}_{ft} = 0$$

6f) $$\frac{\partial\tilde{L}}{\partial\tilde{\mu}_t} = \tilde{M}_{ht} + e_t\tilde{M}_{ft} - p_t\tilde{c}_t = 0$$

TABLE 3-2: BUYER'S CURRENCY PROBLEM

Domestic Agent Problem

$$L=\sum_{t=0}^{\infty}\left[\beta^t\left(\ln(c_t)\right)+\lambda_t\left(p_{t-1}y_{t-1}+e_t\left((1+r_{t-1})b_{t-1}-b_t\right)-M_{ht}\right)+\mu_t\left(M_{ht}-p_tc_t\right)\right]$$

First Order Conditions

1[h]) $\dfrac{\partial L}{\partial c_t}=\dfrac{\beta^t}{c_t}-\mu_t p_t=0$

2[h]) $\dfrac{\partial L}{\partial M_{ht}}=-\lambda_t+\mu_t=0$

3[h]) $\dfrac{\partial L}{\partial b_t}=-\lambda_t e_t+\lambda_{t+1}e_{t+1}\left(1+r_t\right)=0$

4[h]) $\dfrac{\partial L}{\partial \lambda_t}=p_{t-1}y_{t-1}+e_t\left((1+r_{t-1})b_{t-1}-b_t\right)-M_{ht}=0$

5[h]) $\dfrac{\partial L}{\partial \mu_t}=M_{ht}-p_tc_t=0$

TABLE 3-2: BUYER'S CURRENCY PROBLEM (continued)

Foreign Agent Problem

$$\tilde{L}=\sum_{t=0}^{\infty}\left[\beta^{t}\left(\ln\left(\tilde{c}_t\right)\right)+\tilde{\lambda}_t\left(e_t\tilde{p}_{t-1}\tilde{y}_{t-1}+e_t\left(\left(1+r_{t-1}\right)\tilde{b}_{t-1}-\tilde{b}_t\right)-e_t\tilde{M}_{ft}\right)+\tilde{\mu}_t\left(e_t\tilde{M}_{ft}-e_t\tilde{p}_t\tilde{c}_t\right)\right]$$

First Order Conditions

1f) $$\frac{\partial\tilde{L}}{\partial\tilde{c}_t}=\frac{\beta^{t}}{\tilde{c}_t}-\tilde{\mu}_t e_t\tilde{p}_t=0$$

2f) $$\frac{\partial\tilde{L}}{\partial\tilde{M}_{ft}}=-\tilde{\lambda}_t e_t+\tilde{\mu}_t e_t=0$$

3f) $$\frac{\partial\tilde{L}}{\partial\tilde{b}_t}=-\tilde{\lambda}_t e_t+\tilde{\lambda}_{t+1}e_{t+1}\left(1+r_t\right)=0$$

4f) $$\frac{\partial\tilde{L}}{\partial\tilde{\lambda}_t}=p_{t-1}\tilde{y}_{t-1}+e_t\left(\left(1+r_{t-1}\right)\tilde{b}_{t-1}-\tilde{b}_t\right)-e_t\tilde{M}_{ft}=0$$

5f) $$\frac{\partial\tilde{L}}{\partial\tilde{\mu}_t}=e_t\tilde{M}_{ft}-e_t\tilde{p}_t\tilde{c}_t=0$$

IV

An Empirical Investigation of the Seasonal Behavior of Interest Rates and Exchange Rates During the Gold Standard

INTRODUCTION

The purpose of this empirical investigation of the time series behavior of U.S. and British short term nominal interest rates and exchange rates between the United States and Britain during the period from 1883 to 1913 is to determine whether predictable seasonal fluctuations can be identified in the historical record. Previous empirical investigations, discussed in the literature review, have found significant seasonal fluctuations of U.S. and British short term nominal interest rates and the dollar-sterling sight exchange rate. The results of this investigation concur with earlier work. The pattern of seasonal fluctuations is consistent with the traditional stories. Interest rates in both the United States and Britain tended to be highest during the late fall and early winter and tended to be lowest during the late spring and early winter months.

There are some differences in seasonal patterns, however. The two U.S. short term interest rates investigated have very large positive seasonals slightly earlier in the fall than does the British open market discount rate. Both U.S. rates have a large negative seasonal in January, while a small positive seasonal is estimated for the British rate during that month. The amplitude of seasonal fluctuations in the *ex post* implicit interest rate on bankers' long bills of exchange is larger than the amplitude of seasonal fluctuations in any of the other three rates. This implicit interest rate is calculated using data on sight and sixty day sterling bills of exchange in New York and measures the *ex post* interest rate on borrowing in New York by drawing long sterling bills of exchange on London.

Both the dollar-sterling sight exchange rate and the rate on sixty day sterling bills of exchange tended to be highest during the spring and early summer months and lowest during the months of August through December. There appears to have been a significant decline in the amplitude of seasonal fluctuations in both exchange rates during the later half of the period. There was also a significant decline in the amplitude of seasonal fluctuations of the implicit interest rate, but not in any of the other interest rate series.

This chapter begins with an explanation of the univariate time series procedure used here to model seasonality of exchange rates and interest rates. The results of the empirical investigation of the two exchange rate series and four interest rate series are presented in the following section. These results are interpreted and compared with the literature in the final section.

PROCEDURE FOR MODELING SEASONALITY

Many different approaches to the treatment of seasonality in economic time series have been advocated over the years.[1] Most work deals with the issue of "seasonal adjustment," that is with removing the seasonal components in order to make the cyclical movements of the series clearer or to aid in short term forecasting. The focus of this study is on the seasonal fluctuations themselves, not on obtaining an "adjusted" series. The methodology used in this empirical investigation is based on an approach developed by Pierce (1978). In this section, an explanation of the approach developed by Pierce is followed by an outline of the procedures used in this study.

The framework for investigating seasonality adopted here is based on Pierce's (1978) univariate procedure for testing and adjusting for both deterministic and stochastic seasonality. Like many other treatments of seasonality, Pierce's approach assumes that the series which is being studied can be represented as the sum of a trend cycle, a seasonal, and an irregular component:

(1) $$y_t = p_t + s_t + e_t$$

where y_t represents the series, p_t represents the trend cycle component, s_t represents the seasonal component and e_t represents the irregular component. The decomposition in (1) can also be used for a multiplicative framework if logarithms of the series are taken. Pierce allows the trend cycle and seasonal components to have both deterministic and stochastic components:

(2) $$p_t = p_{1t} + p_{2t}$$

(3) $$s_t = s_{1t} + s_{2t}$$

where p_{1t} is the deterministic trend cycle component, p_{2t} is the stochastic trend cycle component, s_{1t} is the deterministic seasonal component and s_{2t} is the stochastic seasonal component.

Pierce's procedure combines two of the major approaches to seasonal adjustment. One approach, using linear regression models, is to treat seasonal fluctuations and trend cycle fluctuations as perfectly predictable components of a series. In this approach, the trend cycle components are captured using powers of a time variable and the seasonal components are captured using periodic variables such as seasonal dummy variables:

(4) $$p_t = p_{1t} = \sum_{i=1}^{I} \alpha_i c_{it}$$

(5) $$s_t = s_{1t} = \sum_{j=1}^{J} \beta_j d_{jt}$$

where the $\{c_{it}\}$ are usually powers of the time variable or variables representing other nonseasonal influences and the $\{d_{jt}\}$ are usually seasonal dummy variables. Equations (4) and (5) are substituted into (1) to obtain the estimated model:

$$y_t = \sum_{i=1}^{I} \alpha_i c_{it} + \sum_{j=1}^{J} \beta_j d_{jt} + e_t .$$

Another major approach models seasonality as essentially a stochastic phenomenon and models a seasonal series using symmetric moving average filters or seasonal ARIMA models. In this approach, the trend cycle and seasonal components are each assumed to be generated by an ARIMA process:

(6) $$\varphi_p(B)\Delta_p(B)p_t = \theta_p(B)\xi_t,\ \mathrm{Var}(\xi_t) = \sigma_\xi^2$$

or

$$\Delta_p(B)p_t = \Psi_p(B)\xi_t,\ \text{where } \Psi_p(B) = \frac{\theta_p(B)}{\varphi_p(B)}$$

(7) $$\varphi_s(B)\Delta_s(B)s_t = \theta_s(B)\varepsilon_t,\ \mathrm{Var}(\varepsilon_t) = \sigma_\varepsilon^2$$

or

$$\Delta_s(B)s_t = \Psi_s(B)\varepsilon_t,\ \text{where } \Psi_s(B) = \frac{\theta_s(B)}{\varphi_s(B)}$$

where B is the backshift operator, $\varphi_p(B)$, $\varphi_s(B)$, $\theta_p(B)$ and $\theta_s(B)$ are polynomials in B, $\Delta(B)$ is a difference operator, and ξ_t and ε_t are white noise. Stochastic trend cycle and seasonal components are not perfectly predictable because the error process which generates the process is not perfectly predictable.

Pierce combines these two approaches and allows the trend cycle and seasonal components to have both stochastic and deterministic elements. If the stochastic cyclical and seasonal components are stationary, his general model can be represented as:

(8) $$y_t = \sum_{i=1}^{I} \alpha_i c_{it} + \sum_{j=1}^{J} \beta_j d_{jt} + \psi_p(B)\xi_t + \psi_s(B)\varepsilon_t + e_t.$$

Deterministic influences are modeled using powers of time variables and seasonal dummy variables. Stochastic influences are modeled using seasonal and nonseasonal autoregressive and moving average terms. For the purposes of this study, the procedure outlined by Pierce provides an appropriate framework for investigating the question of whether or not predictable seasonal fluctuations were a significant characteristic of interest rates and exchange rates because the presence of both deterministic and stochastic seasonality can be tested easily within this framework.

The procedures followed in this study are as follows. The first step in model identification is a test for stationarity using Phillips-Perron unit root tests.[2] The general model estimated for these tests is:

$$y_t = \mu + \beta\left(t - \frac{T}{2}\right) + \alpha y_{t-1} + u_t, \tag{9}$$

where y_t is the series tested, $(t\text{-}T/2)$ is a modified linear trend term, and the residuals u_t can have a very general form. Phillips and Perron have developed test statistics for the presence of a unit root (a test for $\alpha = 1$) and for the significance of the trend term (a test for $\beta = 0$) which account for the very general structure of the residuals.

The next step is to examine the autocorrelation and partial autocorrelation functions of each series to tentatively identify the form and order of the cyclical components of the series. After these model identification steps, the deterministic seasonal and cyclical stochastic components are estimated jointly using a Box-Jenkins transfer function model. Seasonal dummy variables are included to capture the deterministic seasonal effects. The stochastic cyclical effects can be captured using low order autoregressive and/or moving average parameters, where the order of the parameters is too low to capture seasonal movements in the series. The final model is selected on the basis of the significance of the AR and/or MA parameters and the whiteness of the residual series. The Ljung-Box Q statistic is used to test whether the residuals approximate white noise.[3] In all cases, where more than one specification seemed adequate, the simplest specification was chosen.

Significance of seasonal dummy variables is determined using a standard F test for the significance of a subset of variables:

$$F = \frac{\left(SSE_K - SSE_Q\right)/(Q-K)}{SSE/(n-Q)},$$

which is distributed F with Q-K and n-Q-K-1 degrees of freedom, where SSE_Q is the sum of squared residuals in the full regression, SSE_K is the sum of squared residuals in the restricted regression, Q is the number of variables in the full regression, K is the number of variables in the restricted regression and n is the number of observations. Under the null hypothesis of no seasonality, $SSE_K = SSE_Q$ because the seasonal dummy variables should not significantly explain variation in the series. Significant deterministic seasonality is indicated by a large value of the F statistic.

The residuals from the seasonal dummy variable and low order *ARMA* model are tested for stochastic seasonality. Stochastic seasonality is indicated by large positive values of the autocorrelation and partial autocorrelation coefficients of these residuals at seasonal lags. A Q test on the sum of the squared residuals at seasonal lags is used to test for the presence of significant stochastic seasonality:

$$Q_s = n\sum_{k=1}^{m/s}\hat{r}_{sk}^2, \text{ distributed } \chi^2 \text{ with m/s degrees of freedom,}$$

where s is the seasonal span, n is the number of observations, m is the number of autocorrelations used and $\hat{r}_{sk}^2$ is the sample autocorrelation coefficient at lag sk. Small values of this Q statistic indicate that the autocorrelations at seasonal lags are consistent with white noise. Large values would be expected if the process were seasonal. The null hypothesis of no significant autocorrelations at seasonal lags (no stochastic seasonality) is rejected if the value of the Q statistic is large (i.e. the probability value is less than 10%).

The deterministic seasonal pattern is easily recovered from the seasonal dummy variables by finding and subtracting the common mean from each of the 12 dummy variable coefficients. A test for a shift in seasonal pattern after 1896 is conducted by including a second set of seasonal dummy variables defined only for the second half of the period. An F test for the significance of this set of "shift" dummy variables was used as a simple test of shift in seasonal pattern.

One of the most challenging aspects of empirical research on U.S. financial markets in the 19th and early 20th centuries is dealing with money market disturbances and missing data. The approach taken in this chapter is to use dummy variables to control for the occurrence of financial panics and other periods when data are missing or when there is other evidence that published interest rates were not market clearing rates. A set of dummy variables is used to correct for outliers in all series involving U.S. interest rates. This approach, while admittedly *ad hoc* in nature, does allow an examination of seasonality over a time period much longer than would be the case if the time period were limited to periods when no disturbances in financial markets occurred.[4] A more complete explanation of data problems can be found in Appendix 4-3 of this chapter.

The results of the empirical modeling of the behavior of the sight exchange rate, interest rates and interest rate differentials are presented in the next section.

RESULTS OF EMPIRICAL INVESTIGATION

Two sets of series are modeled here using the procedures outlined above.[5] The two exchange rate series are the dollar-sterling sight exchange rate and the dollar price of 60 day sterling bills of exchange. The four short term nominal interest rate series are the 60–90 day U.S. double name commercial paper rate, the 60 day U.S. time loan rate, the 60–90 day British open market discount rate and the *ex post* implicit interest rate on borrowing in the U.S. by drawing finance bills on Britain. The results indicate that all series can be modeled as having a deterministic seasonal component: seasonal dummy variables are significant in every case. The seasonal patterns of interest rates and exchange rates found in this study accord with contemporary accounts and with the findings of other researchers. Interest rates in both the United States and Britain showed strong seasonal fluctuations: they tended to be lowest in the summer months and highest in the autumn and early winter. The sight exchange rate and the rate on 60 day sterling bills of exchange tended to be highest in the late spring and early summer months and to be lowest in the autumn and early winter. A significant shift in seasonal pattern, indicating a weakening of seasonal fluctuations, was found in the case of the two exchange rate series and the implicit interest rate on borrowing abroad using finance bills, but not in the case of the U.S. and British short term nominal interest rate series.

Results for each of the series modeled are discussed in more detail below. The results of unit root tests for stationarity for all the series are presented before a description of the time series models for individual series. A table summarizing the model chosen for the series, graphs of the series and model residuals, graphs of the autocorrelation function and partial autocorrelation function of the series and model residuals, and a graph of the pattern of seasonal fluctuations are presented for each series.[6] In cases where the shift in seasonal pattern is significant, the changes in the seasonal pattern are shown. The results of this investigation are interpreted and compared with the results of other studies in the final section of this chapter.

Unit Root Tests for Stationarity

The results of the Phillips-Perron unit root tests are shown in Table 4-1. As discussed above, the general model estimated for these tests is:

$$y_t = \mu + \beta\left(t - \frac{T}{2}\right) + \alpha y_{t-1} + u_t.$$

In Table 4-1, $Z(t_\alpha)$ is a test statistic for $\alpha = 1$. $Z(t_\beta)$ is the test statistic for $\beta = 1$. $Z(\varphi_s)$ is a test statistic for the joint hypothesis that $\alpha = 1$ and $\beta = 0$. The hypothesis of a unit root is rejected at the 2% level for all series at all lag lengths. This means that none of the series has to be differenced to correct for stochastic nonstationarity. The $Z(t_\beta)$ statistics indicate that there is no significant deterministic trend term in any of the series.

Sight Rate

The dollar-sterling sight exchange rate during the period 1883–1913 is shown in Figure 4-1a and its autocorrelation function and partial autocorrelation function are shown in Figure 4-2a. The persistent peaks of the autocorrelation function of the sight rate at seasonal lags indicate that the sight rate has a strong seasonal component. This is confirmed by the results of the model chosen for the sight rate series for this time period, shown in Table 4-2. The large value of the *F* statistic means that the seasonal dummy variables are significant at the 1% level. The small value of the *Q* statistic for seasonal lags of the residual indicates that the seasonality in the series is adequately represented by the seasonal dummy variables and there is no need to incorporate both stochastic and deterministic seasonality in the model. A fourth order autoregressive process is used to model the cyclical component of the series. An intervention dummy variable for the months of June and July 1893 is used to capture the effects of the panic of 1893 and its aftermath on the exchange rate series.[7]

The seasonal pattern of the sight exchange rate for the period 1883–1913 is shown in Figure 4-3a. The exchange rate tended to be highest during the late spring and early summer months and tended to be lowest during the autumn and early winter. The mean sight rate for the period as a whole is 4.8669.[8] As shown in Table 4-2, the set of dummy variables allowing for a shift in the seasonal pattern of the exchange rate during the period 1897–1913 is significant at the 1% level. The seasonal patterns for the early subperiod (1883–1896) and the later subperiod (1897–1913) shown in Figures 4-3b and 4-3c provide clear evidence of a weakening in the seasonal pattern of the sight rate. There is a noticeable decline in the amplitude of the seasonal fluctuations when the two subperiods are compared. The exchange rate tended to peak in April during the earlier years and in May during the later years. The trough tended to occur in October during the earlier period and in September during the later period. This shift in seasonal pattern was accompanied by a decline in the mean value of the exchange rate: from 4.8707 during 1883–1896 to 4.8640 during 1897–1913. The one troubling aspect of the model incorporating a shift in seasonal pattern is the large value of the Q statistic at seasonal lags of the residuals, also shown in Table 4-2. This is due to large negative autocorrelations at seasonal lags of the residuals. This may be due to the simple specification of the shift in the seasonal pattern of exchange rates used in this model.

The 60 Day Sterling Bill of Exchange

The rate of exchange on sixty day sterling bills for the period 1883–1913 is shown in Figure 4-4a. The autocorrelation and partial autocorrelation functions for this series are shown in Figure 4-5a. The ACF clearly indicates a strong seasonal component for this series. The results of the model chosen for this series are shown in Table 4-3. The set of seasonal dummy variables is significant at the 1% level. The cyclical component is modeled using a fourth order autoregressive process. Intervention dummy variables are used to capture the effect of the 1893 disturbance in financial markets on exchange rates during the months of June and July.

The seasonal pattern of fluctuations is shown in Figure 4-6a. The pattern is very similar to the pattern of fluctuations in the sight rate. Rates tended to be highest in the late spring and early summer months and lowest during the fall and early winter months. As shown in Table 4-3, the set of seasonal dummy variables which allow for a shift in seasonal pattern during the years 1897–1913 is significant at the 1% level. The seasonal patterns for the two subperiods 1883–1896 and 1897–1913 shown in Figures 4-6b and 4-6c provide evidence of a weakening of the seasonal pattern of fluctuations during the latter part of the period. As was the case for the sight rate, the amplitude of seasonal fluctuations decreased after 1896. There is a shift in the peak of the series from April to June and a shift in the trough of the series from October to November. The large value of the *Q* statistic for seasonal lags of the residuals of this model is due to large negative seasonal autocorrelations. Again, this result may be due to the simple specification of the shift in seasonality incorporated into the model.

Implicit Interest Rate

In the absence of transactions costs, the *ex post* implicit interest rate on borrowing abroad by means of drawing a finance bill depends only on the rate at which the finance bill is sold in the New York market and the sight rate which prevails when the bill matures (i.e. when the loan from the British bank has to be paid off):

(10) $$i_{imp}^{k}(t) = \frac{s_{t+k}^{0} - s_{t}^{k}}{s_{t}^{k}},$$

where i^{k}_{imp} is the implicit k period interest rate, s^{0}_{t+k} is the sight rate which prevails at time $t+k$, and s is the dollar price of k period sterling bills of exchange. This *ex post* implicit rate is also the return from investing in sterling bills of exchange. If this implicit interest rate is low, then the cost of borrowing funds abroad is low, or, equivalently, the return on investing in k period bills of exchange is low. The lower the sight rate prevailing at t+k, i.e. the greater the extent of exchange rate appreciation, the cheaper it is to borrow abroad.

The implicit borrowing rate used in this study was constructed using weekly data on sight and 60 day bills of exchange. A three day grace period was allowed on long bills of exchange drawn on British banks. This means that a 60 day bill presented for acceptance in London at time *t* would be due exactly 63 days (9 weeks) later.[9] Given the reasonable assumption that the shipping time for sight and 60 day bills of exchange are the same, a very good proxy for the realized rate of interest on borrowing abroad by means of finance bills can be obtained by using data on sight and 60 day bills of exchange. The implicit rate at time *t* is constructed using the 60 day bill rate at time *t* and the sight rate prevailing 63 days (9 weeks) later. The original weekly series was then sampled to construct the end of month series.

This implicit interest rate is shown in Figure 4-7a. This *ex post* implicit interest rate on borrowing from Britain was negative in 27 months of the period investigated here: 24 months during the earlier period 1880–1896 and only three months during the years 1897–1913. As indicated in the table below, all the cases of negative implicit interest rates occurred during the months of March through August:

Month	March	April	May	June	July	August
# of Negative Rates	1	4	6	6	6	4

This concentration of negative interest rates during the spring and summer months reflects the strong seasonality in this series. This seasonality is confirmed by the autocorrelation and partial autocorrelations functions, shown in Figure 4-8a. The ACF shows clear peaks at seasonal lags.

The results of the model for this series are shown in Table 4-4. The seasonal dummy variables are significant at the 1% level. The cyclical component of the series is modeled using a third order autoregressive process. The mean implicit interest rate for the period as a whole is 3.27%. Dummy variables for the months of April, May, June and July are used to capture the effects of the panic of 1893 on the series.[10] The seasonal pattern shown in Figure 4-9a indicates that the implicit interest rate tended to be lowest during the late spring and early summer months and rose to a peak in November and December.

As shown in Table 4-4, the set of dummy variable which allows for a shift in the seasonal pattern after 1897 is significant at the 10% level, but not at the 5% level. The seasonal patterns for the two subperiods are shown in Figures 4-9b and 4-9c. There is a decrease in amplitude of the seasonal fluctuations from the earlier to the later years, a shift in the trough from June to July and a shift in the peak of the series from December to November. An increase in the mean of the series from 2.985% to 3.52% is associated with the shift in seasonal pattern.

The 60–90 Day British Open Market Discount Rate

The 60–90 day British open market discount rate is shown in Figure 4-10a. The autocorrelation functions and partial autocorrelation functions are shown in Figure 4-11a. As in the cases of the other series discussed previously, the significant peaks of the ACF at seasonal lags indicate that this series has a strong seasonal component. The results of the model chosen for this series are shown in Table 4-5. Seasonal dummy variables are significant at the 1% level and the cyclical component of the series is modeled with a fourth order autoregressive process. The seasonal pattern for the British discount rate is shown in Figure 4-12. The pattern of seasonal fluctuations resembles the seasonal fluctuations in the implicit interest rate: the interest rate tended to be low during the late spring and early summer months and highest during the months of October, November and December. However, the amplitude of fluctuations in the British discount rate is not as large as the amplitude of fluctuations in the implicit interest rate.

The set of seasonal dummy variables which allow for a shift in the seasonal pattern of the British discount rate after 1896 was not significant at the 10% level. The hypothesis of a shift in the seasonal pattern of the British discount rate is rejected.

The United States 60–90 Day Prime Commercial Paper Rate

The U.S. 60–90 day prime commercial paper rate is shown in Figure 4-13a. The effects of disturbances in U.S. financial markets during 1893, 1896 and 1907 are clearly visible as peaks in the series. The volatility of U.S. interest rates during this period is widely known, and presents problems for time series analysis. Table 4-8, found in Appendix 4-3, identifies the months for which normal quotations for commercial paper are not available for one of the following reasons:

(1) the reported quote was entirely nominal, which means that no business was conducted at that rate,

(2) there was no quote reported, or

(3) a commission was charged in addition to the reported interest rate. During times of financial disturbances, interest rates could not always move to clear markets because of the existence of interest rate limits imposed by usury laws. Business was often suspended or curtailed in markets for particular kinds of loans. The approach adopted in this analysis is to use dummy variables to control for times of financial market disturbance. Given that the objective of this study is to investigate seasonal fluctuations of interest rates during the entire period 1883–1913, the decision was made to control the effects of disturbed financial periods using dummy variables rather than to restrict the analysis to periods of time when no disturbances occurred.

The autocorrelation and partial autocorrelation function of the US commercial paper rate are shown in Figure 4-14a. Unlike the previous series examined, the ACF of the commercial paper rate does not show clear seasonal peaks at the first and second seasonal lags (12 or 24 months). There is a significant peak in the ACF at the lag corresponding to 36 months. The estimated model for the U.S. commercial paper rate is summarized in Table 4-6. Despite the weak evidence of seasonality in the ACF of the original series, the seasonal dummy variables are significant at the 1% level.[11] The cyclical component of the series is captured using a first order autoregressive process. An extensive set of dummy variables is used to control for the effects of disturbances in U.S. financial markets. Markets were disturbed for several months during the years of 1893, 1896 and 1907, and for shorter periods during 1890, 1892, 1895, and 1898.

The seasonal pattern of the commercial paper rate is shown in Figure 4-16. The commercial paper rate was lowest during the winter, late spring and summer months and highest during the late summer and autumn. This pattern is similar to the pattern of seasonal fluctuations in the British discount rate, but the U.S. commercial paper rate rises more abruptly and earlier than the British rate. The hypothesis of no shift in the seasonal pattern of the commercial paper rate could not be rejected at the 10% level.

The United States 60 Day Time Loan Rate

The U.S. 60 day time loan rate for the period 1890–1913 is shown in Figure 4-16a. Data on time loan rates were not readily available before 1890. The high interest rates associated with disturbed financial conditions during 1893, 1896 and 1907 show up clearly as peaks in the series. Table 4-9 of Appendix 4-3 shows the months for which normal quotations for the 60 day time loan rate are not available. The 60 day time loan rate was subject to a 6% ceiling due to usury laws throughout this period. High rates are due to commissions charged in addition to interest. Intervention dummy variables were used to control for the effect of disturbed financial conditions in the case of the time loan rate just as they were for the case of the commercial paper rate.

The autocorrelation and partial autocorrelation functions for the 60 day time loan rate are shown in Figure 4-17a. The ACF and PACF do not show clear evidence of seasonality: there are no significant peaks at seasonal lags 12 or 24. However, the seasonal dummy variables are significant at the 1% level for the U.S. time loan rate, just as they were for the U.S. commercial paper rate. The results of the model are shown in Table 4-7. The cyclical component of the series is modeled using a second order autoregressive process. The Q statistic of the residuals at seasonal lags indicates that the seasonality in the series can be modeled adequately as deterministic seasonality, and the seasonal pattern is shown in Figure 4-18. The hypothesis of no shift in the seasonal pattern after 1896 can not be rejected at the 10% level.

SUMMARY AND INTERPRETATION OF EMPIRICAL RESULTS

The results reported here for interest rates are consistent with the results of previous studies. Interest rates in both the United States and Britain tended to be highest during the months of September to December and lowest during the late spring and early summer. Seasonal patterns of the four interest rate series are shown together in Figure 4-19. Some differences in seasonal patterns are apparent. Seasonal fluctuations in the implicit interest rate are much larger than in any of the other three interest rates. The U.S. commercial paper rate tended to show a seasonal increase in August, a month earlier than the other rates. Both the U.S. commercial paper rate and the U.S. time loan rate have a larger positive seasonal during the month of September than does the British discount rate. U.S. rates tend to have a negative seasonal component in January, whereas the British rate has a small positive seasonal. The U.S. commercial paper rate is the only rate which has a large negative seasonal in February. The overall pattern of seasonal fluctuations in the four rates is, however, similar. Rates tended to be lowest in late spring and early summer and highest in the fall of the year.

The findings in this study of significant seasonal fluctuations of exchange rates and a weakening of seasonal fluctuations of exchange rates after 1896 are consistent with the work of Kemmerer, Cole and Morgenstern, as well as with reports in the contemporary literature. The dollar-sterling exchange rate tended to be highest during the late spring and early summer months and lowest during the months of August to December. In addition, this study finds seasonal fluctuations in other series which have a significant exchange rate component: the rate on 60 day bills of exchange and the implicit interest rate. Seasonal fluctuations in these series also appear to have weakened after 1896.

These findings of seasonal movements of exchange rates call into question the assumption made by Officer (1989) that exchange rate speculators believed that every value of the exchange rate between the gold points had an equal probability of occurring at any point in time. The contemporary literature indicates that speculators expected seasonal movements of exchange rates within the gold points and conducted their arbitrage activities in international short term capital markets based in part on those expected seasonal exchange rate movements. Given the persistence of seasonal exchange rate fluctuations found here, it is not clear that the asset market approach advocated by Officer is the best approach for understanding and predicting exchange rate movements during the pre-World War I gold standard. Other factors, such as seasonal movements in the trade balance, may be important in explaining exchange rate movements during this period.

NOTES

1. See Bell and Hilmer (1984) for a survey of approaches to seasonal adjustment.

2. See Perron (1986) for a discussion of these tests.

3. $Q = n(n+2)\left(\sum_{j=1}^{m}\frac{1}{n-j}r_j^2\right)$, where r_j is the *j*th lag sample autocorrelation of the residuals, *m* is the number of autocorrelations used, and *n* is the number of observations. Small values of the Q-statistic indicate that the autocorrelations of the residuals are consistent with white noise.

4. Fishe and Wohar (1990) advocate restricting analysis of U.S. interest rates to time periods when there were no financial market disturbances. As pointed out by Mankiw *et al* (1990), this results in a very short period of analysis. They suggest using month dummies to exclude observations where there are data problems.

5. The original source for all data used in this study is the *Commercial and Financial Chronicle*. See the Appendix 4-3 of this chapter for a more complete description.

6. All tables are included in Appendix 4-1 of this chapter. All figures and graphs are included in Appendix 4-2 of this chapter.

7. Exchange rates were unusually low at the end of June and during the month of July in the aftermath of the stock market collapse of May 1893. During these weeks the *Commercial and Financial Chronicle* reports high U.S. interest rates, large exports of grain due to low grain prices and buying of securities on foreign account as reasons for the low exchange rates. U.S. interest rates remained high through the month of August, with commissions charged in addition to interest in both time loan and commercial paper markets. Widespread suspension of payments by banks caused currency and gold to go to a premium over deposits during the month of August. The premium on gold meant that gold imports were profitable even when exchange rates rose above the gold import point. See Sprague (1910: 153–215) for a description and analysis of the crisis of 1893 and the effect of the currency premium on gold imports.

8. This mean is the mean of all the seasonal dummy variables. The seasonal pattern is derived as the monthly deviations from this common mean.

9. Cross (1923: 137) and Escher (1918a: 40) report that in Britain a 3 day grace period was allowed on time and date bills of exchange, but not on

sight bills of exchange. This grace period was not granted in other European countries.

10. The low exchange rates in June and July caused 4 months of disturbance in the implicit interest rate. Low sight rates in June and July meant the implicit rates in April and May were very low. Low 60 day bill rates in June and July meant that implicit rates were very high.

11. The autocorrelation function of residuals from AR models estimated without seasonal dummy variables had significant peaks at seasonal lags. A reasonable explanation of the lack of significant peaks at seasonal lags of the original series is that the large outliers during times of disturbances in financial markets were obscuring the time series patterns.

APPENDIX 4-1: TABLES FOR CHAPTER 4

TABLE 4-1: RESULTS OF PHILLIPS-PERRON UNIT ROOT TESTS

SERIES	LAG 4	LAG 12	LAG 24	LAG 36
Sight Rate (1883–1913)				
$Z(t_\alpha)$	-9.00*	-9.31*	-9.11*	-7.78*
$Z(t_\beta)$	-0.85	-0.81	-0.84	-1.07
$Z(\varphi_3)$	40.47*	43.33*	41.54*	30.27*
60 Day Bill Rate (1883–1913)				
$Z(t_\alpha)$	-7.19*	-7.15*	-7.11*	-6.43*
$Z(t_\beta)$	-1.07	-1.08	-1.08	-1.23
$Z(\varphi_3)$	25.89*	25.61*	25.30*	20.69*
U.S. Commercial Paper Rate (1883–1913)				
$Z(t_\alpha)$	-6.41*	-6.89*	-4.34*	-4.47*
$Z(t_\beta)$	- 0.21	- 0.19	- 0.38	- 0.36
$Z(\varphi_3)$	20.54*	23.73*	9.43*	10.02*
U.S. 60 Day Time Loan Rate (1890–1913)				
$Z(t_\alpha)$	-8.22*	-8.10*	-6.71*	-5.98*
$Z(t_\beta)$	-0.26	-0.27	-0.37	-0.60
$Z(\varphi_3)$	33.82*	32.79*	22.51*	17.86*
British Discount Rate (1883–1913)				
$Z(t_\alpha)$	-6.27*	-7.43*	-8.03*	-7.74*
$Z(t_\beta)$	2.49	2.03	1.85	1.93
$Z(\varphi_3)$	19.71*	27.61*	32.27*	29.98*
Implicit Borrowing Rate (1883–1913)				
$Z(t_\alpha)$	-9.22*	-9.82*	-10.44*	-9.78*
$Z(t_\beta)$	0.92	0.82	0.75	0.83
$Z(\varphi_3)$	42.53*	48.25*	54.51*	47.83*

*** Significant at the 2% level. ** Significant at the 5% level.**

$Z(t_\alpha)$: test statistic for $\alpha = 1$. $Z(t_\beta)$: test statistic for $\beta = 0$.

$Z(\varphi_3)$: test statistic for $\alpha = 1$ and $\beta = 0$.

TABLE 4-2: SIGHT RATE

	model for 1883–1913		*model with seasonal shift after 1896*	
$\bar{R}^2$	0.57		0.59	
Regression Q statistic[a]	58.82	(0.41)	65.25	(0.21)
F statistic[b]	7.41	(<0.01)	2.51	(<0.01)
Seasonal Q statistic[c]	1.89	(0.86)	9.69	(0.09)
degrees of freedom	355		343	
Variables[d]				
AR1	0.575	(10.95)	0.566	(10.64)
AR2	0.194	(3.24)	0.164	(2.71)
AR3	-0.172	(-2.86)	-0.155	(-2.54)
AR4	0.147	(2.81)	0.164	(3.09)
D93:6–7	-0.460	(-6.20)	-0.047	(-6.27)

a Q statistic for the regression, probability value in parentheses.
b F statistic for the significance of the seasonal dummy variables for the 1883–1913 model and for the seasonal shift dummy variables for the shift model; probability values in parentheses.
c Q statistic for residuals at 5 seasonal lags, probability value in parentheses.
d Variables included in the model other than the seasonal dummy variables, *t* statistics in parentheses.

TABLE 4-3: 60 DAY STERLING BILL OF EXCHANGE RATE

	model for 1883–1913		*model with seasonal shift after 1896*	
$\overline{R}^2$	0.75		0.76	
Regression *Q* statistic[a]	69.51	(0.12)	58.57	(0.42)
F statistic[b]	12.76	(<0.01)	2.92	(<0.01)
Seasonal *Q* statistic[c]	2.15	(0.83)	10.16	(0.07)
degrees of freedom	355		343	
Variables[d]				
AR1	0.626	(11.86)	0.598	(11.17)
AR2	0.239	(3.85)	0.212	(3.41)
AR3	-0.120	(-1.94)	-0.086	(-1.38)
AR4	0.111	(2.10)	0.130	(2.43)
D93:6–7	-0.046	(-6.00)	-0.048	(-6.23)

a *Q* statistic for the regression, probability value in parentheses.
b *F* statistic for the significance of the seasonal dummy variables for the 1883–1913 model and for the seasonal shift dummy variables for the shift model; probability values in parentheses.
c *Q* statistic for residuals at 5 seasonal lags, probability value in parentheses.
d Variables included in the model other than the seasonal dummy variables, *t* statistics in parentheses.

TABLE 4-4: IMPLICIT INTEREST RATE

	model for 1883–1913		*model with seasonal shift after 1896*	
$\bar{R}^2$	0.60		0.61	
Regression Q statistic[a]	61.63	(0.31)	65.53	(0.21)
F statistic[b]	12.15	(<0.01)	1.65	(0.08)
Seasonal Q statistic[c]	2.21	(0.82)	6.02	(0.30)
degrees of freedom	355		343	
Variables[d]				
AR1	0.71	(13.76)	0.70	(13.37)
AR2	-0.38	(-6.37)	-0.40	(-6.67)
AR3	0.23	(4.49)	0.25	(4.79)
D93:6–7	4.25	(3.10)	4.77	(3.45)
D93:4–5	-6.44	(-4.70)	-6.03	(-4.36)

a Q statistic for the regression, probability value in parentheses.
b F statistic for the significance of the seasonal dummy variables for the 1883–1913 model and for the seasonal shift dummy variables for the shift model; probability values in parentheses.
c Q statistic for residuals at 5 seasonal lags, probability value in parentheses.
d Variables included in the model other than the seasonal dummy variables, t statistics in parentheses.

TABLE 4-5: BRITISH 60–90 DAY DISCOUNT RATE

	model for 1883–1913		*model with seasonal shift after 1896*	
$\overline{R}^2$	0.76		0.76	
Regression Q statistic[a]	66.04	(0.19)	79.58	(0.04)
F statistic[b]	10.94	(<0.01)	1.20	(0.28)
Seasonal Q statistic[c]	5.56	(0.35)	13.49	(0.02)
degrees of freedom	356		344	
Variables[d]				
AR1	0.740	(14.05)	0.739	(13.73)
AR2	-0.004	(-0.06)	-0.008	(-0.13)
AR3	0.038	(0.58)	0.031	(0.47)
AR4	0.110	(2.10)	0.101	(1.88)

a Q statistic for the regression, probability value in parentheses.
b F statistic for the significance of the seasonal dummy variables for the 1883–1913 model and for the seasonal shift dummy variables for the shift model; probability values in parentheses.
c Q statistic for residuals at 5 seasonal lags, probability value in parentheses.
d Variables included in the model other than the seasonal dummy variables, t statistics in parentheses.

TABLE 4-6: U.S. 60–90 DAY COMMERCIAL PAPER RATE

	model for 1883–1913		*model with seasonal shift after 1896*	
$\overline{R}^2$	0.88		0.89	
Regression Q statistic[a]	59.26	(0.39)	65.56	(0.20)
F statistic[b]	15.10	(<0.01)	1.31	(0.21)
Seasonal Q statistic[c]	1.84	(0.87)	4.24	(0.516)
degrees of freedom	349		337	
Variables[d]				
AR1	0.894	(37.04)	0.898	(37.19)
D90:10–12	0.877	(2.82)	1.049	(3.33)
D92:12	0.928	(2.97)	1.086	(3.43)
D93:2–3	1.699	(5.45)	1.696	(5.37)
D93:6–8	5.471	(15.26)	5.435	(14.95)
D93:9	2.125	(5.88)	2.080	(5.68)
D95:12-1	1.469	(4.71)	1.464	(4.63)
D96:8,10	4.150	(13.33)	4.034	(12.79)
D96:9	1.527	(3.47)	1.392	(3.12)
D98:4	1.932	(6.18)	1.878	(5.97)
D07:10-12	1.147	(3.69)	1.007	(3.22)

a Q statistic for the regression, probability value in parentheses.
b F statistic for the significance of the seasonal dummy variables for the 1883–1913 model and for the seasonal shift dummy variables for the shift model; probability values in parentheses.
c Q statistic for residuals at 5 seasonal lags, probability value in parentheses.
d Variables included in the model other than the seasonal dummy variables, t statistics in parentheses.

TABLE 4-7: U.S. 60 DAY TIME LOAN RATE

	model for 1891–1913		*model with seasonal shift after 1896*	
$\overline{R}^2$	0.90		0.91	
Regression Q statistic[a]	49.46	(0.42)	61.35	(0.09)
F statistic[b]	11.14	(<0.01)	1.16	(0.31)
Seasonal Q statistic[c]	2.28	(0.81)	8.97	(0.11)
degrees of freedom	251		239	
Variables[d]				
AR1	0.640	(10.20)	0.623	(9.78)
AR2	0.224	(3.62)	0.241	(3.85)
D93:6	13.717	(23.21)	13.642	(21.63)
D93:7	7.883	(12.15)	7.507	(10.88)
D93:8–9	1.959	(3.65)	1.748	(3.06)
D95:12-1	2.981	(6.52)	3.191	(6.61)
D96:8,10	8.046	(16.82)	7.938	(15.50)
D96:9	1.667	(2.71)	1.574	(2.39)
D98:4	2.820	(5.38)	2.811	(5.32)
D02:9,11	1.725	(4.29)	1.649	(4.04)
D06:8–12	1.350	(3.00)	1.225	(2.73)
D07:10-11-11	8.385	(16.58)	8.240	(16.37)
D07:12	5.142	(8.86)	4.982	(8.53)

a Q statistic for the regression, probability value in parentheses.
b F statistic for the significance of the seasonal dummy variables for the 1891–1913 model and for the seasonal shift dummy variables for the shift model; probability values in parentheses.
c Q statistic for residuals at 5 seasonal lags, probability value in parentheses.
d Variables included in the model other than the seasonal dummy variables, *t* statistics in parentheses.

APPENDIX 4-2: FIGURES FOR CHAPTER 4

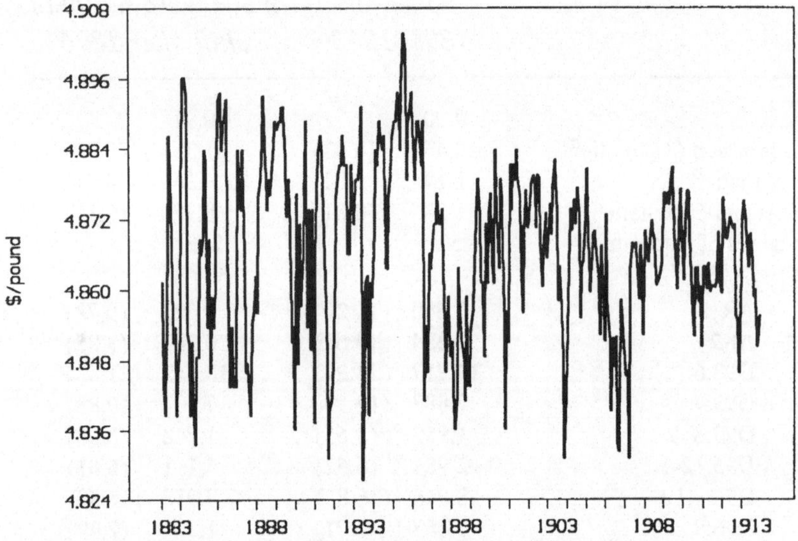

Figure 4-1a: Sight Rate, 1883-1913

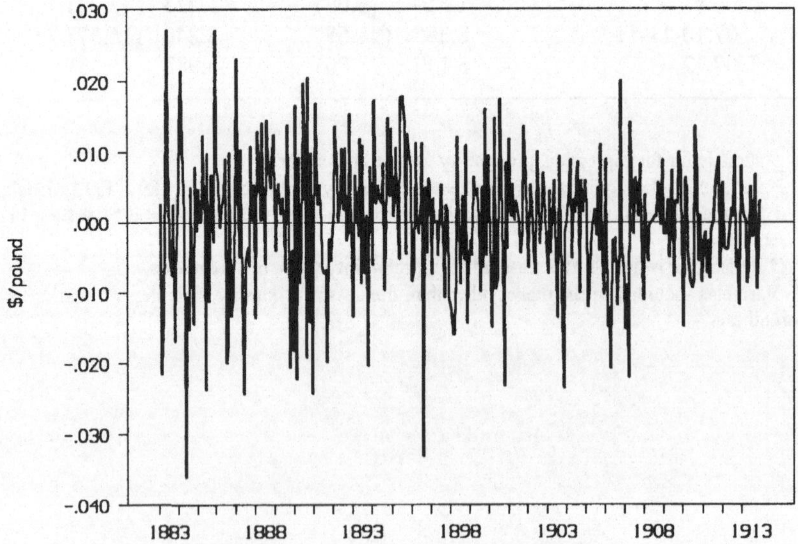

Figure 4-1b: Model Residuals

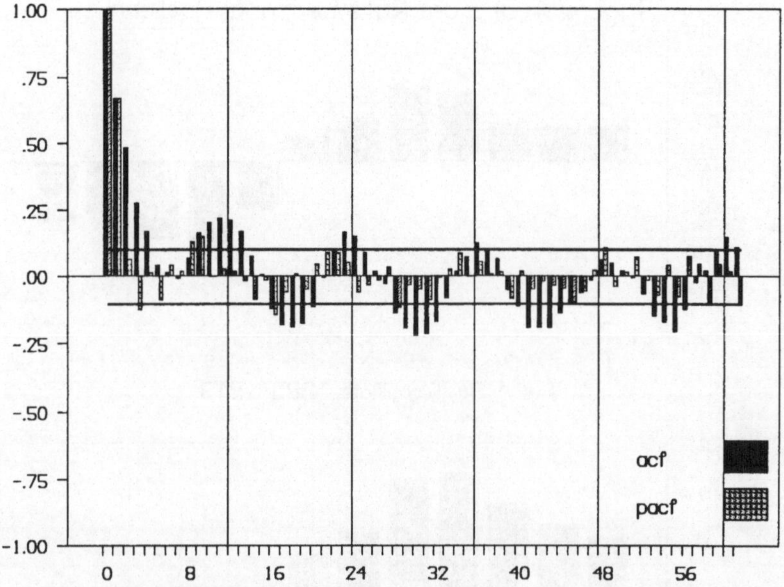

Figure 4-2a: ACF and PACF of Sight Rate

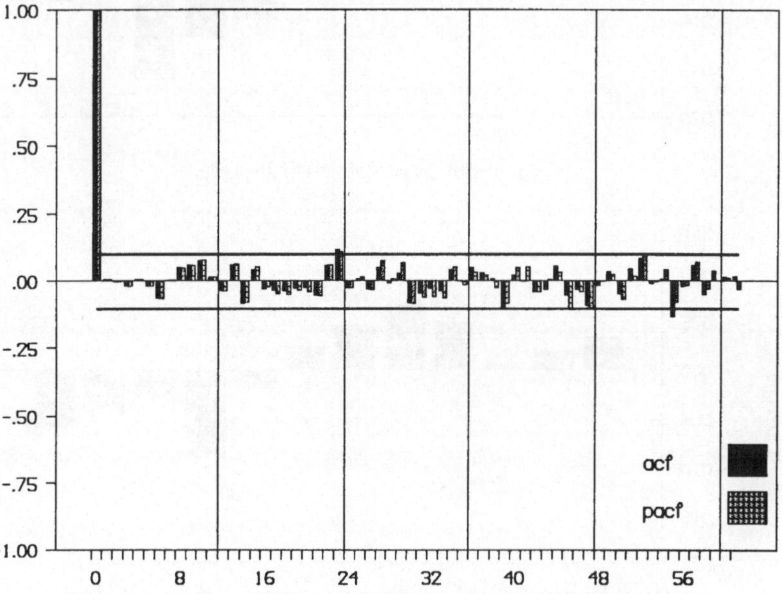

Figure 4-2b: ACF and PACF of Model Residuals

Figure 4-3: Sight Rate Seasonal Pattern

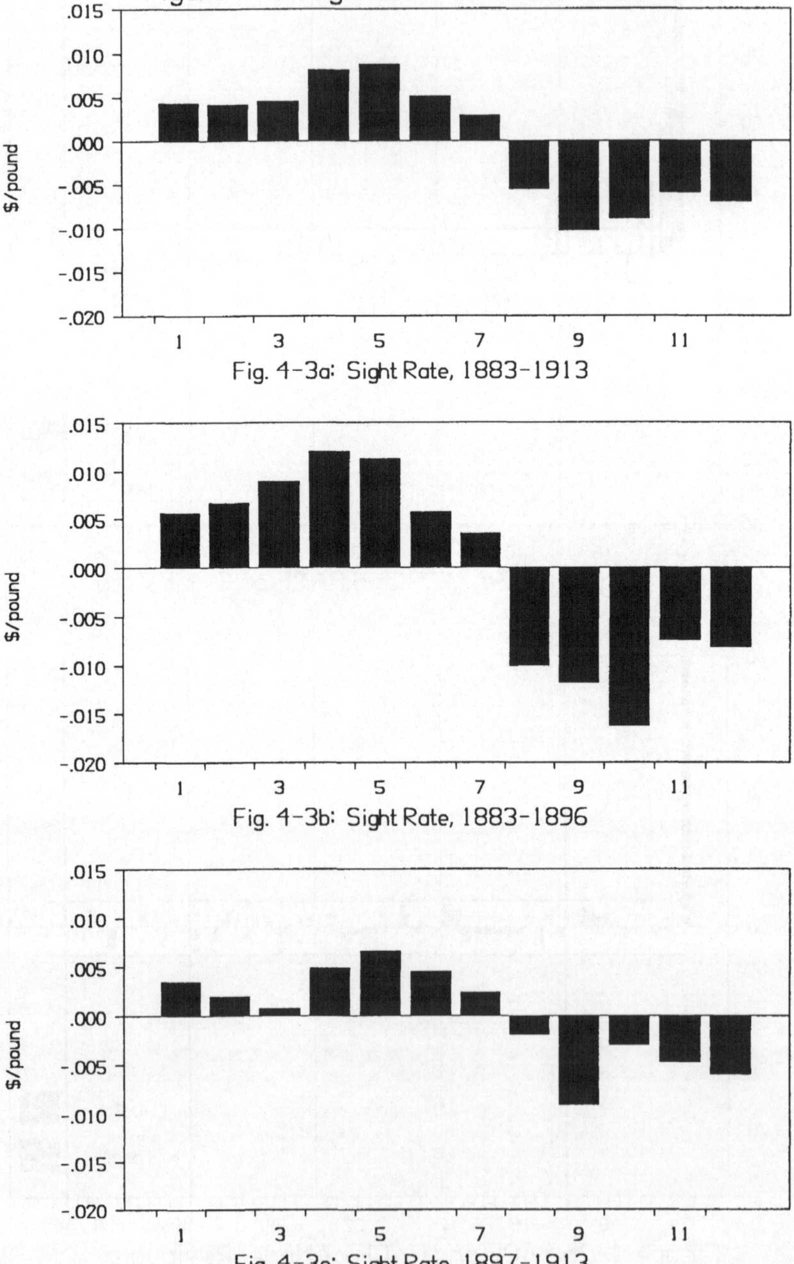

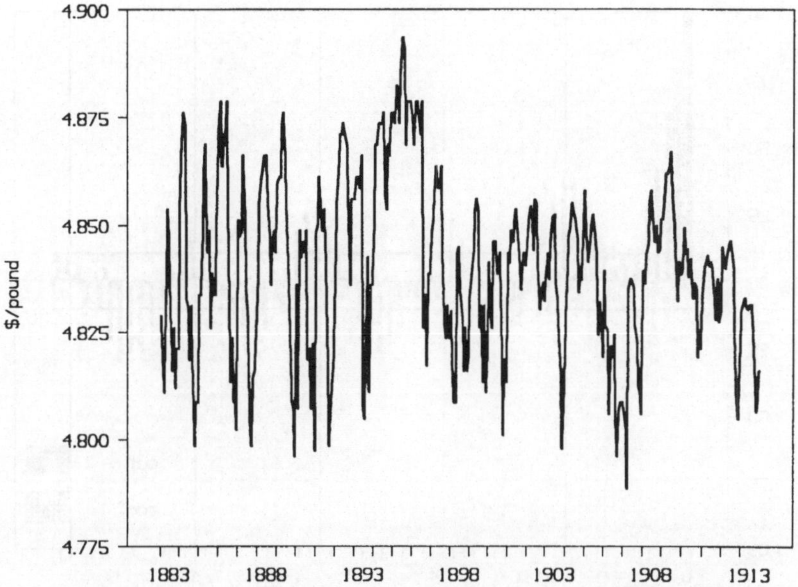

Figure 4-4a: 60 Day Sterling Bill Rate, 1883-1913

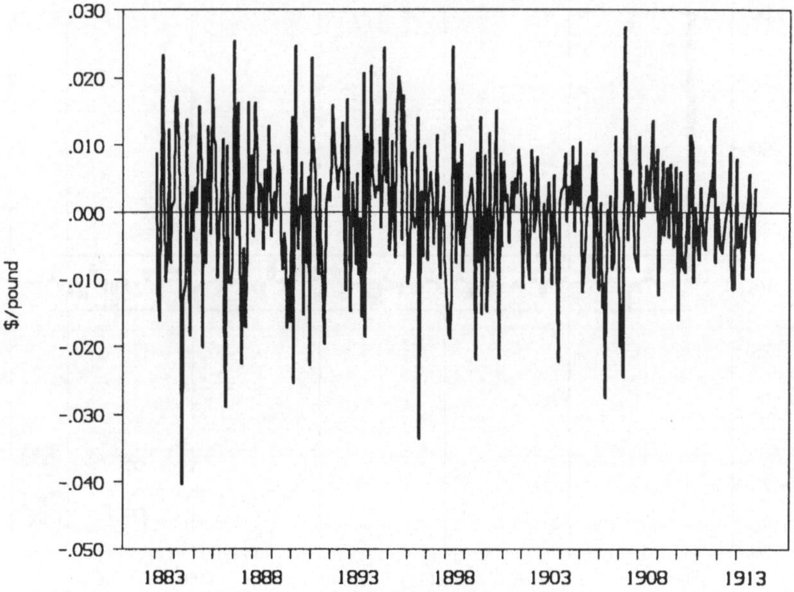

Figure 4-4b: Model Residuals

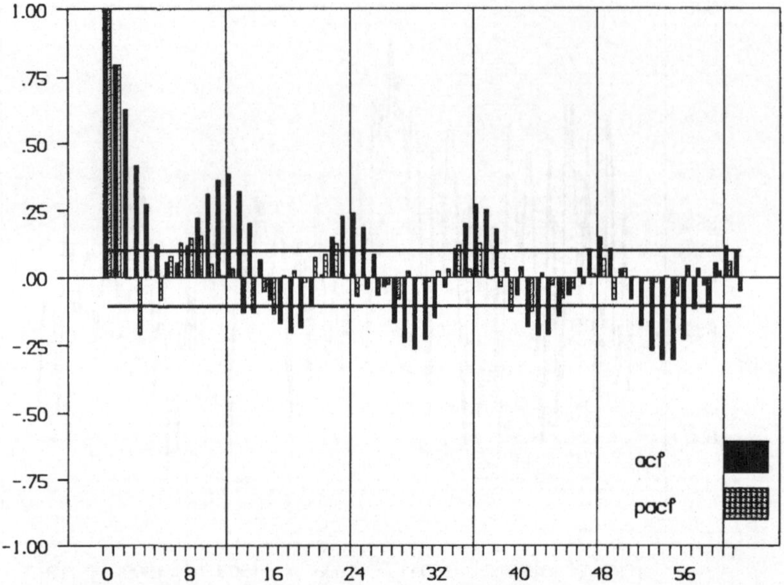

Figure 4-5a: ACF and PACF of 60 Day Sterling Bill Rate

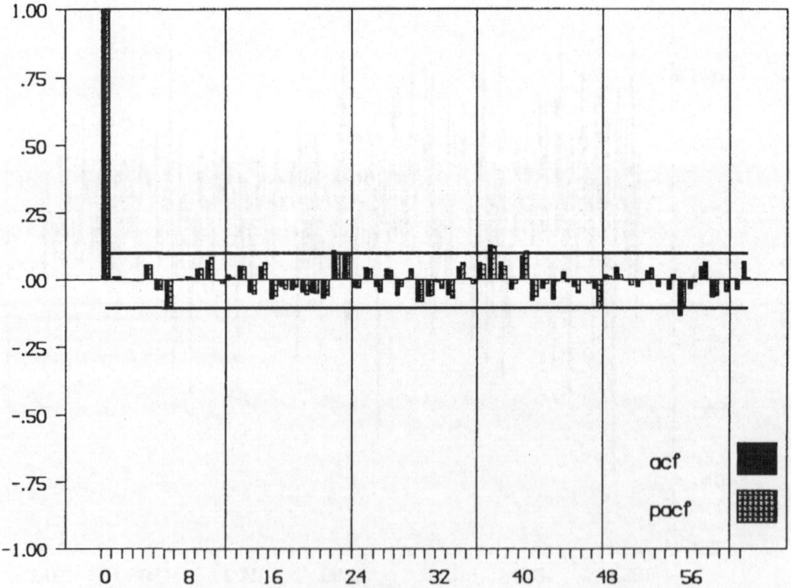

Figure 4-5b: ACF and PACF of Model Residuals

Figure 4-6: 60 Day Sterling Bill Rate Seasonal Pattern

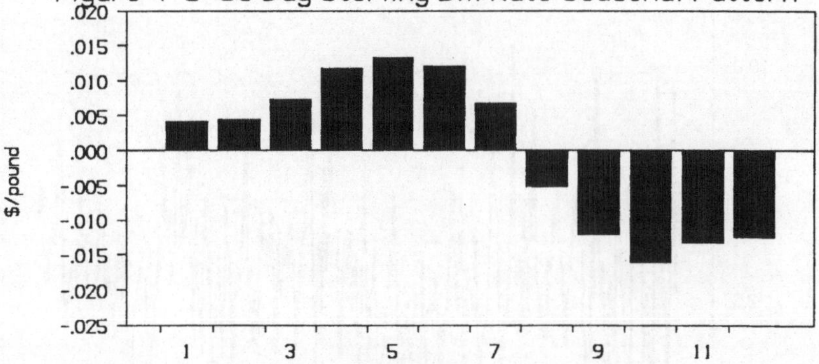

Fig. 4-6a: 60 Day Bill Rate, 1883-1913

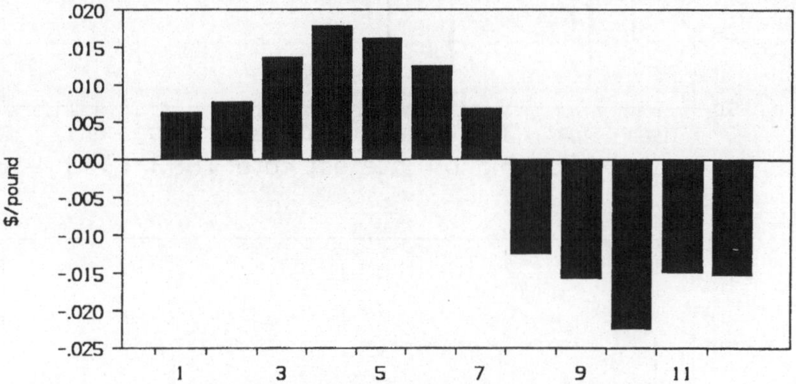

Fig. 4-6b: 60 Day Bill Rate, 1883-1896

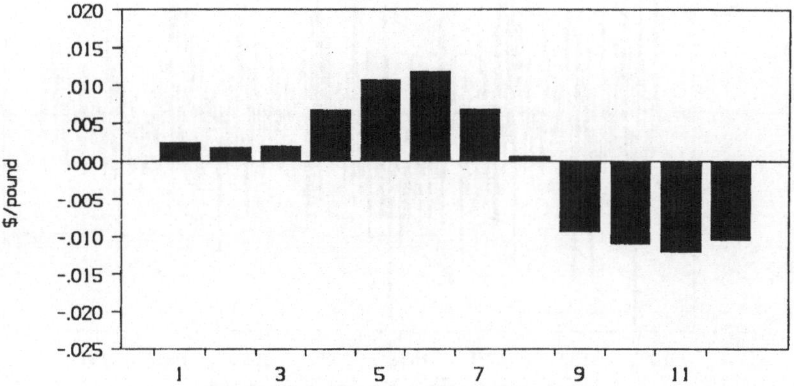

Fig. 4-6c: 60 Day Bill Rate, 1897-1913

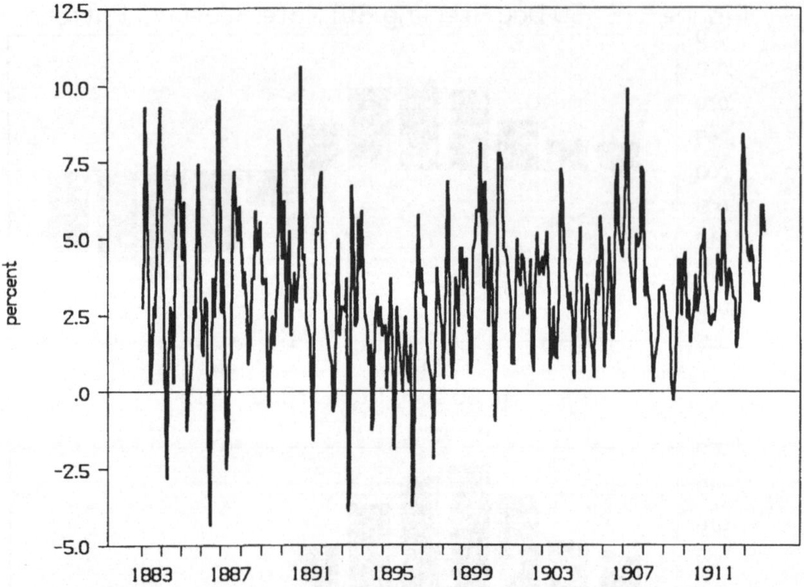

Figure 4-7a: Implicit Interest Rate, 1883-1913

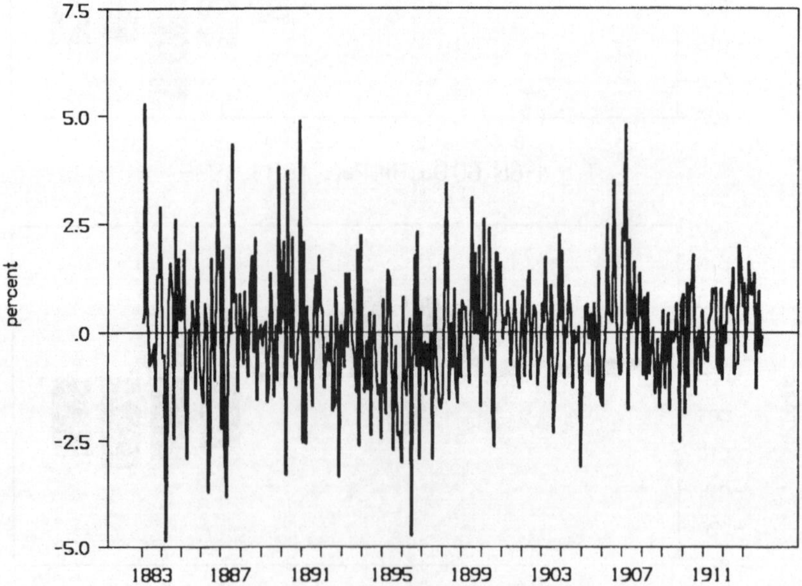

Figure 4-7b: Model Residuals

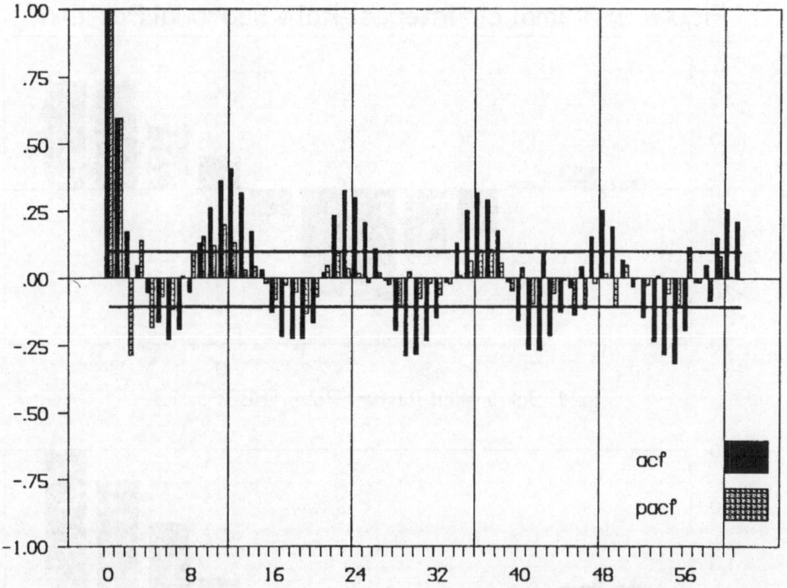

Figure 4-8a: ACF and PACF of Implicit Interest Rate

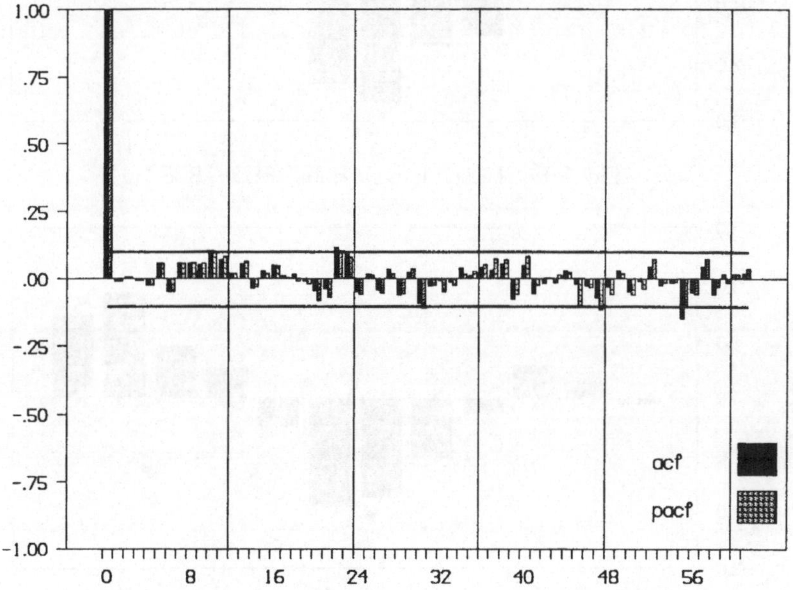

Figure 4-8b: ACF and PACF of Model Residuals

Figure 4-9: Implicit Interest Rate Seasonal Pattern

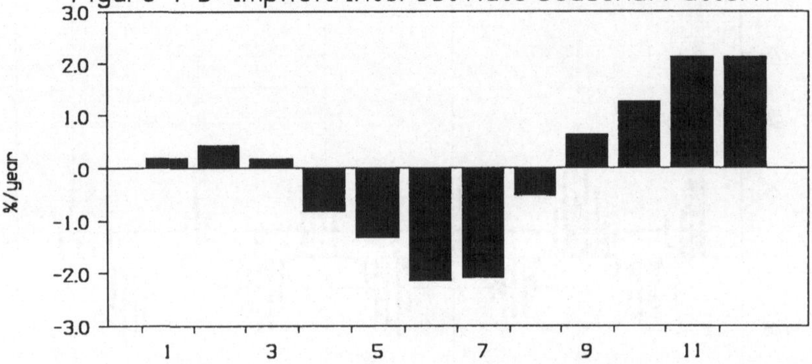

Fig. 4-9a: Implicit Interest Rate, 1883-1913

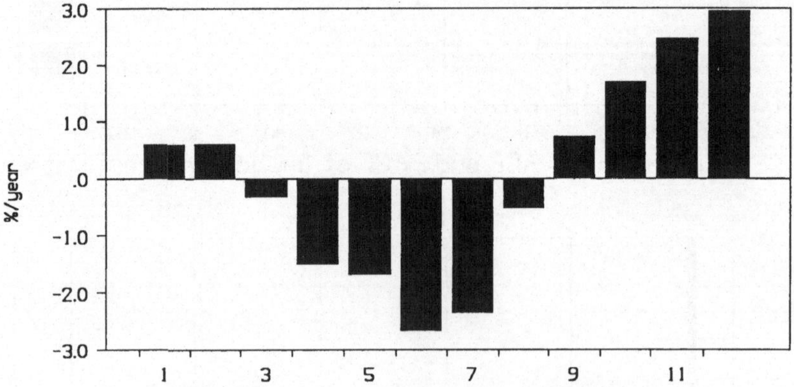

Fig. 4-9b: Implicit Interest Rate, 1883-1896

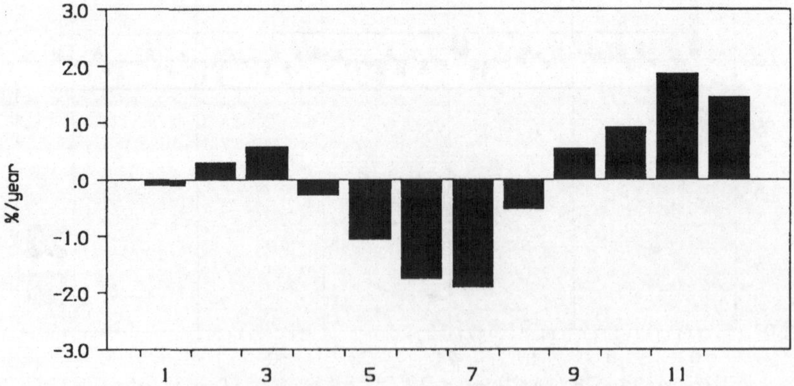

Fig. 4-9c: Implicit Interest Rate, 1897-1913

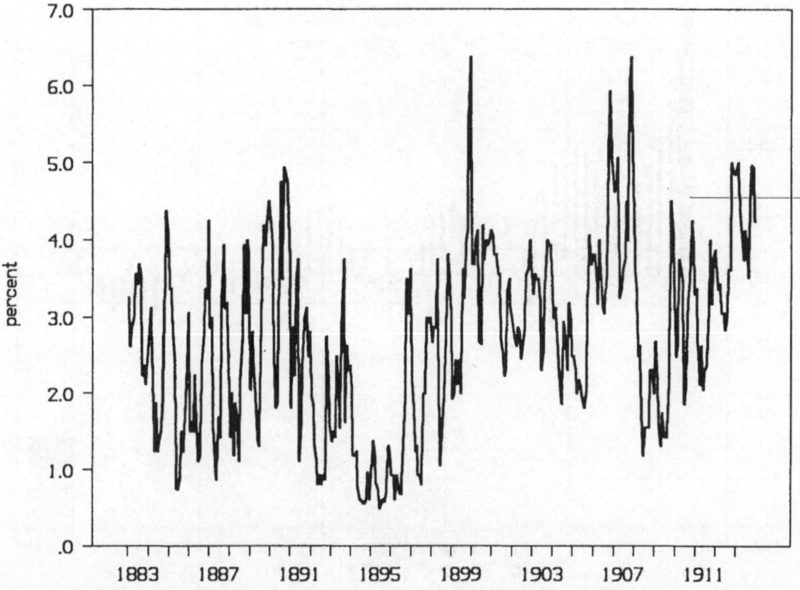

Figure 4-10a: British Discount Rate, 1883-1913

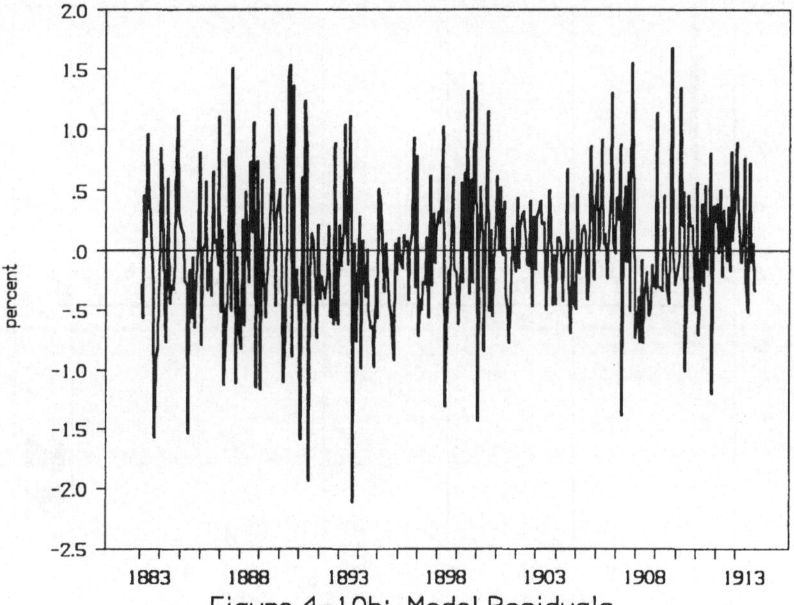

Figure 4-10b: Model Residuals

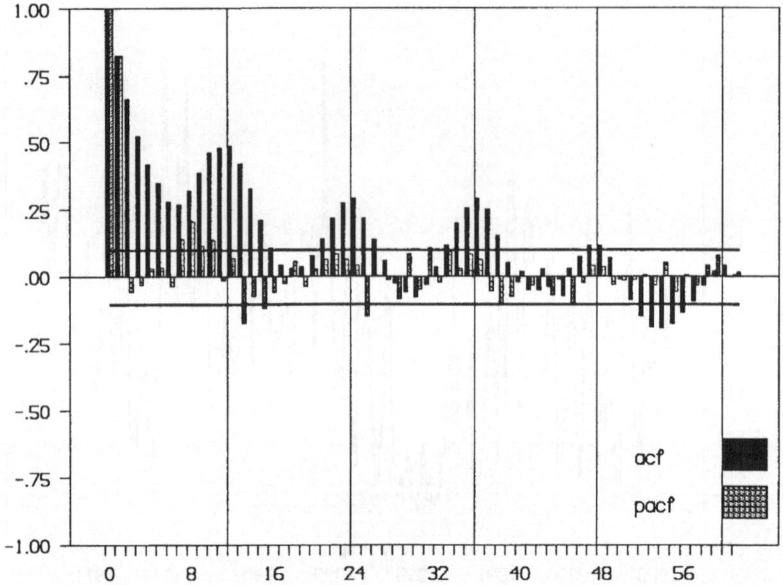

Figure 4-11a: ACF and PACF of British Discount Rate

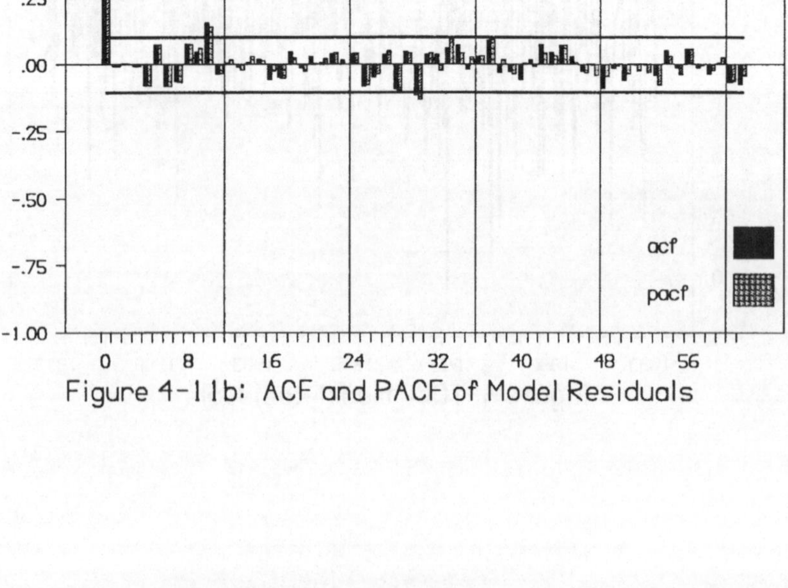

Figure 4-11b: ACF and PACF of Model Residuals

Figure 4-12: British Discount Rate Seasonal Pattern
1883-1913

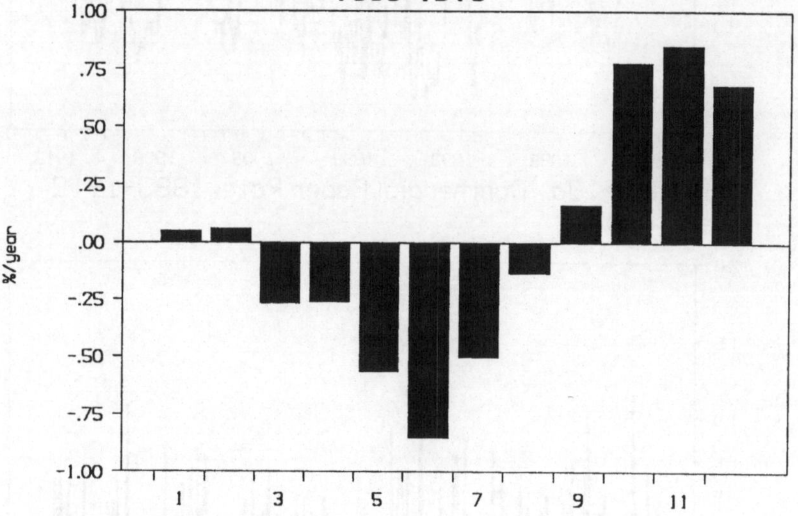

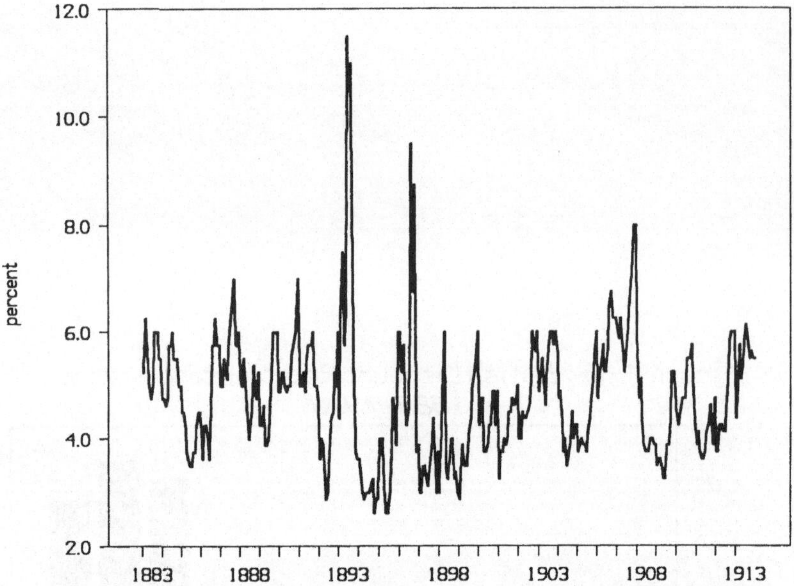

Figure 4-13a: Commercial Paper Rate, 1883-1913

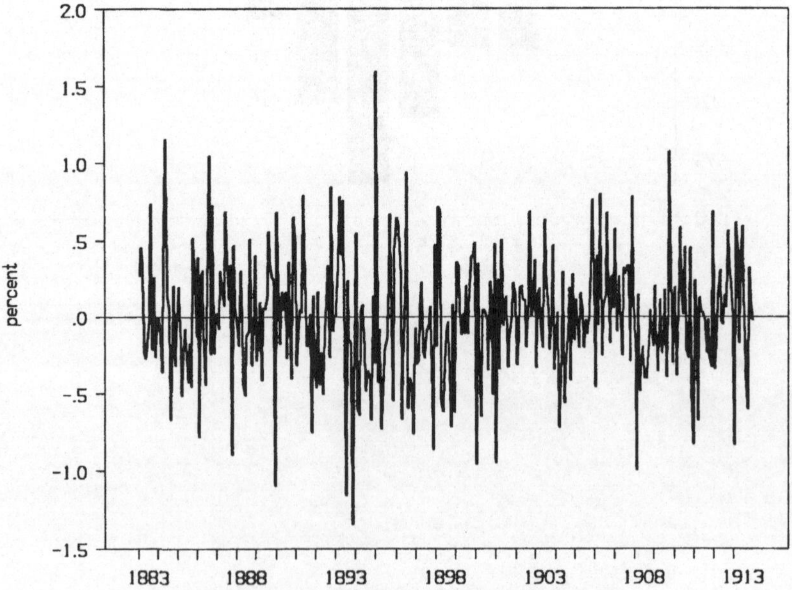

Figure 4-13b: Model Residuals

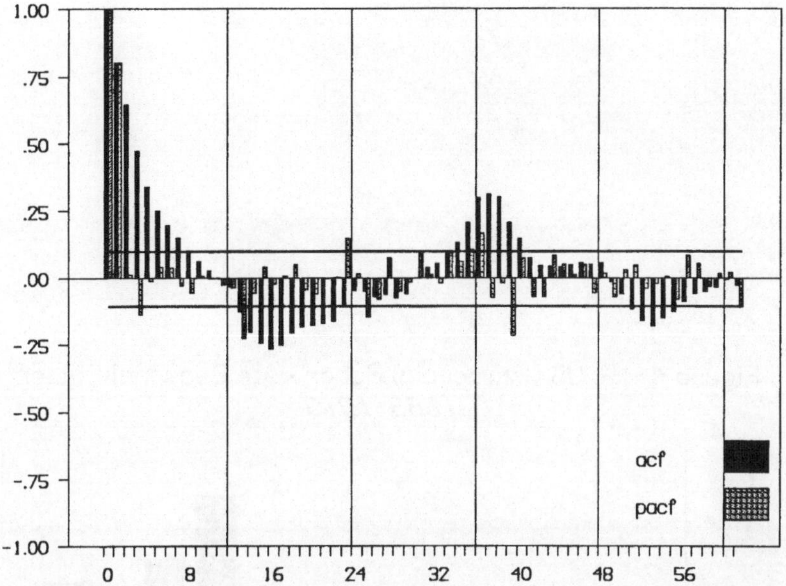

Figure 4-14a: ACF and PACF of Commercial Paper Rate

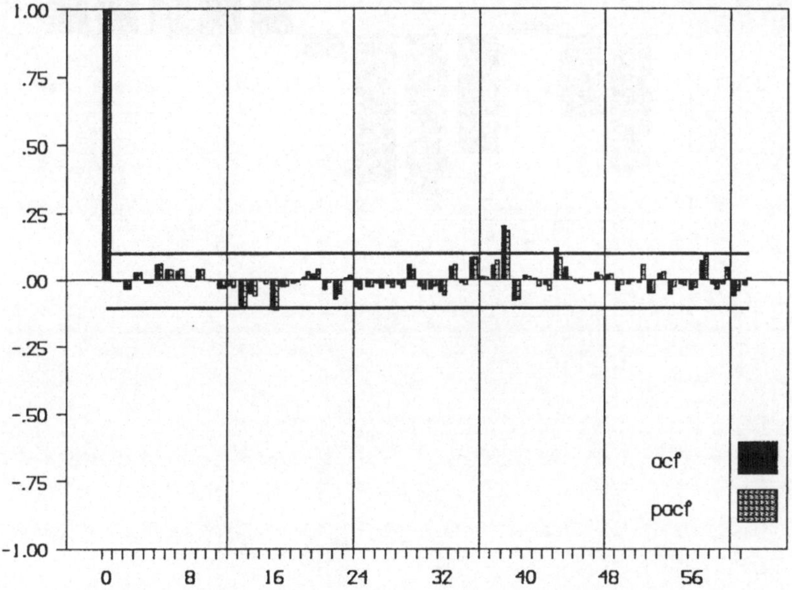

Figure 4-14b: ACF and PACF of Model Residuals

Figure 4-15: US Commercial Paper Rate Seasonal Pattern
1883-1913

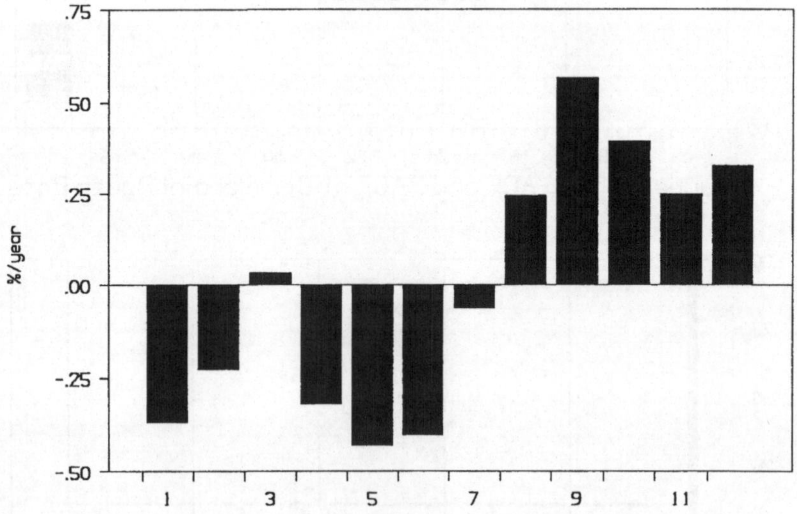

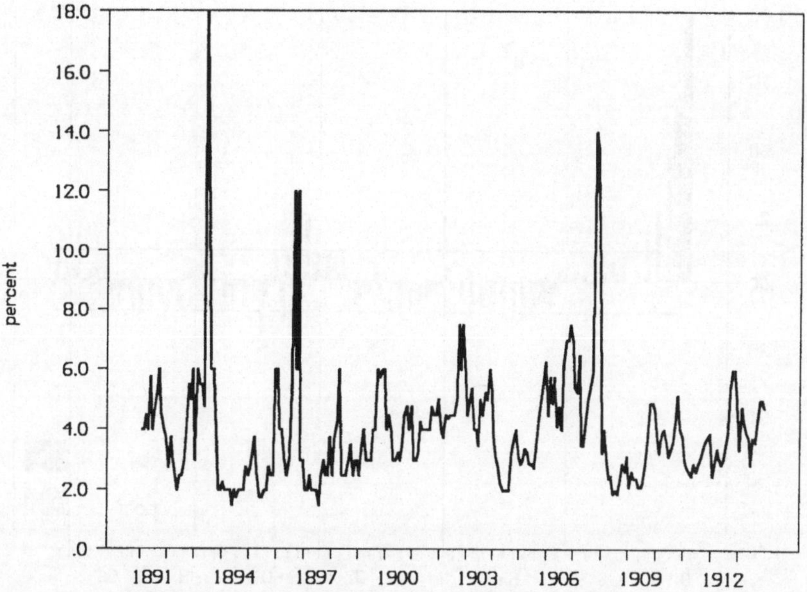

Figure 4-16a: 60 Day Time Rate, 1891-1913

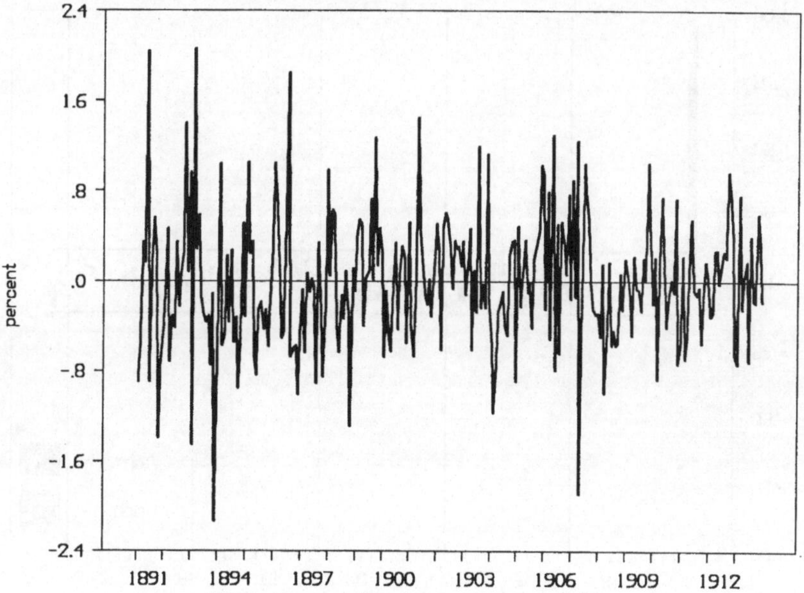

Figure 4-16b: Model Residuals

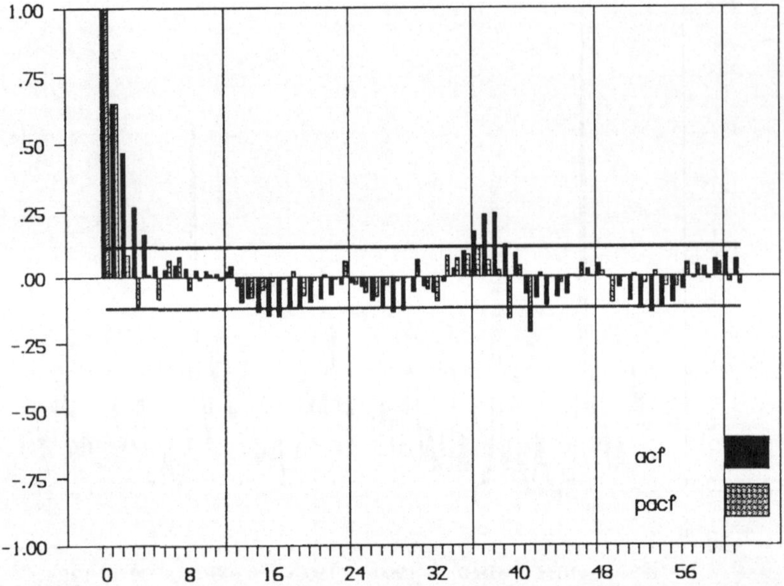

Figure 4-17a: ACF and PACF of 60 Day Time Loan Rate

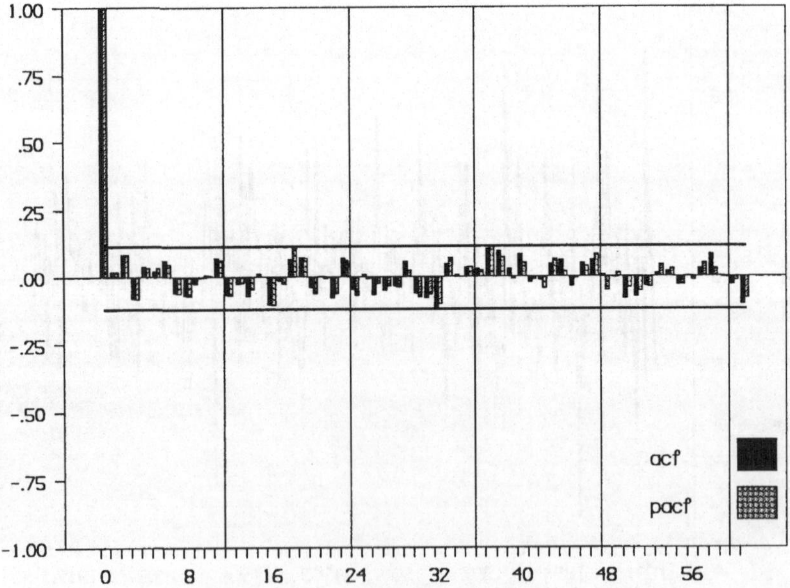

Figure 4-17b: ACF and PACF of Model Residuals

Figure 4-18: US Time Loan Rate Seasonal Pattern
1890-1913

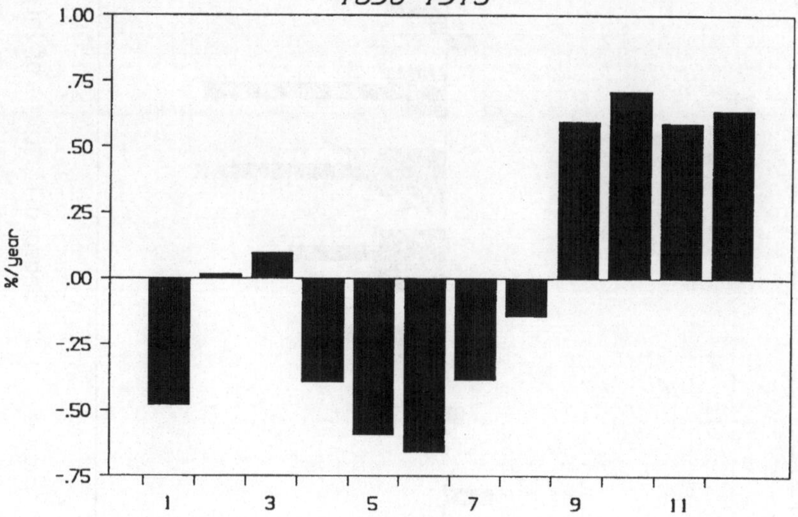

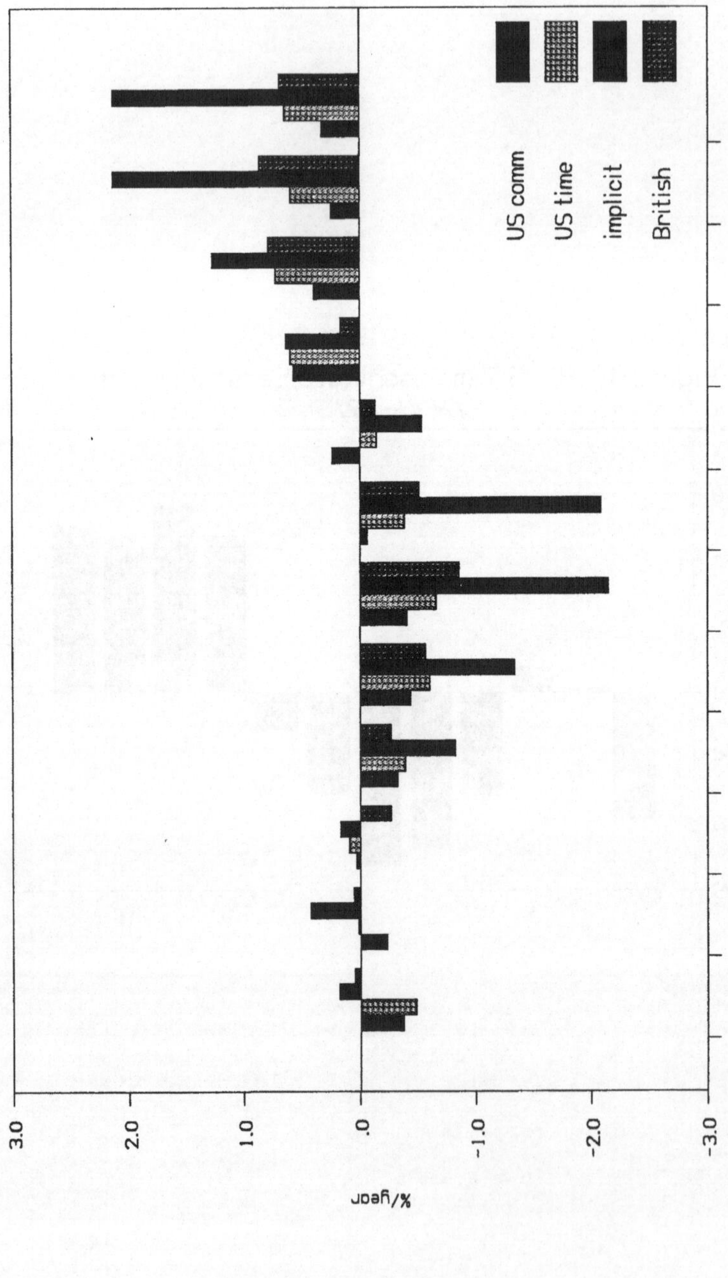

Figure 4-19: Seasonal Patterns of Interest Rates

APPENDIX 4-3: DATA SOURCES AND NOTES

The original source for all data used in this study is the Commercial and Financial Chronicle. Data for the sterling sight exchange rate, the sterling 60 day prime bill of exchange rate and the British 60–90 day open market discount rate were obtained directly from weekly issues of the *Commercial and Financial Chronicle.*[1] The data sources used for the U.S. 60–90 day commercial paper rate and the 60 day time loan rate are:

1880: *The Financial Review.* 1881, p. 19.
1881–1884: *The Commercial and Financial Chronicle*
1885–1889: *The Financial Review.* 1893, p. 30
1890–1909: Andrew (1910) Table 29, pp. 119–138
1910–1914: *The Financial Review.* years 1911–1915.

The 60 day time loan rate was not available before 1890. Before 1890, the commercial paper rate used was referred to as "prime paper". The term of this paper is not explicitly stated. After 1890, the quote used is for double names, choice 60 to 90 day commercial paper. For all the data, end of month series were created from the weekly data. Whenever a range of rates is given, the midpoint of the range is used in the empirical work.

The occurrence of disturbances in United States financial markets and the existence of usury laws in the United States mean that the U.S. commercial paper and time loan rates during this period are sometimes either not available or do not represent market clearing rates. Tables 4-8 and 4-9 below show the months for which normal quotations for commercial paper and time loan rates were not available because: (1) the reported quote was entirely nominal, (2) there was no quote reported, or (3) a commission was charged in addition to the reported rate. In cases where a nominal quote was given, that nominal quote is used in the data series. In cases where no quote is reported, the quote for an adjacent week or an adjacent maturity is used. In cases where a commission rate was charged in addition to a reported rate, an estimated effective annual rate of interest is used which takes the commission into account.

TABLE 4-8: MONTHS FOR WHICH A NORMAL QUOTATION RANGE IS NOT AVAILABLE FOR THE 60–90 DAY COMMERCIAL PAPER RATE

Month	Problem With Quote	Quote Used
Dec. 1892	no quote	use 6% nominal quote
July 1893	range stated is 9–6+1% c	convert to annual rate of 9–12%
Aug. 1896	9–10 % for best, other grades unquotable	use 9–10%
Sep. 1902	nominal quote	use 6% nominal quote
Oct. 1907	no quote, no business	use 7.5% nominal quote for adjacent weeks

TABLE 4-9: MONTHS FOR WHICH A NORMAL QUOTATION RANGE IS NOT AVAILABLE FOR THE 60 DAY TIME LOAN RATE

Month	Problem With Quote	Quote Used
May 1890 week and 4	no quote	quote of 5% for previous month rate used
July 1890	no quote	90 day rate of 4.5–5% used
Aug. 1890	6% nominal rate	use 6%
Nov. 1890	6% + com	use 6%, commission rate not listed
Mar. 1891	no quote	use April 4 rate of 4.5%
June 1893	6+2% c	convert to 18% effective annual rate
July 1893	6+1% c	convert to 12% effective annual rate
Jan. 1896	6% nominal rate	use 6%
Aug. 1896	6+1% c	convert to 12% effective annual rate
Oct. 1896	some business at 12%	use 12%
Nov. 1899	no quote	use 6% quote for adjacent weeks and maturities
Mar. 1902	no quote	use 4.25–4.75% range quoted for 4 month rate
May 1902	no quote	use 5 % quote for 60 day rate for week of May 23
July 1902	no quote	use 4.25% quote for July 25
Sep. 1902	no quote	use range for 90 day rate: 6+.25% c, converted to effective annual rate of 7.5%
Nov. 1902	6+.25% c	convert to 7.5% effective annual rate
Dec. 1902	no quote	use December 26 quote of 6%
Nov. 1907	no quote	use 90 day range of 12–15%

NOTES

1. Exchange rate data are also available in various issues of *The Financial Review* and in Andrew (1910: 188–208), Tables 13 and 14. For the years before 1896, the data included in these sources is for posted rates of exchange, not actual rates of exchange. After 1896, the published data are for actual rates of exchange. Posted rates of exchange were rates used for small transactions and were usually above the actual rates charged for large transactions. Both actual and posted rates of exchange for the entire period are published in the weekly issues of the *Commercial and Financial Chronicle*. In order to construct a consistent data series for the entire period, data on actual rates of exchange were taken from weekly issues of the *Commercial and Financial Chronicle.*

End of month data on British three month prime bills of exchange is also available in Capie and Webber (1985: 507–514), Table III.(10) column V. The original source for this series is *The Economist.* An alternative series constructed from the rates published weekly in the *Commercial and Financial Chronicle* is used instead in this study because these rates are probably more representative of rates charged for bills of exchange originating in the United States. Given that these rates are rates for 60–90 day bills, the term of the bill is also better suited for the purposes of this study. On occasion, separate rates were quoted for 60 and for 90 day bills. Whenever this happened, the rate used is the rate for 60 day bills.

V

An Empirical Investigation of the Seasonal Behavior of Interest Rate Differentials During the Gold Standard

INTRODUCTION

This empirical investigation of interest rate differentials between the United States and Britain is designed to address two questions which arise from reports in the contemporary literature of systematic opportunities for profit by borrowing in London and investing in the United States during the late spring and summer months. First, how similar were the seasonal patterns of interest rate fluctuations in the United States and Britain? Second, did seasonal movements in exchange rates tend to increase or decrease the profit opportunities afforded by borrowing in Britain and investing in the United States during the late spring and early summer months? Uncovered interest parity suggests that movements in exchange rates should offset interest rate differentials between the United States and Britain. Neither of these questions have been satisfactorily addressed in the empirical literature.

As discussed in the literature review, empirical investigations of seasonal fluctuations in interest rate differentials between the United States and Britain have not produced consistent results. Clark (1982) found no significant seasonal pattern in the differential between New

York and British mid-month call loan rates. Morgenstern (1959) found a significant seasonal pattern in the differential between the average monthly New York commercial paper rate and the average monthly London discount rate that was different from the seasonal pattern Goodhart (1969) identified for the difference between average monthly U.S. time loan rates and average monthly London discount rates. In this study, significant seasonal fluctuations were found in all six interest rate differential series investigated.[1] Based upon the seasonal patterns identified here, interest rate differentials tended to increase in the late spring and summer months and were lowest during the late fall and early winter months. Seasonal fluctuations are greater for interest rate differentials which take account of exchange rate fluctuations than for "pure" interest rate differentials which ignore exchange rate movements. These results indicate that exchange rate movements may have increased profit opportunities associated with drawing finance bills during the late spring and summer months. Seasonal fluctuations in several of the interest rate differential series appear to have weakened after 1897.

This chapter begins with a discussion of the six interest rate differential series investigated in this study. The results of the univariate time series models are presented in the next section. The methodology followed here is the same as in the last chapter. The series are first tested for stationarity using Phillips-Perron unit root tests. Based upon an approach developed by Pierce (1978), univariate time series models which allow for deterministic seasonal and cyclical movements in the series are then estimated.[2] In the following section, the out-of-sample forecast performance of seasonal and nonseasonal time series models are compared in order to determine whether seasonal fluctuations remain significant through the end of the period. The next section discusses whether the seasonal fluctuations in interest rate differentials found in this study constitute unexploited profit opportunities. This chapter concludes with a summary and interpretation of the empirical results.

CONSTRUCTION OF THE INTEREST RATE DIFFERENTIAL SERIES

Six interest rate differential series between the United States and Britain are investigated here. The choice of these series reflects the dual objectives of this empirical study: to determine how similar the patterns of seasonal fluctuations in interest rates in the United States and Britain were and to determine whether seasonal movements in exchange rates tended to increase or decrease the profit opportunities afforded by borrowing in Britain during the late spring and summer months. In order to address the first issue, two interest rate differentials between U.S. and British short term nominal interest rate series are examined: the differential between the U.S. 60–90 day double name commercial paper rate and the British discount rate and the differential between the U.S. 60 day time loan rate and the British discount rate. In order to investigate the existence of short term profit opportunities from drawing finance bills on London and investing the proceeds in the United States, it is necessary to take both interest rates and exchange rate movements into account. The uncovered interest parity condition (UIP) says that, after accounting for expected changes in the exchange rate, the returns from investing at home or abroad should be equal. This parity condition assumes that investors are risk neutral, there are no transactions costs and assets are perfect substitutes. Uncovered interest rate parity implies that it should not be possible to make systematic profits by borrowing in one country and investing in the other country. Interest rates at home and abroad can differ, however, if expected exchange rate movements offset the interest rate differential. In this chapter, uncovered interest parity during the pre-World War I gold standard is tested by investigating the behavior of the differential between the U.S. commercial paper rate and the *ex post* implicit borrowing rate and the differential between the U.S. time loan rate and the *ex post* implicit borrowing rate.[3] Uncovered interest rate parity implies that these *ex post* returns from borrowing in Britain and investing in the United States should be unpredictable.[4] In the context of this study, simple uncovered interest parity will be rejected if significant seasonal fluctuations in these *ex post* returns are found. As discussed more fully below, two additional interest rate differential series—the differential between the U.S.

commercial paper rate and the interest rate on 60 day sterling bills in New York and the differential between the U.S. time loan rate and the interest rate on 60 day sterling bills in New York—are investigated in order to determine whether the greater amplitude of seasonal fluctuations of interest rate differentials constructed with the *ex post* implicit borrowing rate are due to seasonal movements of exchange rates or to seasonal movements in the differential between the British discount rate and the discount rate on sterling bills in New York.

There is some dispute in the literature concerning which U.S. interest rate is most appropriate for international comparisons. Morgenstern (1959:119) claimed that the U.S. commercial paper rate was "one of the most important American short term rates, at least up to 1914, at which a large volume of domestic and foreign business was transacted." Goodhart (1969: 47–51) argued that Morgenstern erred in his assessment of the importance of commercial paper rates, claiming that the market was relatively insignificant during the pre-World War I period and that U.S. commercial paper was not regarded as an acceptable form of investment by most foreign bankers. He chooses time rates over commercial paper rates as the relevant rates for international comparisons. Much U.S. paper was "single name" paper, that is paper which was accepted by only one individual. Most European paper was "double name" paper, that is paper which was accepted by two individuals and so was more secure than single name paper. It is not clear, however, that arbitrage activities were restricted to the time loan market. Escher (1918a:90–98) explains that currency loans (loans made where foreign bankers accepted the exchange risk) were usually, but not always, made against high quality collateral. However, prior to the panic of 1907 the standing of the borrower, and not the quality of the collateral, was the most important consideration for the foreign banker. In the case of finance bills (loans made where a U.S. bank accepted the exchange risk), the bills were sometimes, but not always covered by collateral. Escher's remarks indicate that funds obtained by borrowing from London were not restricted to a particular market within the United States. This position is clearly supported by Withers (1918: 122) who states that the proceeds of finance bills drawn by a great American financial house on an "equally eminent English house" could be invested in " . . . the stock-markets or the produce markets or any other outlet that American ingenuity can devise." Johnson (1905: 95) describes an example where high interest rates in New York would cause London bankers to have their correspondents draw long bills on them and invest the proceeds in good commercial paper in New York.

Both differentials between the U.S. commercial paper rate and the British discount rate and differentials between the U.S. 60 day time loan rate and the British discount rate are investigated in this study for several reasons. First, the commercial paper rate used here was the rate for the highest quality double name commercial paper, which was generally quoted at a lower rate than single name paper and would be more comparable to British bills of exchange than the single name paper. Second, although British investors may have preferred the time loan market, there appears to be no reason why an American investor could not borrow in Britain by means of finance bills and then invest the proceeds in the U.S. commercial paper market. Third, rates on commercial paper are readily available for the entire period under investigation, but time loan rates are only available from 1890. Finally, as discussed in Appendix 4-3, the time loan rate series has more missing observations and problems than the commercial loan rate series.

The differential between call loan rates in the United States and Britain is not investigated in this study for two reasons. First, call loans can be renegotiated by either party at any time and therefore have no definite time to maturity. Second, U.S. call loan rates were the most volatile of all the U.S. interest rate series, and tended to soar during times of financial panics. The problem of outliers is therefore greater in the case of call loan rates than with either U.S. time loan or commercial paper rates.

In order to investigate arbitrage opportunities between the New York and London money markets, it is necessary to take exchange rate movements as well as interest rates in both countries into account. Observers of New York financial and foreign exchange markets during the pre-World War I gold standard reported that seasonal fluctuations of exchange rates often created profit opportunities from drawing finance bills on London in the late spring and summer months.[5] These reports of systematic profit opportunities are at odds with the uncovered interest parity hypothesis, which says that it should not be possible to make systematic profits by borrowing in one country and investing in another. An important empirical issue is whether seasonal fluctuations in the differentials between U.S. interest rates and the *ex post* implicit rate on borrowing by drawing finance bills on London reflect seasonal fluctuations of exchange rates or reflect a difference in the seasonal patterns of short term nominal interest rates in the two countries. This issue can be addressed by comparing the pattern of seasonal fluctuations in the implicit borrowing rate differentials with the pattern of seasonal fluctuations in the "pure" differentials between U.S. and British short term interest rates. It is possible that seasonal fluctuations in exchange rates were working to offset the effects of different patterns of seasonal fluctuations in U.S. and British short term interest rates. In this case, we would expect seasonal fluctuations of interest rate differentials which do not take exchange rate movements into account to be much larger than the seasonal fluctuations of interest rate differentials which do take exchange rate movements into account. As shown below, differentials between the *ex post* implicit borrowing rate and U.S. interest rates do take account of both interest rate movements and exchange rate movements.

The *ex post* implicit interest rate on borrowing in London using finance bills was defined in the last chapter as:

$$(1) \qquad i_{k,t} = \frac{s^0_{t+k} - s^k_t}{s^k_t},$$

where $i_{k,t}$ is the implicit k period interest rate at time t (not annualized), s^0_{t+k} is the sight rate at time $t+k$, and s is the dollar price of k period sterling bills of exchange at time t. This implicit borrowing rate can be decomposed into a discount rate component and a dollar depreciation component. In order to see this, we need to define:

$$(2) \qquad s^k_t = \frac{s^0_t}{1+i^*_{k,t}},$$

where $i^*_{k,t}$ is the k-period discount rate in New York on sterling bills (not annualized). The rate used to discount sterling bills in the New York market should be almost equal to the British discount rate because sterling bills of exchange sold in New York were sent to London for acceptance and ultimately discounted in the London discount market. However, this discount rate may differ slightly from the British (London) discount rate at time t because of time lags, the allowance for payment of the British stamp tax, and other frictions.[6] The sight exchange rate at time $t+k$ is equal to the sight exchange rate at time t plus the *ex post* rate of dollar depreciation:

$$s^0_{t+k} = s^0_t\left(1 + x_{t,}\right) \tag{3}$$

where $x_t = \dfrac{s^0_{t+k} - s^0_t}{s^0_t}$ is the *ex post* rate of dollar depreciation during period k (not annualized). Substitution of (2) and (3) into (1) above shows that the *ex post* implicit borrowing rate is approximately equal to the discount rate on sterling bills in New York plus the rate of depreciation on the dollar:

$$i_{k,t} = \left(1 + x_t\right)\left(1 + i^*_{k,t}\right) - 1 \approx x_t + i^*_{k,t}. \tag{4}$$

As long as exchange rate movements are limited by the gold points, the implicit borrowing rate can differ from the discount rate on k-period sterling bills in New York by at most the maximum dollar depreciation allowed by the gold points.[7] The discount rate on sterling bills in New York can be written as:

$$i^*_{k,t} = i^{uk}_{k,t} + d_t, \tag{5}$$

where $i^{uk}_{k,t}$ is the British discount rate on sterling bills and d_t is the difference between the two rates. Substituting (5) into (4), we have:

$$i_{k,t} = i^{uk}_{k,t} + x_t + d_t. \tag{6}$$

Equation (6) shows that if d_t is small, then the major difference in differentials between U.S. interest rates and the *ex post* implicit borrowing rate and differentials between U.S. interest rates and the British discount rate should be due to exchange rate depreciation. In the case where d_t is small, a comparison of the seasonal patterns identified for these two series will indicate whether exchange rate movements tended to increase or decrease profit opportunities for drawing finance bills in the late spring and summer months.

The differential between the London discount rate and the discount rate on sterling bills in New York was much smaller than the differential between U.S. rates and the British discount rate, but it did vary substantially throughout the period 1883 to 1913.[8] In order to eliminate the possibility that variations in this component (d_t) were causing the greater seasonal fluctuations in the differentials with the *ex post* implicit borrowing rate, the seasonal fluctuations in differentials between the two U.S. short term interest rates and the discount rate on 60 day bills in New York are also examined. The discount rate in New York on sixty day sterling bills of exchange can be calculated from data on the dollar prices of sight and sixty day sterling bills of exchange in New York:

$$i^*_{k,t} = \frac{s_t^0 - s_t^k}{s_t^k}, \tag{7}$$

where s_t^0 is the sight exchange rate at time t, and s_t^k is the price of sterling sixty day bills of exchange in New York at time t.[9] Equation (4) above shows that the difference between differentials involving the *ex post* implicit rate and differentials involving the New York discount rate on sterling bills should be due to the rate of depreciation of the dollar.

All interest rate series were matched with respect to the period of the loans as closely as possible. The original source for all series is the *Commercial and Financial Chronicle* and all data refer to the Friday closest to the end of each month. End-of-month data rather than monthly average data were used in order to obtain a series which reflected potential arbitrage opportunities at particular points in time. The loans do differ with respect to quality and riskiness. Dummy variables are used to control for periods of financial market disturbances. The procedure followed was to allow periods of disturbance in either one of the constituent series to affect the differential. Only significant dummy variables are included in the final model.

RESULTS OF EMPIRICAL INVESTIGATION

The results of the empirical modeling of interest rate differentials are presented in this section. All six interest rate differential series investigated here are found to have significant deterministic seasonal components. The pattern of seasonal fluctuations of interest rate differentials between the United States and Britain indicate that seasonal fluctuations of interest rates were more pronounced in Britain than in the United States. In the last chapter, it was found that both U.S. and British short term nominal interest rates tended to be highest in the fall and lowest in the spring and summer months. The seasonal patterns estimated in this chapter indicate that, in general, the differential between U.S. and British rates was highest during the late spring and summer months and lowest in the late fall and early winter months. The amplitude of seasonal fluctuations of differentials which take exchange rate fluctuations into account is greater than the amplitude of the fluctuations in the "pure" interest rate differential series. This finding does not support uncovered interest parity: seasonal exchange rate movements were not working to offset seasonal interest rate differentials between the two countries. The results of this investigation support the existence of profit opportunities from drawing finance bills during the late spring and summer months. There is evidence of weakening, but not of a complete disappearance of seasonal fluctuations in the later part of the period for the three interest rate differential series which involve the U.S. commercial paper rate.

Results for each of the six differential series modeled are discussed in more detail below. The results of unit root tests for stationarity are presented before a description of the time series models for individual series. A table summarizing the model chosen for each series, graphs of the series and model residuals, graphs of the autocorrelation function and partial autocorrelation function of the series and model residuals and a graph of the pattern of seasonal fluctuations are presented for each series.[10] In cases where the shift in seasonal pattern is significant, the changes in the seasonal pattern are shown. Out-of-sample forecast performance for seasonal and nonseasonal models of several interest rate differential series and the sight exchange rate are discussed in the fourth section. The fifth section of this chapter discusses whether these findings of significant seasonal fluctuations can be interpreted as evidence of unexploited profit opportunities. The results of this investigation are summarized and compared with the results of other studies in the final section of this chapter.

Unit Root Tests for Stationarity

The results of the Phillips-Perron unit root tests are shown in Table 5-1. As discussed in the last chapter, the general model estimated for these tests is:

$$y_t = \mu + \beta\left(t - \frac{T}{2}\right) + \alpha y_{t-1} + u_t.$$

In Table 5-1, $Z(t_\alpha)$ is a test statistic for $\alpha = 1$. $Z(t_\beta)$ is the test statistic for $\beta = 1$. $Z(\varphi_s)$ is a test statistic for the joint hypothesis that $\alpha = 1$ and $\beta = 0$. The hypothesis of a unit root is rejected at the 2% level for all series at all lag lengths. This means that none of the series has to be differenced to correct for stochastic nonstationarity. The $Z(t_\beta)$ statistics indicate a significant deterministic trend term in the case of two series: the differential between the U.S. 60 day time loan rate and the British discount rate and the differential between the U.S. 60 day time loan rate and the discount rate on 60 day sterling bills in New York. A time trend will be included in the univariate models for these two series. The hypothesis that $\beta = 0$ (no deterministic trend) was also rejected at the 5% level for the differential between the U.S. commercial paper rate and the British discount rate at lag length 4. When longer lag lengths were used, however, the significance disappeared and so no deterministic trend term was included in the estimated models for these series.

The U.S. Commercial Paper Rate - the British Discount Rate (CMUK)

The differential between the 60–90 day U.S. commercial paper rate and the 60–90 day British discount rate is shown in Figure 5-1a. In general, the U.S. commercial paper rate is higher than the British discount rate. The effects of high commercial paper rates in 1893 and 1896 are evident in the strong peaks in the differential series. The effects of the 1907 episode are not clearly evident. The results of the modeling procedure are shown in Table 5-2. Intervention dummy variables used to capture the effects of disturbances in 1893 and 1896 are significant, but intervention dummy variables for 1907 are not and were dropped from the model.

The autocorrelation function of this differential series is shown in Figure 5-2a and exhibits significant peaks at seasonal lags. The seasonal dummy variables are significant at the 1% level. The seasonal pattern of this series is shown in Figure 3a. This interest rate differential tended to be highest during the months of March and June through September, and lowest during the fall and winter. The mean difference between the two series for the period as a whole is 1.99%. As reported in Table 5-2, the dummy variables allowing for a shift in the seasonal pattern during the years 1897–1913 are significant at the 1% level. The seasonal pattern implied for the years 1883–1896 is shown in Figure 5-3b and the pattern implied for the years 1897–1913 is shown in Figure 5-3c. There is a decline in the amplitude of the seasonal fluctuations and a marked decrease in the differential between the rates during the month of March. There was also a marked decline in the mean of the two series from 2.543% in the early subperiod to 1.527% in the later subperiod. During the early 1890's, there were several periods of uncertainty concerning whether the United States would be able to remain on the gold standard. This decrease in mean value after 1897 could be due to the elimination of a risk premium in U.S. short term interest rates to compensate for the risk that the United States would go off gold.

The 60–90 Day U.S. Commercial Paper Rate - the Implicit Rate (CMIMP)

The differential between the U.S. commercial paper rate and the implicit rate of interest is shown in Figure 5-4a and the autocorrelation function and the partial autocorrelation function for this series are shown in Figure 5-5a. The ACF of this series shows clear evidence of seasonality: autocorrelations at seasonal lags are consistently significant. The results of the model for this series are shown in Table 5-3. The seasonal dummy variables are significant at the 1% level. Dummy variables are used to control for disturbances during 1893 and 1896. The cyclical component of this series is modeled using an AR3 process.

The seasonal pattern of the differential between the commercial paper rate and the implicit interest rate is shown in Figure 5-6a. The amplitude of the seasonal fluctuations of this series is much greater than the amplitude of seasonal fluctuations between the commercial paper rate and the British discount rate. This differential, which takes both exchange rate movements and interest rates into accounts, becomes larger during the late spring and summer months, and decreases sharply from September to December. The mean difference between the two series for the period 1883–1913 is 1.39%. As shown in Table 5-3, the seasonal dummy variables which allow for a shift in the seasonal pattern during the years 1897–1913 are significant at the 1% level. The seasonal pattern implied by the dummy variables for the period 1883–1896 is shown in Figure 5-6b and the seasonal pattern for the period 1897–1913 is shown in Figure 5-6c. There is a decline in the amplitude of the fluctuations and a shift in timing. The seasonal pattern becomes positive in March during the earlier years, but does not become positive until April during the later years. The size of the April seasonal during the later period is much smaller than during the earlier period. There is also a marked decline in the mean of the differential series during the period: from 1.743% during 1883–1896 to 1.102% during 1897–1913. This decline in mean is consistent with the disappearance of a currency risk premium on dollar-denominated assets after 1897.

The 60 Day U.S. Time Loan Rate - the British Discount Rate (TMUK)

Figure 5-7a shows the differential between the 60 day U.S. time loan rate and the British discount rate. Disturbances in the time loan market show up clearly as peaks in the series during 1893, 1896, and 1907. In general, the U.S. time loan rate is higher than the British discount rate. The autocorrelation and partial autocorrelation functions of this series are shown in Figure 5-8a. There are no clear significant peaks in the ACF at 12 or 24 months. However, as shown in Table 5-4, the seasonal dummy variables for this series are significant at the 1% level. The Phillips-Perron unit root tests indicated the presence of a deterministic trend term in this series, and a linear trend variable is significant. Intervention dummy variables are used to control for disturbances in the time loan market in 1893, 1896, 1902, 1906 and 1907. The cyclical component of the series is modeled using a fourth order autoregressive process.

The seasonal pattern implied by the dummy variables, shown in Figure 5-9, is much more erratic than that for the differential between the U.S. commercial paper rate and the British discount rate. The seasonal in this differential is positive in March, June, July, August and September. The lowest difference between the two series tended to occur in January. The weak negative seasonal components in this differential series during the fall of the year are atypical when compared with other interest rate differential series. The mean differential for period as a whole is 2.77%. As shown in Table 5-4, the dummy variables allowing for a shift in seasonal pattern from 1897–1913 are not significant. This finding should be interpreted cautiously, however, because of the limited number of years in the early 1891–1896 subperiod. Two of those six years are years of serious disturbances in financial markets.

The 60 Day U.S. Time Loan Rate - the Implicit Rate (TMIMP)

The differential between the 60 day U.S. time loan rate and the implicit interest rate is shown in Figure 5-10a. Disturbances in the time loan market in 1893, 1896 and 1907 show up clearly . The autocorrelation function and partial autocorrelation function for this series are shown in Figure 5-11a. Evidence of seasonality is stronger in the case of this series than in the case of the difference between time loan rates and the British discount rate: autocorrelations at the first three seasonal lags are significant. However, the pattern of the ACF is not clearly seasonal. At longer lags the peaks in the series occur close to, but not at the seasonals.

As shown in the results presented in Table 5-5, the seasonal dummy variables are significant at the 1% level. Intervention dummy variables are used to control for time loan disturbances in 1893, 1896 and 1907. A third order autoregressive process is used to model the cyclical component of the series. The mean difference between the rates is .477%, which is lower than the mean difference between the U.S. time loan rate and the British discount rate. The seasonal pattern derived from the dummy variables is shown in Figure 5-12. As was true for the differential constructed using the U.S. commercial paper rate, the amplitude of seasonal fluctuations of the series constructed with the implicit borrowing rate is much greater than the amplitude of seasonal fluctuations of the series constructed using the British discount rate. April, May, June, July and August are months when the seasonal component is positive. The size of the April and May seasonals are very small. The seasonal component becomes negative during the fall of the year, and stays negative through the month of March. Seasonal dummy variables allowing for a shift in the seasonal pattern during the years 1897–1913 are not significant at the 10% level. In this case, as in the case of other differentials with the U.S. time loan rate, the result of no shift in seasonal pattern is not a strong one. There certainly is the possibility that a disappearance of currency risk after 1897 could have caused a change in the time series behavior of the interest rate differential.

The U.S. Commercial Paper Rate - Discount Rate on Sterling Bills in New York (CMNYSTER)

The differential between the U.S. commercial paper rate and the discount rate on sterling bills in New York is shown in Figure 5-13a. The effects of high commercial paper rates in 1893 and 1896 are evident in the strong peaks in the series. The autocorrelation function and partial autocorrelation function for the series are shown in Figure 5-14a. The autocorrelation coefficients at seasonal lags 12, 24, and 36 are significant.

The results of the modeling procedure are shown in Table 5-6. Cyclical movements in the series are modeled using a first order autoregressive process. Intervention dummy variables are used to capture the effects of disturbances in 1893 and 1896. The seasonal dummy variables are significant at the 1% level. The seasonal pattern for the entire period is shown in Figure 5-15a. The seasonal in this differential is positive in the months of March through September, and is negative in the months of October through February. The mean differential is 1.44%. As shown in Table 5-6, the dummy variables allowing for a shift in the seasonal pattern during the years 1897–1913 are significant at the 1% level. The seasonal pattern implied for the years 1883–1896 is shown in Figure 5-15b, and the pattern implied for the years 1897–1913 is shown in Figure 5-15c. There is a decline in the amplitude of the seasonal fluctuations and a marked decrease in the mean differential from 1.826% in the earlier subperiod to 1.133% in the later subperiod. As in the case of other interest rate differentials with the U.S. commercial paper rate, this decrease could be due to the disappearance of a currency risk premium on dollar-denominated assets after 1897.

The U.S. 60 Day Time Loan Rate - Discount Rate on Sterling Bills in New York (TMNYSTER)

Figure 5-16a shows the differential between the 60 day U.S. time loan rate and the discount rate on sterling bills in New York. Disturbances in the time loan market show up clearly as peaks in the series during 1893, 1896 and 1907. The autocorrelation and partial autocorrelation functions of this series are shown in Figure 5-17a. As was the case for the differential between the U.S. time loan rate and the British discount rate, there are no significant peaks in the ACF at the seasonal lags 12 or 24 months. However, as shown in Table 5-7, the seasonal dummy variables for this series are significant at the 1% level. The Phillips-Perron unit root tests, shown in Table 5-1, indicate the presence of a deterministic trend term in this series, and a linear trend variable is significant. Intervention dummy variables are used to control for disturbances in the time loan market in 1893, 1895, 1896, 1902 and 1907. The cyclical component of the series is modeled using a fourth order autoregressive process.

The seasonal pattern implied by the seasonal dummy variables, shown in Figure 5-18, is very similar to the seasonal pattern of the differential between the U.S. time loan rate and the British discount rate. The seasonal peaks in the month of September, and is positive during the months of March, June, July and August as well. The seasonal is most negative in the month of January. The mean differential for this series is 1.812%. The dummy variables allowing for a shift in seasonal pattern during the period 1897–1913 are not significant.

Comparison of Seasonal Patterns of Interest Rate Differential Series

All the interest rate differential series investigated here have significant deterministic seasonal components as well as cyclical autoregressive components. Figure 5-19 summarizes the seasonal patterns of all interest rate differential series. The seasonal patterns of the three differential series with the commercial paper rate are shown for the period as a whole and for the two subperiods 1883–1896 and 1897–1913. Because there was not a significant shift in seasonal pattern for any of the three differential series with the time loan rate, only the seasonal pattern for the period as a whole is shown for these series.

The seasonal patterns of the differentials between the U.S. rates and the British discount rate (CMUK, TMUK) and the differentials between the U.S. rates and the discount rate on sterling bills in New York (CMNYSTER, TMNYSTER) are very similar. In all cases, the amplitude of seasonal fluctuations of the interest rate differentials with the implicit borrowing rate (CMIMP, TMIMP), shown by solid black bars, are greater than the amplitude of seasonal fluctuations of the "pure" interest rate differentials. As discussed above in section II, the interest rate differentials constructed between U.S. rates and the implicit borrowing rate have both an interest rate component and an exchange rate depreciation component. The greater amplitude of seasonal fluctuations in differentials involving the implicit borrowing rate clearly indicates that exchange rate movements tended to increase, rather than offset, seasonal differences in U.S. and British interest rates. This result suggests that uncovered interest parity did not hold during the gold standard.

The amplitude of seasonal fluctuations of the differential between the U.S. commercial paper rate and the implicit borrowing rate (CMIMP) is greater than the amplitude of the differential between the U.S. time loan rate and the implicit borrowing rate (TMIMP). Seasonal fluctuations in both series peak in July and are lowest during the months of November and December. The April and May seasonals are much smaller in the case of TMIMP than in the case of CMIMP. The mean differentials for TMIMP are also smaller than for CMIMP.

These differences in means and seasonal patterns suggest the existence of lower rates of return from drawing finance bills and investing in time loans rather than U.S. commercial paper.

OUT-OF-SAMPLE FORECAST PERFORMANCE

Although significant seasonal fluctuations were identified for all interest rate differential series, it is not clear whether these seasonal fluctuations remained significant up to the end of the period. Out-of-sample forecasting results suggest that they did. A comparison of out-of-sample forecasting performance for the years 1911 to 1913 of seasonal and nonseasonal models of four interest rate differential series indicates that the seasonal movements identified for the years 1897–1910 help improve predictions of movements in each series at the end of the period. In order to determine whether seasonal movements of exchange rates remained important at the end of the period, the out-of-sample forecast performance of seasonal and nonseasonal models of the sight exchange rate are also compared in this section.[11]

The procedure followed in this comparison of out-of-sample forecast performance is to identify and estimate both an autoregressive seasonal model and an autoregressive nonseasonal model for each series for the period 1897–1910. The time period for model estimation was restricted to the years when there was no uncertainty that the United States would leave the gold standard. Forecast errors for the years 1911–1913 were evaluated for forecast horizons from one month to fourteen months ahead. The seasonal models estimated are summarized in Table 5-8. The nonseasonal models estimated are summarized in Table 5-9. Because all of these series have a significant deterministic seasonal component, none of the nonseasonal autoregressive models was completely satisfactory. The selection of the final nonseasonal model for each series was based upon the best forecast performance. In the case of three series—the differential between the U.S. commercial paper rate and the British discount rate (CMUK), the differential between the U.S. time loan rate and the implicit borrowing rate (TMIMP) and the differential between the U.S. time loan rate and the British discount rate (TMUK)—the order of the seasonal model is the same as the order of the nonseasonal model. In the case of the other two series–the differential between the U.S. commercial paper rate and the implicit borrowing rate (CMIMP) and the sight rate–the order of the nonseasonal model is lower than of the seasonal model. For these two series, the forecast errors were smaller in the case of the simpler nonseasonal autoregressive models.

Tables 5-10a through 5-10e present the mean absolute errors (MAE), the root mean square errors (RMSE), and Theil's U statistics for seasonal and nonseasonal models of each series. The Theil's U statistic compares the root mean square error from forecasts of the specified model to the root mean square error of the simplest possible forecast, a naive forecast of no change in the series (a random walk forecast). A value less than one indicates that the specified model has a smaller root mean square error than the random walk model. A value greater than one indicates that the random walk model tend to forecast better than the specified model. Forecast errors for the years 1911–1913 were evaluated for forecast horizons from one month to fourteen months ahead.

The seasonal model has a smaller root mean square error than the nonseasonal model for all series at all forecast horizons. The nonseasonal model had a smaller mean absolute error than the seasonal model at the one month forecast horizon for four of the five series: the sight rate, the differential between the U.S. commercial paper rate and the implicit interest rate, the differential between the U.S. time loan rate and the implicit interest rate and the differential between the U.S. time loan rate and the British discount rate. The seasonal model had a smaller mean absolute error than the nonseasonal model at all other forecast horizons for these four series. The seasonal model also had a smaller mean absolute error at all forecast horizons in the case of the differential between the U.S. commercial paper rate and the British discount rate.

Because none of these series were identified as nonstationary, we would expect that both the seasonal and nonseasonal autoregressive models would forecast better than the naive random walk model.[12] If this is true, then all the Theil's U statistics should be less than one. However, for all five series, the Theil's U statistic is close to or greater than one for the nonseasonal autoregressive model at forecast horizons of twelve months. One explanation of this pattern is that the nonseasonal autoregressive models are forecasting more poorly than the random walk model because the random walk forecast of no change in the series accounts for the seasonal movements of the series better than the nonseasonal autoregressive model at a one year forecast horizon. The superior forecast performance of the seasonal models in almost all cases indicates that seasonal fluctuations remained important for all series through the end of the period.

SEASONAL FLUCTUATIONS OF INTEREST DIFFERENTIALS: UNEXPLOITED PROFIT OPPORTUNITIES?

The foregoing results indicate that there may indeed have been systematic profit opportunities associated with drawing finance bills during the late spring and summer months, and suggest that uncovered interest parity may not have held during this period. The differentials between U.S. interest rates and the interest rate on borrowing from Britain using finance bills clearly did not fluctuate randomly, but rather tended to increase systematically during the late spring and summer months. As has been noted in other studies of uncovered interest parity during more recent historical periods, a rejection of the simple uncovered interest parity hypothesis does not necessarily mean that unexploited profit opportunities exist. There are three reasons why the profits identified in this study may be overstated. First, the relevant rate for determining whether or not to draw finance bills is not the *ex post* implicit rate calculated and used here, but an *ex ante* implicit rate which depends on the expected future value of the sight rate and which includes an allowance for transactions costs. Second, interest rate differentials may include a time varying seasonal risk premium to compensate arbitrageurs for exchange rate risk and/or the greater riskiness associated with U.S. assets. Third, it is not clear that published rates for sixty day bills of exchange were the rates at which finance bills could be drawn "at the margin." If prices of sixty day bills of exchange offered to exchange rate speculators were lower than the published rates, then profits on drawing finance bills would be lower.

As explained above, the implicit rate used in this investigation is the *ex post* implicit interest rate, calculated using actual sight rates and rates on sixty day bills of exchange. In the absence of transactions costs, the *ex post* implicit interest rate on borrowing abroad by means of drawing a finance bill depends only on the rate at which the finance bill is sold in the New York market and the sight rate which prevails when the bill matures (i.e. when the loan from the British bank has to be paid off):

$$i_{imp}^{k}(t) = \frac{s_{t+k}^{0} - s_{t}^{k}}{s_{t}^{k}}.$$

However, the relevant rate for determining whether or not to draw finance bills is of course not this *ex post* implicit rate, but an *ex ante* implicit rate which depends on expected sight rate and includes transactions costs:

$$i_{eximp}^{k}(t) = \frac{E_t\left(s_{t+k}^{0}\right) - s_{t}^{k}}{s_{t}^{k}} + c,$$

where i_{eximp}^{k} is the *ex ante* implicit *k*-period interest rate, $E_t\left(s_{t+k}^{0}\right)$ is the time *t* expectation of the sight rate at time *t*+*k*, s_t^k is the dollar price of *k*-period sterling bills of exchange in New York at time *t*, and *c* is the transactions costs of drawing finance bills expressed in annual percentage terms. There are two reasons why this *ex ante* implicit interest rate differs from the *ex post* implicit interest rate: (1) the actual sight rate at time *t*+*k* may differ from its time *t* expectation, and (2) the existence of transactions costs which are not incorporated into the price of long bills of exchange.

If expectations are rational, then the actual spot rate at time *t*+*k* should be an unbiased predictor of the time *t* expectation of the spot rate at *t*+*k*:

$$s_{t+k}^{0} = E_t\left(s_{t+k}^{0}\right) + e_t$$

where e_t is a random forecast error. If the actual spot rate at *t*+*k* differs from its time *t* expectation only by a random forecast error, then the *ex post* implicit rate should be an unbiased estimate of the *ex ante* implicit rate. There were periods in the early 1890's when there was considerable uncertainty concerning whether or not the United States would remain on the gold standard.[13] The assumption that forecast errors were random may not hold: expected depreciation of the dollar may well have been greater than actual depreciation, and the *ex post* implicit rate may underestimate the *ex ante* implicit rate during those times of speculation that the United States would be forced to leave the gold standard.

There were two transactions costs involved in drawing finance bills: the acceptance commission, which is the London bank's return for guaranteeing payment of the bill, and the British stamp tax. Allowance for the payment of the stamp tax is included in the price of long bills of exchange. Based upon the range of rates available in the literature, a range of 0.5–1.5% is a reasonable range for estimates of additional transactions costs on finance bills.[14] In cases where the American bank and the London bank were acting on joint account, or where the London bank was accepting the exchange risk and the American bank was acting as an agent of the London bank, the explicit transactions costs of drawing finance bills could well be lower.

The seasonal pattern of interest rate differentials is not affected by higher transactions costs associated with drawing finance bills. Higher transactions costs imply a higher implicit borrowing rate and a downward shift in interest rate differentials calculated using the implicit interest rate. If transactions costs are increased by 0.5–1.5 %, the apparent profit opportunities from drawing finance bills are reduced, but do not disappear completely. This can be seen by examining Table 5-11a and Table 5-11b, which show the sample monthly means of realized *ex post* returns for the differential between the U.S. commercial paper rate and the implicit interest rate (CMIMP) and the differential between the U.S. time loan rate and the implicit interest rate (TMIMP). Although the large standard deviations indicate the returns each month are variable, the mean monthly differentials are greater than the upper bound transactions cost estimate of 1.5% for the months of April through May in the case of CMIMP and for the months of July and August for TMIMP. These actual *ex post* returns during the months which were identified as profitable one for drawing finance bills based upon seasonal patterns are shown in more detail in Figure 5-20 and Figure 5-21. Figure 5-20 shows the differential between the U.S. commercial paper rate and the implicit interest rate during the years 1883–1913 for the months of April, May, June, July and August. Figure 5-21 shows the differential between the U.S. time loan rate and the implicit interest rate during the years 1890–1913 for the months of May, June, July and August.

Table 5-12 is designed to show the variability of returns and the significance of transactions costs during the months identified as months of seasonal profit opportunities. Table 5-12a shows the number of times the differential between the U.S. commercial paper rate and the implicit borrowing rate was negative, less than 0.5%, less than 1.0%, and less than 1.5% during the months of April, May, June, July and August. Returns were most certain during the months of June and July. The differential was negative only once during July out of the 31 years in the period investigated. It was less than 1.5% only six times during the month of June and only three times during the month of July. This indicates that even though transactions costs at the upper bound estimate of 1.5% would eliminate many of the profitable opportunities for drawing finance bills during the months of April, May and August, transactions costs would not eliminate many of the profitable opportunities during the months of June and July.

Table 5-12b shows the number of months when the differential between the U.S. time loan rate and the implicit borrowing rate was negative, less than 0.5%, less than 1%, and less than 1.5% during the months of May, June, July and August. This differential was negative only in two out of twenty two years during the month of July, and was less than 1.5% only five times. Transactions costs of 1.5% would, however, eliminate almost all the positive returns from borrowing using finance bills and investing in the New York time loan market during the month of May. This level of transactions costs would also eliminate more than one half of the positive returns during the months of August and more than one third of the positive returns during June. Once again, July is identified as the month when returns from drawing finance bills were consistently the highest. In the cases of both the U.S. commercial paper market and the U.S. time loan market, transactions costs would eliminate some, but by no means all of the profit opportunities from drawing finance bills.

There is another reason why the predictable seasonal fluctuations in interest rate differentials must be interpreted cautiously as evidence that drawing finance bills in the late spring and summer months provided systematic profit opportunities. The published actual rate for 60 day bills of exchange may not represent the rate at which an arbitrageur could draw finance bills "at the margin." American finance bills were viewed as "prime bank acceptances" by the London discount market as long as the volume of such bills was not too large. Escher (1918: 85–98) points out that the London discount market effectively limited the loans made to the American market by its willingness to discount bankers long bills originating in the United States. Rates charged to financial houses which drew "too many" finance bills would increase. Withers (1918:125) says that the willingness of the London discount market to absorb finance bills placed limits on the creation of the bills:

> *A bill drawn on London is of no use if the London discount market will not buy it, and though it is exceedingly rare for bills drawn on a well-known London name to be looked on askance, it does sometimes happen, and the accepting houses know that their lives depend on not putting their names to more paper than the discount market thinks enough for them.*

Withers emphasizes the importance of reputation to the London acceptance houses, whose business could suffer for years if they accepted too many bills. If a risk averse London discount market prevented exchange rate speculators from drawing finance bills at prevailing discount rates, then the *ex post* implicit interest rate does not represent a market rate at which additional funds could be borrowed. The observed seasonal profit opportunities constitute profit opportunities only on "inframarginal" units borrowed from London. In this case, all profit opportunities would be exploited at the margin because rates of discount for bills drawn by arbitrageurs were higher than the published rates.

The existence of transactions costs, the potential for systematic exchange rate forecast errors, the possibility of an exchange-risk premium and/or a risk premium on U.S. loans, and limits imposed by the London discount market all mean that the seasonal profit opportunities identified in this paper may be overstated. It is impossible, however, to quantify these factors exactly. Based on estimates of transactions costs for this period available in the literature, transactions costs alone are clearly not large enough to eliminate all the *ex post* returns identified in this study. During times of uncertainty the U.S. would not be able to remain on the gold standard, arbitrageurs may have persistently expected the dollar to depreciate past the gold export point. This uncertainty was largely eliminated after 1896, yet seasonal fluctuations of exchange rates and *ex post* profit opportunities persisted throughout the period. Although there is a possibility that an exchange-risk premium and/or a risk premium on U.S. loans existed during this period, it is not clear why those premia should fluctuate seasonally in a way which could explain the seasonal fluctuations in *ex post* returns. Liquidity constraints, in the form of limits imposed by the London discount market on the amount of finance bills drawn, stand out as the most likely explanation of the persistence of seasonal profit opportunities over time. These liquidity constraints could have prevented arbitrageurs from drawing finance bills in sufficient quantities such that published market exchange rates and interest rates moved to eliminate all systematic profit opportunities. This is a case in which all profit opportunities for arbitrageurs would be eliminated at the margin, but positive profits could be realized on all inframarginal units of finance bills drawn.

Rejection of the simple uncovered interest parity hypothesis is consistent with tests conducted by Morgenstern (1959) and Officer (1986). In both of these studies, short term interest rate differentials were found to be too large to be consistent with uncovered interest parity, given the limits on exchange rate fluctuations implied by the gold points. Results of this study contradict the finding of Calomiris and Hubbard (1987), who argue that gold interest rate parity held during the gold standard. In studies of uncovered interest parity during more recent historical periods, the results are mixed. Some studies have found support for the simple uncovered interest parity condition, while many others have rejected uncovered interest parity. These studies of uncovered interest rate parity for more recent historical periods can be divided into two categories: those that assume covered interest parity holds and then test uncovered interest parity by testing the unbiasedness of the forward rate, and those that test uncovered interest parity without assuming that covered interest parity holds. There is a wide range of methods and results found in this literature, and the definitive explanation of when and why uncovered interest parity holds or does not hold has yet to be developed. Both categories of tests of uncovered interest parity are briefly reviewed here.

A test for the unbiasedness of the forward rate is a test of uncovered interest parity if covered interest parity is assumed to hold.[15] Covered interest parity states that there should be no riskless profit opportunities from borrowing in one currency and investing in assets denominated in another currency. In logarithmic form, this condition is:

(8) $$\ln(F_{k,t}) - \ln(S_t) = R_{k,t} - R*_{k,t},$$

where $F_{k,t}$ is the k-period forward rate at time t, S_t is the spot exchange rate defined as the domestic currency price of foreign currency, and $R_{k,t}$ ($R*_{k,t}$) is the nominal rate of return on a k-period domestic (foreign) asset. This differs from the uncovered interest parity condition, which states that the difference between domestic and foreign rates of return should be equal to the expected rate of change of the exchange rate:

(9) $$\ln(E_t(S_{t+k})) - \ln(S_t) = R_{k,t} - R*_{k,t}.$$

If covered interest parity hold, equations (8) and (9) imply that the forward rate should be equal to the expected future spot rate:

$$F_{k,t} = E_t(S_{t+k}).$$

A test of uncovered interest parity is a test of unbiasedness of the forward rate. Frenkel (1981) tests uncovered interest parity by testing the hypothesis that $a = 0$ and $b = 1$ in the regression:

$$\ln(S_{t+1}) = a + b(\ln(F_{1,t})) + v_{t+1}.$$

He finds that he can not reject the maintained hypothesis of unbiasedness of the forward rate, a result which suggests that uncovered interest parity is supported by the data. Many other studies, including Cumby and Obstfeld (1984), point out econometric problems with this simple test of uncovered interest parity in level form using ordinary least squares: estimation and testing need to take account of both the nonstationarity of the spot and forward rates and the heteroskedasticity of the residuals. Tests of unbiasedness of the forward rate which correct for these problems generally reject the unbiasedness hypothesis and so conclude that the simple uncovered interest parity hypothesis is not supported by the data.

Two explanations for this finding that the forward rate is biased are most common in this literature: the existence of an exchange-risk premium and the peso problem. An exchange-risk premium can be expected if agents are risk averse and exchange rate speculation entails systematic risk. It has, however, proven extremely difficult to model this exchange-risk premium. Cumby (1988) notes that *ex ante* nominal returns to exchange rate speculation are clearly not constant, but fluctuate over time and often change sign. He points out that previous attempts to model exchange risk have been unsuccessful, and also finds that real returns to exchange rate speculation can not be satisfactorily explained by the consumption based model of the risk premium which he develops in his study.

Another potential explanation for the rejection of the unbiasedness hypothesis using standard econometric tests is the "peso problem." Krasker (1980) shows that in cases where an event with a small probability of occurring could cause a large change in the exchange rate, then conventional tests of the efficiency of the forward market are not valid. The expectation of a devaluation which had a small probability of occurring but which did not occur could cause forward rates to consistently overestimate the future spot rate.[16] In a small sample, forward rates appear to be biased even though exchange markets are efficient given the expectation of a possible devaluation. This "peso problem" has been noted as a possible factor which could explain, or at least partially explain, the rejection of the unbiasedness hypothesis in more recent studies as well (Cumby and Obstfeld (1984), Cumby (1988)).

It is also possible to test uncovered interest parity without assuming that covered interest parity holds. Rather than testing the unbiasedness of the forward rate, studies which do not assume covered interest parity take one of several approaches. Some studies investigate the time series behavior of the *ex post* returns from uncovered interest arbitrage (Cumby and Obstfeld (1981), Gregory (1987)). Several others test cross equation implied by rational expectations in a simple exchange rate, a vector autoregression, or a frequency domain model (Gregory (1987), Taylor (1987), Ito (1987), Ito and Quah (1989)). McAvinchey and MacDonald (1990) use a direct approach and test the hypothesis that $\alpha = 0$ and $\beta = 1$, and investigate the error structure of the residuals in the following regression:

(10) $$\Delta s_{t+1} = \alpha + \beta(i_t - i^*_t) + v_{t+1},$$

where Δs_{t+1} is the actual change in the logarithm of the exchange rate from period t to period $t+1$, i (i^*) is the domestic (foreign) one period interest rate, and v_{t+1} is an error process assumed to be orthogonal to all information known at time t. The results of these different approaches are discussed in turn below.

Using weekly data on spot exchange rates, the one week forward rate and one week Eurodeposit rates for the period July 1974–June 1980, Cumby and Obstfeld (1981) reject the simple uncovered interest parity hypothesis on the grounds that the *ex post* returns from uncovered interest arbitrage are not white noise during this period. They note that their results are consistent with the existence of an exchange-risk premium. In a test of the efficiency of the Canadian dollar-U.S. dollar exchange market, Gregory (1987) finds that when the spot rate and interest rate differentials are defined in level form, results for the 1970's are similar those reported by Cumby and Obstfeld (1981): simple uncovered interest parity is rejected. However, results for the 1980's are quite different: *ex post* returns do resemble white noise and uncovered interest parity can not be rejected. Gregory is not able to reject uncovered interest parity for any part of the 1972–1985 period when all the variables are first differenced. He also finds that he can not reject the cross equation restrictions implied by rational expectations in a simple model of exchange rate determination based on uncovered interest rate parity. He concludes that uncovered interest parity does characterize foreign exchange markets in the 1980's.

Taylor (1987) tests uncovered interest parity by testing the cross equation restrictions implied by rational expectations in a vector autoregression model. He finds that using end-of-month exchange rate data and Eurodeposit interest rates during the period 1979–1986, uncovered interest parity is rejected for the dollar-sterling, mark-sterling, yen-sterling, guilder-sterling, yen-dollar, franc-dollar, lira-dollar and guilder-dollar exchange rates. Rational expectations cross equation restrictions were accepted only in the cases of the lira-sterling and the mark-sterling exchange rates. Taylor points to exchange-risk premia as the most likely explanation of deviations from uncovered interest parity and calls for more research into modeling foreign exchange risk.

Using a similar methodology to Taylor, Ito (1987) tests uncovered interest parity for the yen-dollar exchange rate, a Japanese domestic interest rate and the Eurodollar interest rate. He finds that uncovered interest parity is rejected for the years 1973–1977, a period when strict capital controls were in effect, but is not rejected for the years 1981–1985, a period of free capital mobility. He points out that the existence of capital controls in the 1970's meant that the Japanese domestic asset was not comparable to Eurodollar deposits. After capital controls were eliminated at the end of 1980, uncovered interest rate parity holds for the yen-dollar rate, a result which suggests that there was no exchange-risk premium in this market for this time period. Ito and Quah (1989) develop tests of rational expectation cross equation restrictions for a frequency domain model. This enables them to use higher frequency (weekly) data than was tractable in a vector autoregression model. Using this methodology, they find that they can not reject uncovered interest parity for the yen-dollar exchange rate, the three month Eurodollar deposit rate and the three month Euroyen deposit rate during the period 1975–1984.

In summary, tests of uncovered interest parity for recent historical periods have not produced consistent results. At this time, there is a consensus among investigators that the forward rate is a biased predictor of the future spot rate, which suggests that the simple uncovered interest parity hypothesis does not hold. Explanations of this focus primarily on the existence of exchange-risk premia, but the peso problem is also noted as a potential explanation. Tests of uncovered interest parity which do not assume covered interest parity have produced mixed results. Ito (1987) finds that the existence of capital controls in Japanese domestic financial markets explains the failure of uncovered interest parity in the 1970's. He finds that uncovered interest parity holds in the 1980's when capital controls are removed. His work suggests the importance of using comparable assets in tests of uncovered interest parity. Indeed, Ito and Quah (1989) find that they are unable to reject uncovered interest parity for the yen and the dollar for the entire period 1975–1984 when Euroyen and Eurodollar deposit rates are used. Gregory (1987) also is not able reject uncovered interest parity for Canada and the United States for the years 1972–1985. Other studies, including Cumby and Obstfeld

(1981), Taylor (1987) and McAvinchey and MacDonald (1990), all obtain results which suggest that uncovered interest parity may not hold for many currencies. The failure of uncovered interest parity to hold in these studies is attributed to the existence of exchange-risk premia, pointing to the need for more research into modeling exchange risk in financial markets.

The factors discussed as reasons for the failure of uncovered interest parity in studies of more recent periods may help explain the rejection of the simple uncovered interest parity hypothesis during the gold standard. The peso problem is certainly relevant during periods of uncertainty in the early 1890's that the U.S. would leave the gold standard. An exchange-risk premium may well have existed during the gold standard. However, in order to explain deviations from uncovered interest parity, that risk premium would have to fluctuate seasonally. Developing a model which would generate a seasonal exchange-risk premium is an area for future research.

Two of the factors discussed above as possible explanations for deviations from uncovered interest parity–transactions costs and liquidity constraints–have received more attention in the covered interest arbitrage literature than in the uncovered arbitrage literature. Frenkel and Levich (1975, 1977) show how transactions costs determine a neutral band around the uncovered interest parity condition. Their studies also indicate the significance of asset comparability. Transactions costs explain close to 100% of the deviations from covered interest parity when Eurosterling and Eurodollar interest rates are used, but a much smaller percentage of deviations from covered interest parity when U.S. and British treasury bill rates are used. This difference in results is attributed to factors such as differential risk, differential tax treatment and governmental controls that arise when securities issued in different countries are compared.

More recent studies of covered interest parity have used improved data sets to measure transactions costs and arbitrage opportunities facing traders at a particular point in time.[17] Although deviations from covered interest parity are found, the consensus is that those deviations are generally small and transitory. Covered interest parity is generally accepted as holding in international financial markets. Taylor (1989) investigates covered interest parity during turbulent time using a data set obtained from the Bank of England which represents actual prices at which trades took place several times a day, and offers qualified support for covered interest parity. Like the earlier study by Frenkel and Levich (1977), Taylor finds that persistent profit opportunities tend to appear in times of uncertainty and turbulence. He also finds that the frequency, size and persistence of profitable deviations from covered interest parity tend to increase with the length of the maturity investigated. He suggests that the existence of liquidity constraint on traders conducting covered arbitrage operations could explain this finding. Liquidity constraints were discussed above as a potentially important explanation for the persistence of seasonal profit opportunities from drawing finance bills during the gold standard. Taylor's work suggests that liquidity constraints may still explain the persistence of covered interest arbitrage profit opportunities in longer maturities.

CONCLUSION

Significant seasonal fluctuations are found in all interest rate differential series investigated here: both differential series which do not take account of exchange rate fluctuations and those which do. The amplitude of seasonal fluctuations in series which take account of exchange rate movements is much greater than the amplitude of series which do not take account of exchange rate movements. This result tends to support the traditional story that seasonal fluctuations in exchange rates created arbitrage opportunities. Based upon the differentials between the United States commercial paper rate and the implicit interest rate, it appears that there were seasonal incentives to draw finance bills from April through August when the entire period 1883–1913 is used as a point of reference and to draw finance bills from May to August when the seasonal pattern is estimated for the later subperiod 1897–1913. When the U.S. time loan rate is used to calculate the differential, it appears to be profitable to draw finance bills from May through August. The seasonal patterns identified here are consistent with contemporary accounts and with Sprague's (1915) observation that the large volume of finance bills outstanding at the outbreak of World War I in the summer of 1914 could be attributed to the fact that borrowing in London during those months often cost the

U.S. borrower little or nothing. They also support Goodhart's (1969) position that interest rates and exchange rates between the United States and Britain moved in a way that encouraged short term capital flows to the New York money market from London during the spring and summer months and from New York to London during the fall of the year.

The finding of significant seasonal fluctuations in *ex post* returns means that the simple uncovered interest parity hypothesis is rejected in this study and suggests that unexploited profit opportunities may have existed in the pre-World War I period. This rejection of the simple uncovered interest parity hypothesis does not, however, necessarily mean that unexploited profit opportunities existed. There are several other possible explanations of deviations from uncovered interest parity. As discussed in studies of covered interest parity such as Frenkel and Levich (1975, 1977), McCormick (1979) or Clinton (1988), the existence of transactions costs establishes a neutral band around an interest parity condition. Some, but by no means all, deviations from uncovered interest parity during the gold standard can be explained by the existence of positive transactions costs. Reasonable estimates of these transactions costs for the gold standard indicate that they are not large enough to account for all seasonal profit opportunities.

Studies which find deviations from uncovered interest parity in more recent periods often cite exchange-risk premia as an explanation for those deviations.[18] It has proven difficult, however, to develop a satisfactory model of exchange-risk premia in financial markets. In order to explain seasonal deviations from uncovered interest parity, a model of the exchange-risk premium for the gold standard would have to generate seasonal fluctuations in exchange risk. Investigating the existence and nature of an exchange-risk premium during the gold standard stands as a challenge for future research.

Krasker (1980) points out that when there is a small probability of an event occurring which could have a large impact on exchange rates, agents may appear to make systematic exchange rate forecast errors in a small sample, when in fact those forecasts are completely consistent with the agents' information sets. This "peso problem" can probably explain some of the large measured deviations from uncovered interest parity which occurred in the early 1890's during times of uncertainty that the United States would go off the gold standard. The "peso problem" can not, however, explain all the seasonal profit opportunities identified in this study because these seasonal profit opportunities persisted into the early twentieth century, many years after the uncertainty whether the United States would remain on the gold standard had subsided.

Liquidity constraints imposed by the London discount market stand out as the most interesting and potentially the most important explanation for the persistence of seasonal profit opportunities from borrowing by means of finance bills. Taylor (1989) suggests that liquidity constraints affecting covered interest arbitrage operations might explain the positive relation he finds between the frequency, size and persistence of profitable arbitrage opportunities and the length of maturity examined. There is much anecdotal evidence that a risk averse London discount market imposed limits on the amount of finance bills drawn by arbitrageurs during the gold standard. Such liquidity constraints could have prevented exchange rates and interest rates from moving to eliminate all seasonal profit opportunities. In this case, profit opportunities would be exploited at the margin, but arbitrageurs would make profits on the inframarginal units of finance bills drawn. This scenario is consistent with reports in the literature that there were seasonal opportunities for profit from drawing finance bills due to seasonal fluctuations in exchange rates between the gold points.

NOTES

1. Interest rate differentials are always defined as the U.S. rate minus the British rate.

2. See the second section of chapter 4 for a more detailed discussion of the modeling procedure.

3. The construction of the *ex post* implicit borrowing rate is discussed in the last chapter. This rate is the realized rate at which funds in New York were borrowed by drawing long bills of exchange on London.

4. This approach follows that of Cumby and Obstfeld (1981), who pointed out that uncovered interest parity and rational exchange rate expectations jointly imply that *ex post* returns should be unpredictable. They used weekly observations on exchange rates and one week Eurocurrency deposits, and test whether the *ex post* return process defined below is white noise:

$$\ln\left(s_{t+1}\right) - \ln\left(s_t\right) - r_t - r^*_t = \varepsilon_t,$$

where s_t is the spot exchange rate at time t, defined as the domestic currency price of foreign exchange, r_t (r^*_t) is the one week domestic (foreign) currency yield, and ε_t is the *ex post* return process. In Cumby and Obstfeld's specification of the model, ε_t is the exchange rate forecast error, which should be white noise given rational expectations and nonoverlapping data.

5. See the literature review chapter for a more in depth discussion of these accounts.

6. The British discount rate is recognized as the major factor determining the spread between the sight rate and the long rate on sterling bills of different maturities. However, the spread rate at time t is not exactly equal to the British discount rate at time t. Whitaker (1926: 258) explicitly states that the buying price of a 60 day sight bill purchased to be discounted upon arrival in London depend on three factors: the sight rate that day, the London arrival discount rate for 60 day bills, and the stamp tax. U.S. banks could avoid the risk of a change in the London discount rate while the bills were in transit by using the "arrival" discount rate, a rate guaranteed by their correspondent banks in London, rather that the discount rate prevailing in London at the time of the sale of the bill in New York. The *Commercial and Financial Chronicle* does occasionally quote the arrival rate of discount for 60–90 day bills in the later part of the period, but a continuous time series is not available, and it is not clear when London banks began to guarantee arrival discount rates.

7. There were periods in the early 1890's when there was considerable uncertainty concerning whether or not the United States would remain on the gold standard (Friedman and Schwartz 1963: 104–119). Because of this peso problem, the assumption that forecast errors were random may not hold during these periods: expected depreciation of the dollar may have been greater than actual depreciation, and the *ex post* implicit borrowing rate may underestimate the *ex ante* implicit rate during those times of speculation that the United States would be forced to leave the gold standard. Calomiris and Hubbard (1987) discuss the possibility of a premium included in U.S. interest rates during this period because of "silver risk." Even though the United States did not pass the Gold Standard Act until 1900, speculation that the U.S. would leave gold ended after the defeat of Bryan in the 1896 election and the increase in world gold stocks in the late 1890's.

8. Figure 5-22 shows that the discount rate on sterling bills in New York and in London did move together. Figure 5-23 shows that the differential between the two rates was generally small, especially after 1897. However, the differential did vary considerably during the period and was larger and more variable during the early part of the period than in later years.

9. This discount rate can be expressed in annual percentage terms by multiplying by 600.

10. All tables are included in Appendix 5-1 of this chapter. All figures and graphs are included in Appendix 5-2 of this chapter.

11. Seasonal patterns of the sight exchange rate were estimated and discussed in the last chapter.

12. The hypothesis of a unit root and the hypothesis of a deterministic trend are both rejected for all series for the period 1897–1910 according to Phillips-Perron unit root tests.

13. See footnote 6. Krasker (1980) discusses the implications of the "peso problem" for tests of unbiasedness of the forward rate. He points out that forecast errors will be correlated if a "peso problem" exists.

14. A more detailed discussion of estimates of transactions costs is found in the literature review chapter.

15. This derivation is standard in the literature. See, for example, Cumby and Obstfeld (1984: 135–136) or McAvinchey and MacDonald (1990: 62). The notation used here follows Cumby and Obstfeld (1984).

16. This assumes that the exchange rate is defined as the domestic price of foreign currency so that a devaluation of the domestic currency means that the spot exchange rate would increase.

17. These include McCormick (1979), Clinton (1988) and Taylor (1989).

18. See, for example, Cumby and Obstfeld (1981, 1984), Cumby (1988), Taylor (1987), and McAvinchey and MacDonald (1990).

APPENDIX 5-1: TABLES FOR CHAPTER 5

TABLE 5-1: RESULTS OF PHILLIPS-PERRON UNIT ROOT TESTS

SERIES	LAG 4	LAG 12	LAG 24	LAG 36
US Commercial Paper - Implicit Rate (1883–1913)				
$Z(t_\alpha)$	-8.91*	-9.06*	-9.00*	-8.92*
$Z(t_\beta)$	- 1.14	- 1.11	- 1.13	- 1.14
$Z(\varphi_3)$	39.71*	41.04*	40.47*	39.82*
US Commercial Paper Rate - British Discount Rate (1883–1913)				
$Z(t_\alpha)$	-7.53*	-9.16*	-9.56*	-9.42*
$Z(t_\beta)$	-3.22**	-2.47	-2.34	-2.38
$Z(\varphi_3)$	28.34*	41.91*	45.72*	44.33*
U.S. 60 Day Time Loan Rate - Implicit Rate (1890–1913)				
$Z(t_\alpha)$	-8.14*	-8.39*	-7.15*	-6.71*
$Z(t_\beta)$	-1.99	-1.89	-2.62	-3.46
$Z(\varphi_3)$	33.18*	35.23*	25.61*	22.54*
U.S. 60 Day Time Loan Rate - British Discount Rate (1890–1913)				
$Z(t_\alpha)$	-10.08*	-10.16*	-9.62*	-8.55*
$Z(t_\beta)$	-3.17**	-3.11**	-3.46**	-4.94*
$Z(\varphi_3)$	50.77*	51.67*	46.33*	36.60*
U.S. Commercial Paper Rate - N.Y. Sterling Bill Discount Rate (1883–1913)				
$Z(t_\alpha)$	-7.90*	-9.82*	-10.29*	-10.37*
$Z(t_\beta)$	-1.98	-1.48	-1.39	-1.38
$Z(\varphi_3)$	31.25*	48.17*	52.97*	53.73*
U.S. 60 Day Time Loan Rate - N.Y. Sterling Bill Discount Rate (1890–1913)				
$Z(t_\alpha)$	-10.79*	-11.67*	-10.41*	-9.31*
$Z(t_\beta)$	-2.78	-2.62	-2.98	-4.12*
$Z(\varphi_3)$	58.27*	62.42*	54.35*	43.36*

* Significant at the 2% level. ** Significant at the 5% level.

$Z(t_\alpha)$: test statistic for $\alpha = 1$. $Z(t_\beta)$: test statistic for $\beta = 0$.

$Z(\varphi_3)$: test statistic for $\alpha = 1$ and $\beta = 0$.

TABLE 5-2: 60–90 DAY U.S. COMMERCIAL PAPER - BRITISH DISCOUNT RATE

	model for 1883–1913		*model with seasonal shift after 1896*	
$\overline{R}^2$	0.75		0.76	
Regression Q-statistic[a]	52.04	(0.66)	50.26	(0.72)
F-statistic[b]	6.30	(<0.01)	2.99	(<0.01)
Seasonal Q-statistic[c]	3.36	(0.65)	8.83	(0.12)
degrees of freedom	349		337	
<u>*Variables*</u>[d]				
AR1	.791	(23.37)	.696	(17.05)
D93:4–5	-1.437	(-2.22)	-1.015	(-1.60)
D93:6	4.812	(5.90)	5.351	(6.77)
D93:7	2.965	(3.44)	3.555	(4.28)
D93:8	3.232	(3.96)	3.708	(4.67)
D93:9	2.529	(3.85)	2.872	(4.37)
D95:12–1	1.529	(2.97)	1.675	(3.20)
D96:7	1.737	(2.69)	1.810	(2.78)
D96:8	5.406	(6.95)	5.412	(7.05)
D96:9	2.481	(3.19)	2.430	(3.17)
D96:10	3.922	(6.09)	3.646	(5.63)

a *Q*-statistic for the regression, probability value in parentheses.
b *F*-statistic for the significance of the seasonal dummy variables for the 1883–1913 model and for the significance of the seasonal shift dummy variables in the shift model; probability values in parentheses.
c *Q*-statistic for residuals at 5 seasonal lags, probability value in parentheses.
d Variables included in the model other than the seasonal dummy variables, *t*-statistics in parentheses.

TABLE 5-3: U.S. 60–90 DAY COMMERCIAL PAPER RATE - IMPLICIT INTEREST RATE

	model for 1883–1913		*model with seasonal shift after 1896*	
$\bar{R}^2$	0.62		0.67	
Regression Q-statistic[a]	54.54	(0.57)	59.60	(0.38)
F-statistic[b]	8.77	(<0.01)	2.62	(<0.01)
Seasonal Q-statistic[c]	2.52	(0.77)	7.53	(0.18)
degrees of freedom	351		339	
Variables[d]				
AR1	0.700	(13.29)	0.673	(12.59)
AR2	-0.404	(-6.67)	-0.427	(-7.11)
AR3	0.189	(3.59)	0.204	(3.83)
D93:4–5	6.866	(5.39)	6.636	(5.22)
D93:8	6.672	(4.74)	6.248	(4.44)
D93:9	5.335	(3.82)	5.084	(3.65)
D95:12–1	3.946	(3.14)	4.465	(3.56)
D96:6–7	5.085	(3.77)	4.650	(3.50)
D96:8	3.526	(3.05)	3.192	(2.78)

a Q-statistic for the regression, probability value in parentheses.
b F-statistic for the significance of the seasonal dummy variables for the 1883–1913 model and for the significance of the seasonal shift dummy variables in the shift model; probability values in parentheses.
c Q-statistic for residuals at 5 seasonal lags, probability value in parentheses.
d Variables included in the model other than the seasonal dummy variables, t-statistics in parentheses.

TABLE 5-4: U.S. 60 DAY TIME LOAN RATE - BRITISH DISCOUNT RATE

	model for 1891–1913		*model with seasonal shift after 1896*	
$\overline{R}^2$	0.86	0.86		
Regression Q-statistic[a]	46.09	(0.55)	52.82	(.29)
F-statistic[b]	5.14	(<0.01)	1.32	(.21)
Seasonal Q-statistic[c]	6.96	(.22)	13.19	(.02)
degrees of freedom	248		236	
Variables[d]				
AR1	0.577	(8.77)	0.548	(8.17)
AR2	0.116	(1.56)	0.140	(1.85)
AR3	-0.102	(-1.38)	-0.086	(-1.14)
AR4	0.135	(2.08)	0.112	(1.70)
TREND	-0.006	(-3.28)	-0.004	(-1.77)
D93:6	14.252	(21.57)	14.046	(19.87)
D93:7	7.260	(9.71)	6.652	(8.41)
D93:8–9	1.247	(1.99)	0.998	(1.50)
D95:12–1	3.096	(5.80)	3.289	(5.84)
D96:8	7.973	(11.47)	8.065	(10.87)
D96:9	1.611	(2.14)	1.249	(1.576)
D96:10	7.834	(11.31)	7.540	(10.29)
D02:9,11	1.370	(3.10)	1.383	(3.06)
D06:8–12	1.279	(2.67)	1.171	(2.44)
D07:10-11	6.877	(11.46)	6.739	(11.36)
D07:12	4.573	(6.91)	4.367	(6.55)

a Q-statistic for the regression, probability value in parentheses.
b F-statistic for the significance of the seasonal dummy variables for the 1891–1913 model and for the significance of the seasonal shift dummy variables in the shift model; probability values in parentheses.
c Q-statistic for residuals at 5 seasonal lags, probability value in parentheses.
d Variables included in the model other than the seasonal dummy variables, t-statistics in parentheses.

TABLE 5-5: U.S. 60 DAY TIME RATE - IMPLICIT INTEREST RATE

	model for 1891–1913		*model with seasonal shift after 1896*	
$\overline{R}^2$	0.71		0.71	
Regression Q-statistic[a]	46.16	(.55)	59.29	(.13)
F-statistic[b]	3.55	(<0.01)	1.46	(0.15)
Seasonal Q-statistic[c]	7.66	(0.18)	12.79	(0.03)
degrees of freedom	248		236	
Variables[d]				
AR1	0.748	(12.15)	0.719	(11.11)
AR2	-0.369	(-5.07)	-0.313	(-4.11)
AR3	0.163	(2.64)	0.121	(1.90)
D93:2–3	2.761	(2.38)	2.017	(1.63)
D93:4–5	9.448	(7.60)	9.290	(6.98)
D93:6	11.540	(8.69)	10.667	(7.42)
D93:7	5.445	(4.20)	4.202	(2.98)
D93:8–9	4.274	(3.58)	3.665	(2.88)
D95:12–1	4.473	(4.11)	4.932	(4.30)
D96:6–7	5.367	(4.49)	4.446	(3.49)
D96:8	6.595	(6.23)	6.066	(5.26)
D96:10	5.166	(5.30)	5.643	(5.31)
D02:9,11	1.517	(2.60)	1.595	(2.62)
D07:10	8.076	(6.59)	8.115	(6.63)
D07:11	6.404	(4.25)	6.494	(4.37)
D07:12	2.969	(2.43)	2.83	(2.32)

a Q-statistic for the regression, probability value in parentheses.
b F-statistic for the significance of the seasonal dummy variables for the 1891–1913 model and for the significance of the seasonal shift dummy variables in the shift model; probability values in parentheses.
c Q-statistic for residuals at 5 seasonal lags, probability value in parentheses.
d Variables included in the model other than the seasonal dummy variables, t-statistics in parentheses.

TABLE 5-6: 60–90 DAY U.S. COMMERCIAL PAPER - N.Y. DISCOUNT RATE ON STERLING BILLS

	model for 1883–1913		*model with seasonal shift after 1896*	
$\bar{R}^2$	0.71		0.73	
Regression Q-statistic[a]	57.55	(0.45)	74.77	(0.06)
F-statistic[b]	6.20	(<0.01)	2.99	(<0.01)
Seasonal Q-statistic[c]	5.01	(0.41)	10.26	(0.07)
degrees of freedom	350		338	
Variables[d]				
AR1	0.717	(19.09)	0.678	(16.88)
D93:6	5.892	(8.89)	5.976	(9.11)
D93:7	3.451	(4.39)	3.592	(4.65)
D93:8	3.453	(4.39)	3.741	(4.84)
D93:9	2.772	(4.19)	3.130	(4.77)
D95:12–1	1.463	(2.75)	1.559	(2.94)
D96:7	1.773	(2.67)	1.800	(2.74)
D96:8	5.407	(6.87)	5.537	(7.17)
D96:9	2.400	(3.05)	2.546	(3.30)
D96:10	4.343	(6.56)	4.070	(6.22)

a Q-statistic for the regression, probability value in parentheses.
b F-statistic for the significance of the seasonal dummy variables for the 1883–1913 model and for the significance of the seasonal shift dummy variables in the shift model; probability values in parentheses.
c Q-statistic for residuals at 5 seasonal lags, probability value in parentheses.
d Variables included in the model other than the seasonal dummy variables, t-statistics in parentheses.

TABLE 5-7: U.S. 60 DAY TIME LOAN RATE - N.Y. DISCOUNT RATE ON STERLING BILLS

	model for 1891–1913		*model with seasonal shift after 1896*	
$\bar{R}^2$	0.85		0.85	
Regression Q-statistic[a]	42.80	(0.68)	48.69	(0.45)
F-statistic[b]	5.07	(<0.01)	1.25	(0.24)
Seasonal Q-statistic[c]	4.30	(0.51)	10.13	(0.07)
degrees of freedom	247		235	
Variables[d]				
AR1	0.534	(8.07)	0.516	(7.64)
AR2	0.089	(1.19)	0.115	(1.52)
AR3	-0.026	(-0.36)	-0.018	(-0.23)
AR4	0.134	(2.07)	0.123	(1.83)
TREND	-0.004	(-2.22)	-0.003	(-1.08)
D93:2–3	2.129	(3.44)	1.908	(2.87)
D93:4–5	1.362	(1.95)	1.448	(1.95)
D93:6	14.978	(18.91)	14.971	(17.72)
D93:7	7.673	(9.90)	7.105	(8.62)
D93:8–9	1.328	(2.11)	1.292	(1.93)
D95:12–1	2.890	(5.34)	2.794	(4.90)
D96:8	7.897	(11.40)	8.101	(10.98)
D96:9	1.590	(2.13)	1.340	(1.70)
D96:10	8.136	(11.76)	7.826	(10.71)
D02:9,11	1.489	(3.37)	1.451	(3.23)
D07:10–11	6.729	(11.44)	6.605	(11.37)
D07:12	3.863	(5.88)	3.677	(5.58)

a Q-statistic for the regression, probability value in parentheses.

b F-statistic for the significance of the seasonal dummy variables for the 1883–1913 model and for the significance of the seasonal shift dummy variables in the shift model; probability values in parentheses.

c Q-statistic for residuals at 5 seasonal lags, probability value in parentheses.

d Variables included in the model other than the seasonal dummy variables, t-statistics in parentheses.

TABLE 5-8: SUMMARY OF SEASONAL MODELS FOR 1897–1910[a]

SERIES	SIGHT	CMIMP	CMUK	TMIMP	TMUK
January	4.866	0.787	1.045	0.025	0.344
	(0.004)	(0.394)	(0.203)	(0.392)	(0.234)
February	4.865	0.446	1.274	-0.189	0.664
	(0.0035)	(0.394)	(0.202)	(0.392)	(0.234)
March	4.8642	0.385	1.628	-0.307	0.926
	(0.004)	(0.394)	(0.202)	(0.391)	(0.233)
April	4.869	1.251	1.514	0.432	0.677
	(0.004)	(0.394)	(0.202)	(0.391)	(0.232)
May	4.871	1.793	1.541	0.851	0.591
	(0.004)	(0.394)	(0.202)	(0.391)	(0.232)
June	4.869	2.543	2.004	1.579	1.043
	(0.004)	(0.394)	(0.202)	(0.391)	(0.232)
July	4.866	3.079	2.027	1.859	0.807
	(0.004)	(0.394)	(0.202)	(0.391)	(0.232)
August	4.862	1.769	2.007	0.744	0.976
	(0.004)	(0.394)	(0.202)	(0.391)	(0.232)
September	4.854	0.977	2.013	0.402	1.453
	(0.004)	(0.394)	(0.202)	(0.392)	(0.233)
October	4.861	0.806	1.067	0.422	0.749
	(0.004)	(0.394)	(0.202)	(0.399)	(0.235)
November	4.860	-0.050	1.004	-0.256	0.772
	(0.004)	(0.394)	(0.202)	(0.407)	(0.237)
December	4.858	0.319	1.437	0.115	1.113
	(0.004)	(0.394)	(0.202)	(0.399)	(0.236)
AR1	0.628	0.729	0.635	0.827	0.578
	(0.079)	(0.078)	(0.079)	(0.080)	(0.081)
AR2	0.013	-0.482	-0.088	-0.546	0.029
	(0.093)	(0.090)	(-0.091)	(0.092)	(0.088)
AR3	-0.100	0.263	0.157	0.246	0.023
	(0.092)	(0.078)	(0.067)	(0.074)	(0.063)
AR4		0.239			.085
		(0.078)			(0.056)

TABLE 5-8: SUMMARY OF SEASONAL MODELS FOR 1897–1910[a] (continued)

SERIES	SIGHT	CMIMP	CMUK	TMIMP	TMUK
D02:9,11				1.572	1.31
				(0.490)	(0.399)
D07:10[b]				7.731	6.789
				(1.150)	(0.565)
D07:11				6.175	
				(1.480)	
D07:12				2.727	4.395
				(1.150)	(0.611)
$\overline{R}^2$	0.54	0.51	0.52	0.59	0.71
Q-statistic[c]	35.3	45.5	47.0	40.2	41.5
	(0.50)	(0.13)	(0.10)	(0.29)	(0.24)
F-statistic[d]	4.69	4.18	4.99	2.76	3.89

a Standard errors in parentheses.
b In the case of TMUK, this dummy variable is for 1907:10 and 1907:11. *c* *Q*-statistic for the regression; probability values in parentheses.
d *F*-statistic for the significance of the seasonal dummy variables; the probability value is less than 1 % in all cases.

TABLE 5-9: SUMMARY OF NONSEASONAL MODELS FOR 1897–1910[a]

SERIES	SIGHT	CMIMP	CMUK	TMIMP	TMUK
Constant	4.864	1.183	1.548	0.488	0.848
	(0.002)	(0.174)	(0.139)	(0.190)	(0.143)
AR1	0.657	0.744	0.645	0.839	0.500
	(0.059)	(0.074)	(0.077)	(0.078)	(0.079)
AR2		-0.328	-0.114	-0.505	0.044
		(0.074)	(0.088)	(0.092)	(0.083)
AR3			0.123	0.184	0.077
			(0.068)	(0.073)	(0.064)
AR4					.007
					(0.058)
D02:9,11				1.328	1.600
				(0.514)	(0.436)
D07:10[b]				7.649	6.534
				(1.19)	(0.590)
D07:11				5.310	
				(1.53)	
D07:12				2.441	4.651
				(1.18)	(0.656)
$\overline{R}^2$	0.43	0.38	0.38	0.54	0.65
Q stat[c]	62.50	82.20	70.50	47.40	87.10
	(0.004)	(0.000)	(0.001)	(0.100)	(0.000)

a Standard errors in parentheses.

b In the case of TMUK, this dummy variable is for 1907:10 and 1907:11. *c* *Q*-statistic for the regression; probability values in parentheses.

d *F*-statistic for the significance of the seasonal dummy variables; the probability value is less than 1 % in all cases.

TABLE 5-10: FORECAST PERFORMANCE STATISTICS

Table 5-10a: Sight Rate

Forecast Step	Mean Absolute Error		Root Mean Square Error		Theil's U Statistic		NOBS
	SEAS	NONSEAS	SEAS	NONSEAS	SEAS	NONSEAS	
1	.00447	.00429	.00573	.00585	.862	.881	36
2	.00526	.00561	.00679	.00714	.765	.805	35
3	.00553	.00599	.00691	.00759	.683	.751	34
4	.00554	.00654	.00693	.00779	.618	.694	33
5	.00536	.00659	.00666	.00773	.589	.684	32
6	.00499	.00667	.00628	.00772	.556	.682	31
7	.00534	.00681	.00668	.00779	.573	.669	30
8	.00554	.00690	.00691	.00789	.570	.650	29
9	.00563	.00695	.00693	.00796	.589	.676	28
10	.00555	.00712	.00672	.00807	.588	.705	27
11	.00524	.00714	.00631	.00811	.691	.887	26
12	.00537	.00733	.00646	.00825	.781	.998	25
13	.00553	.00747	.00668	.00839	.663	.832	24
14	.00537	.00729	.00656	.00822	.635	.796	23

Table 5-10b: Commercial Paper Rate - Implicit Rate

Forecast Step	Mean Absolute Error SEAS	Mean Absolute Error NONSEAS	Root Mean Square Error SEAS	Root Mean Square Error NONSEAS	Theil's U Statistic SEAS	Theil's U Statistic NONSEAS	NOBS
1	.791	0.735	0.925	1.031	.752	.838	36
2	.923	1.035	1.135	1.358	.619	.740	35
3	.919	1.127	1.143	1.411	.537	.663	34
4	.918	1.142	1.149	1.424	.493	.610	33
5	.920	1.172	1.142	1.470	.497	.640	32
6	.927	1.217	1.148	1.510	.511	.672	31
7	.929	1.249	1.154	1.536	.504	.671	30
8	.898	1.283	1.129	1.560	.484	.669	29
9	.856	1.277	1.083	1.563	.485	.700	28
10	.871	1.297	1.098	1.585	.568	.820	27
11	.903	1.332	1.118	1.614	.790	1.139	26
12	.856	1.253	1.064	1.508	.819	1.162	25
13	.860	1.236	1.074	1.508	.663	.926	24
14	.894	1.269	1.097	1.501	.626	.873	23

Table 5-10c: Commercial Paper Rate - British Discount Rate

Forecast Step	Mean Absolute Error		Root Mean Square Error		Theil's U Statistic		NOBS
	SEAS	NONSEAS	SEAS	NONSEAS	SEAS	NONSEAS	
1	.425	.459	.519	.601	.786	0.910	36
2	.407	.524	.536	.677	.679	0.858	35
3	.429	.555	.561	.722	.640	0.824	34
4	.478	.603	.597	.769	.588	0.757	33
5	.465	.604	.583	.771	.567	0.750	32
6	.495	.625	.613	.786	.561	0.720	31
7	.496	.633	.618	.790	.588	0.751	30
8	.503	.643	.632	.795	.679	0.854	29
9	.509	.656	.642	.807	.753	0.945	28
10	.483	.653	.608	.807	.724	0.961	27
11	.507	.662	.623	.819	.833	1.096	26
12	.504	.638	.619	.790	.938	1.197	25
13	.500	.638	.623	.797	.885	1.132	24
14	.486	.605	.609	.760	.842	1.051	23

Table 5-10d: U.S. Time Loan Rate - Implicit Rate

Forecast Step	Mean Absolute Error		Root Mean Square Error		Theil's U Statistic		NOBS
	SEAS	NONSEAS	SEAS	NONSEAS	SEAS	NONSEAS	
1	0.761	0.704	0.910	0.954	.885	.926	36
2	0.979	0.990	1.214	1.288	.805	.854	35
3	1.031	1.081	1.259	1.354	.712	.766	34
4	1.034	1.089	1.269	1.361	.682	.731	33
5	1.072	1.118	1.288	1.382	.724	.777	32
6	1.133	1.166	1.325	1.409	.763	.811	31
7	1.155	1.213	1.348	1.437	.755	.805	30
8	1.131	1.245	1.329	1.461	.697	.767	29
9	1.094	1.222	1.291	1.444	.687	.768	28
10	1.094	1.222	1.297	1.451	.729	.816	27
11	1.127	1.256	1.320	1.478	.881	.986	26
12	1.093	1.199	1.288	1.407	.915	1.000	25
13	1.078	1.172	1.280	1.387	.828	.897	24
14	1.100	1.179	1.302	1.400	.845	.908	23

Table 5-10e: U.S. Time Loan Rate - British Discount Rate

Forecast Step	Mean Absolute Error		Root Mean Square Error		Theil's U Statistic		NOBS
	SEAS	NONSEAS	SEAS	NONSEAS	SEAS	NONSEAS	
1	.500	.471	0.669	0.677	0.921	0.932	36
2	.517	.549	0.724	0.768	0.896	0.951	35
3	.597	.651	0.773	0.839	0.869	0.943	34
4	.666	.738	0.841	0.907	0.853	0.920	33
5	.718	.774	0.854	0.925	0.977	1.058	32
6	.768	.832	0.918	0.982	0.874	0.935	31
7	.813	.870	0.959	1.011	0.921	0.970	30
8	.858	.907	0.991	1.038	0.931	0.975	29
9	.876	.923	1.013	1.056	0.910	0.949	28
10	.845	.908	0.965	1.042	0.913	0.986	27
11	.874	.931	0.987	1.062	1.001	1.077	26
12	.892	.940	1.004	1.074	1.126	1.204	25
13	.889	.946	1.005	1.085	1.132	1.221	24
14	.866	.903	0.986	1.031	1.155	1.208	23

TABLE 5-11: SAMPLE MONTHLY MEANS AND STANDARD DEVIATIONS OF INTEREST RATE DIFFERENTIALS

Table 5-11a: Sample Monthly Means and Standard Deviations of Interest Rate Differentials for Entire Period

	CMIMP (1883–1913)		TMIMP (1890–1913)	
MONTH	*Sample Mean*	*Standard Deviation*	*Sample Mean*	*Standard Deviation*
January	0.922	1.497	-0.038	1.684
February	0.800	1.402	0.103	1.518
March	1.303	2.079	0.400	1.699
April	2.159	2.399	0.935	2.020
May	2.505	2.192	0.962	2.030
June	3.178	1.858	2.188	2.619
July	3.453	1.789	2.516	2.090
August	2.472	2.154	1.456	2.243
Sept.	1.447	1.595	0.755	1.481
October	0.716	1.395	0.834	2.459
November	-0.428	1.866	-0.038	2.381
December	-0.274	2.163	-0.115	2.476

Table 5-11b: Sample Monthly Means and Standard Deviations of Interest Rate Differentials, 1897–1913

MONTH	CMIMP (1897–1913) *Sample Mean*	*Standard Deviation*	TMIMP (1897–1913) *Sample Mean*	*Standard Deviation*
January	0.728	1.486	-0.052	1.490
February	0.515	1.361	-0.118	1.492
March	0.506	1.587	-0.258	1.380
April	1.164	0.799	0.274	0.837
May	1.673	1.094	0.681	1.183
June	2.411	1.176	1.315	1.359
July	2.956	1.290	1.677	1.291
August	1.801	1.649	0.691	1.482
Sept.	1.096	1.473	0.544	1.379
October	0.669	1.355	0.735	2.494
November	-0.341	1.734	-0.091	2.550
December	0.174	1.360	0.019	1.682

TABLE 5-12A: DIFFERENTIAL BETWEEN THE U.S. COMMERCIAL PAPER RATE AND THE IMPLICIT RATE, 1883–1913

Differential less than	# TIMES DURING PERIOD 1883–1913 APRIL	MAY	JUNE	JULY	AUGUST
0.0%	2	3	1	1	3
0.5%	5	4	1	1	4
1.0%	9	6	3	2	9
1.5%	17	12	6	3	12

TABLE 5-12B: DIFFERENTIAL BETWEEN THE U.S. TIME LOAN RATE AND THE IMPLICIT RATE, 1890–1913

Differential less than	# TIMES DURING PERIOD 1890–1913 MAY	JUNE	JULY	AUGUST
0.0%	8	5	2	6
0.5%	11	7	4	11
1.0%	18	7	5	14
1.5%	19	8	5	15

APPENDIX 5-2: FIGURES FOR CHAPTER 5

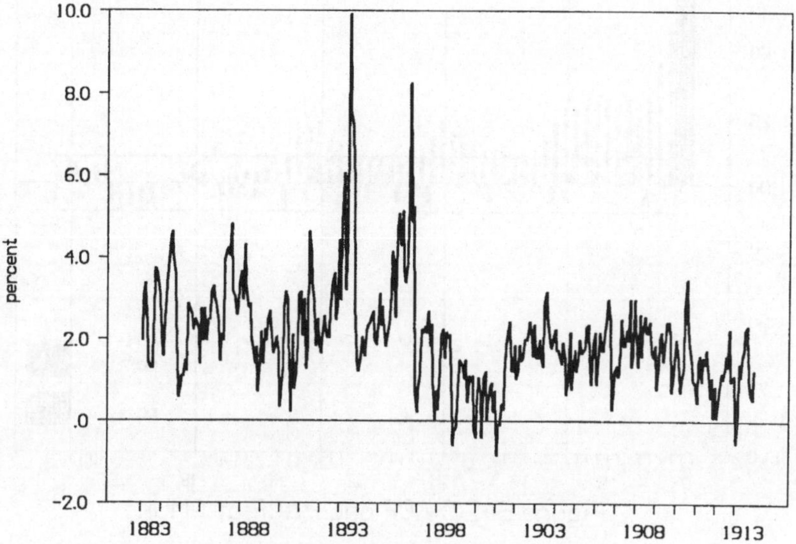

Figure 5-1a: CMUK, 1883-1913

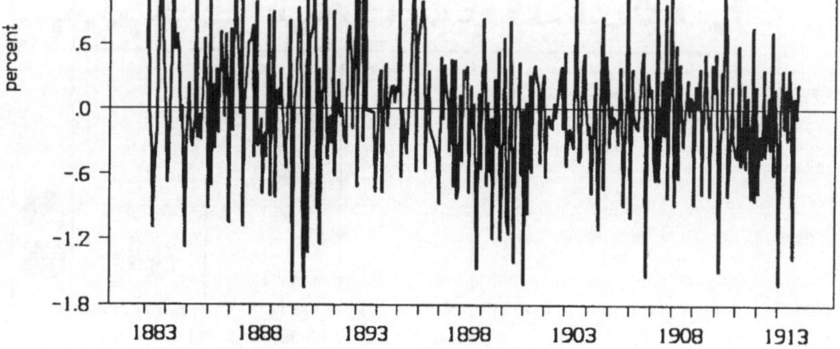

Figure 5-1b: Model Residuals

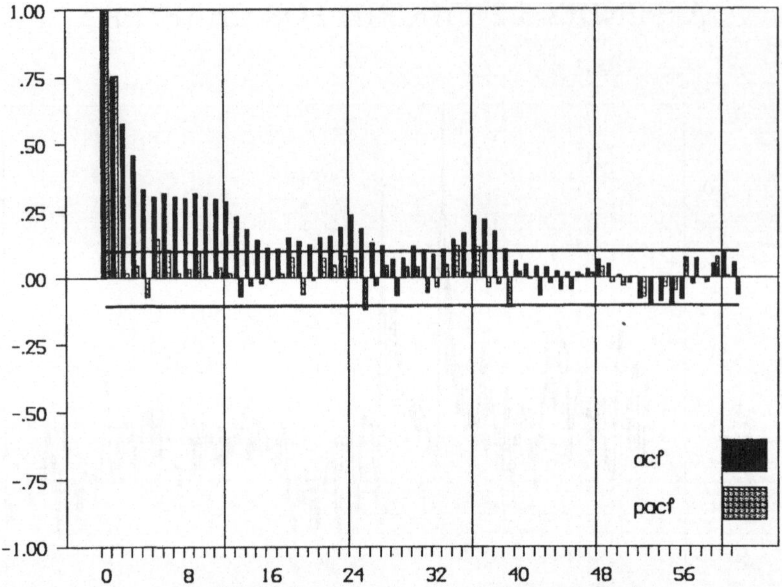

Figure 5-2a: ACF and PACF of CMUK

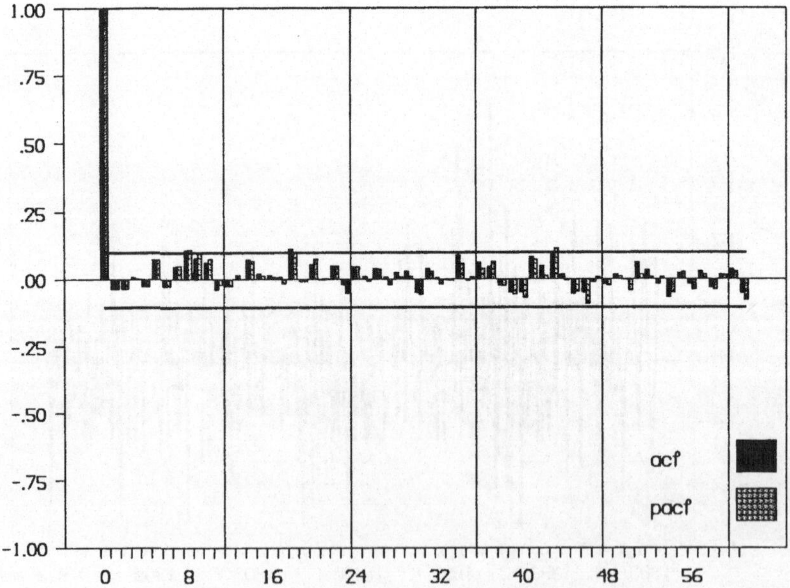

Figure 5-2b: ACF and PACF of Model Residuals

Figure 5-3: Seasonal Pattern of Interest Rate Differential

US Commercial Paper Rate - British Discount Rate

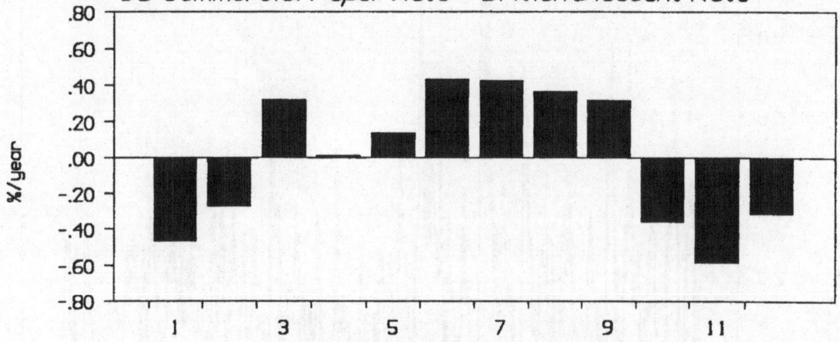

Figure 5-3a: CMUK, 1883-1913

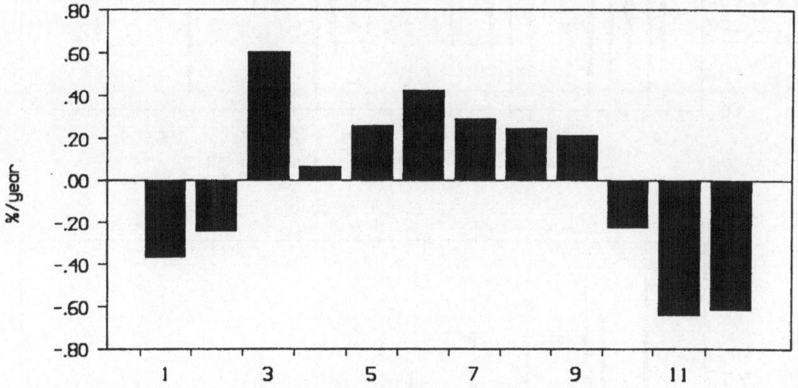

Figure 5-3b: CMUK, 1883-1896

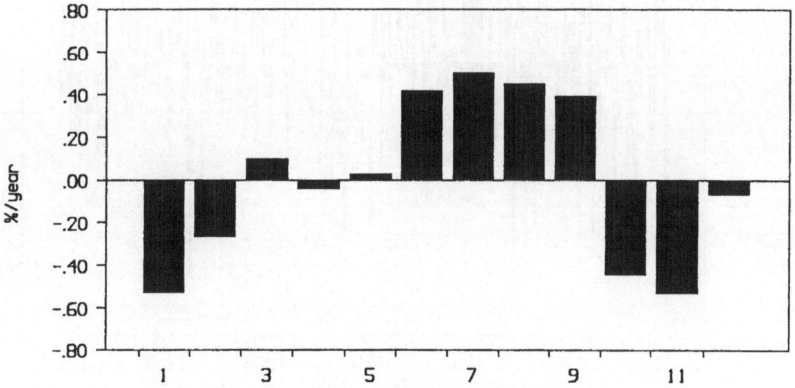

Figure 5-3c: CMUK, 1897-1913

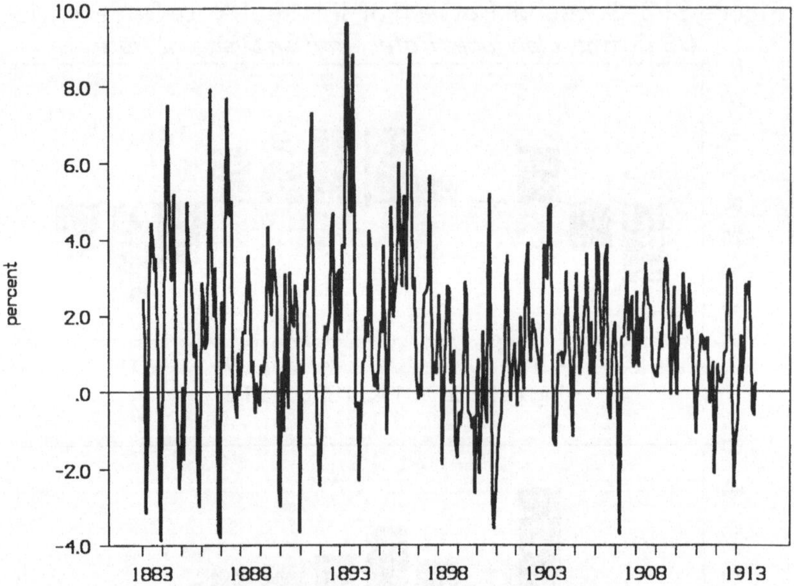

Figure 5-4a: CMIMP, 1883-1913

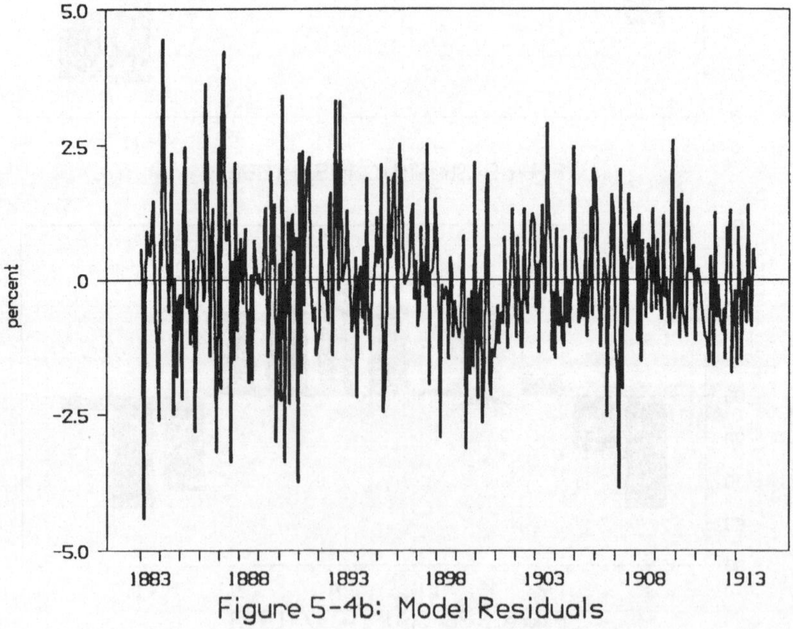

Figure 5-4b: Model Residuals

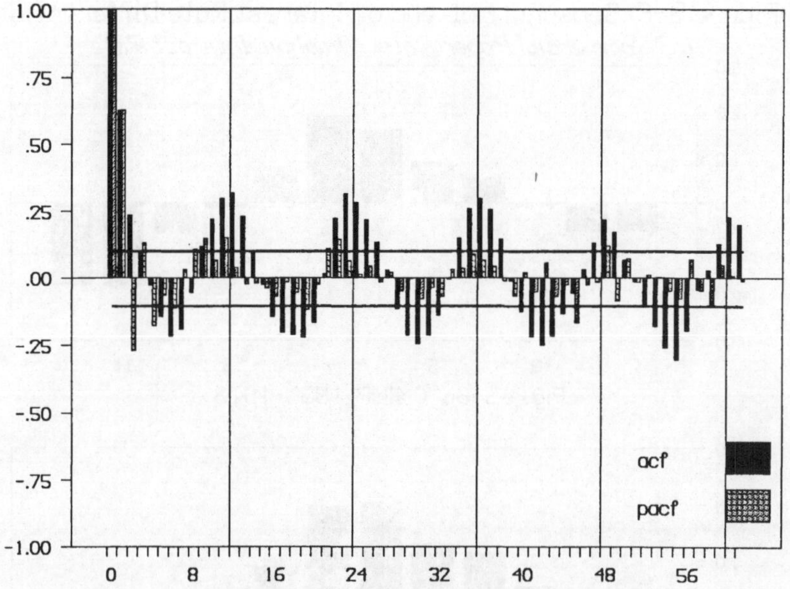

Figure 5-5a: ACF and PACF of CMIMP

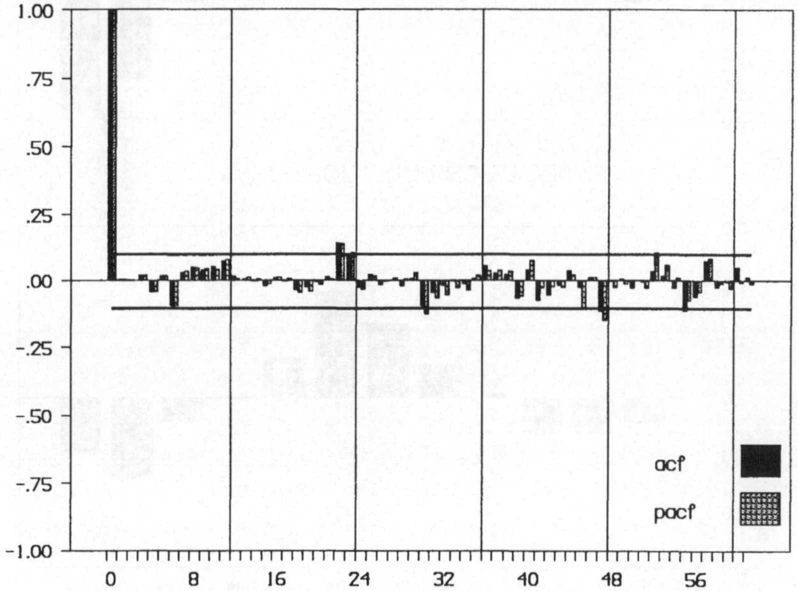

Figure 5-5b: ACF and PACF of Model Residuals

Figure 5-6: Seasonal Pattern of Interest Rate Differential

US Commercial Paper Rate - Implicit Interest Rate

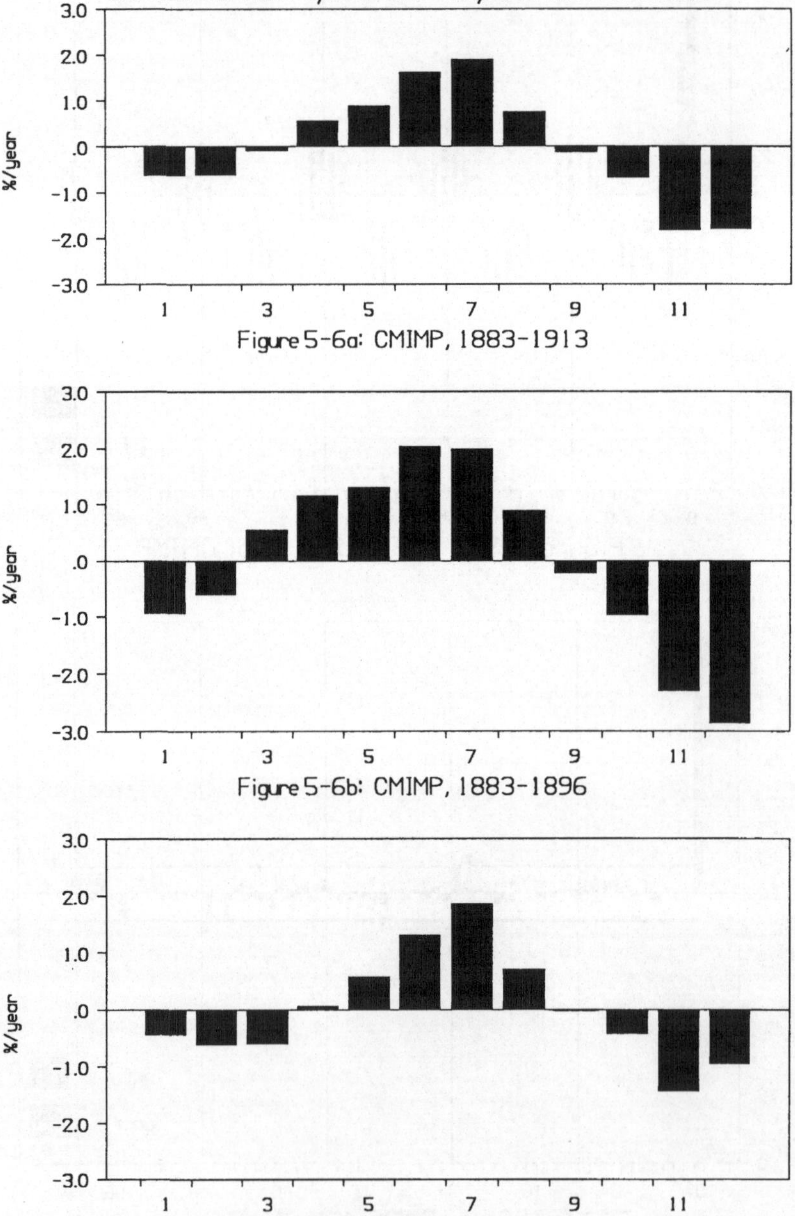

Figure 5-6a: CMIMP, 1883-1913

Figure 5-6b: CMIMP, 1883-1896

Figure 5-6c: CMIMP, 1897-1913

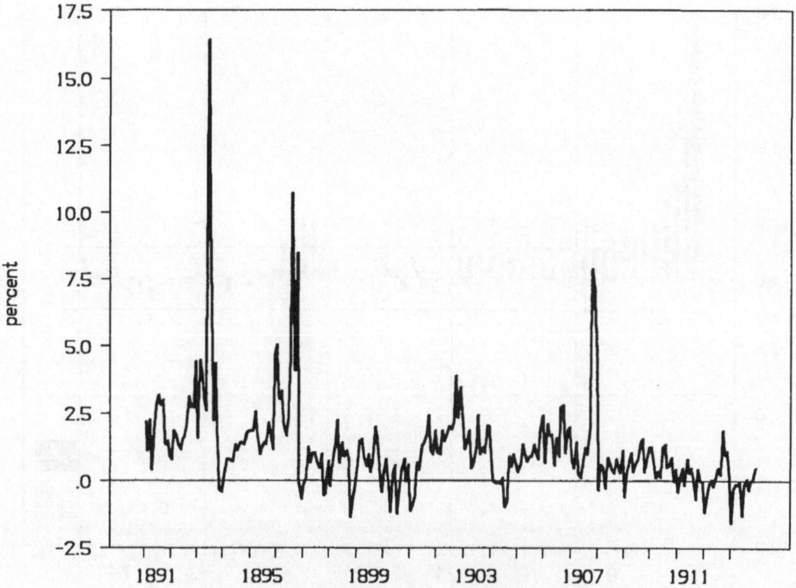

Figure 5-7a: TMUK, 1891-1913

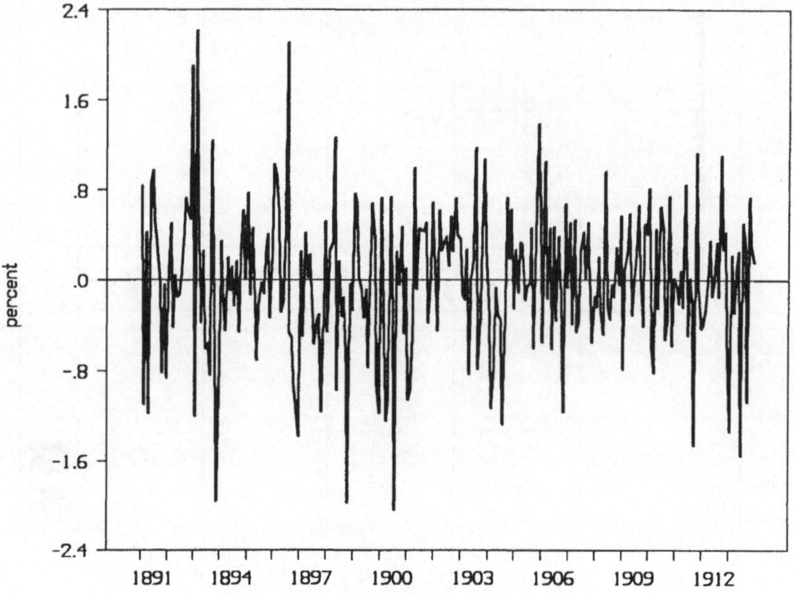

Figure 5-7b: Model Residuals

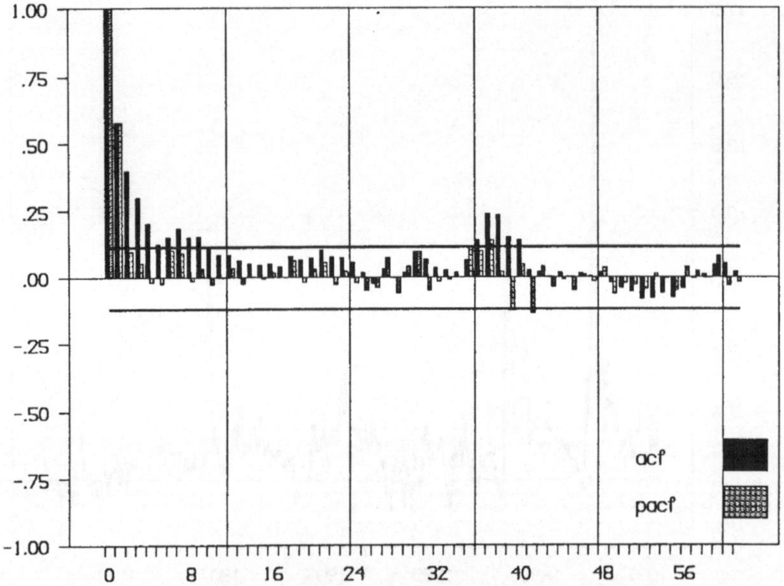

Figure 5-8a: ACF and PACF of TMUK

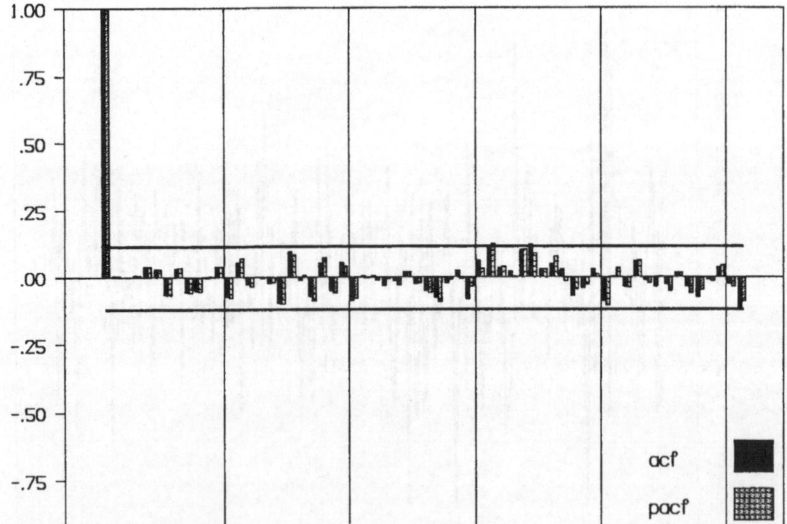

Figure 5-8b: ACF and PACF of Model Residuals

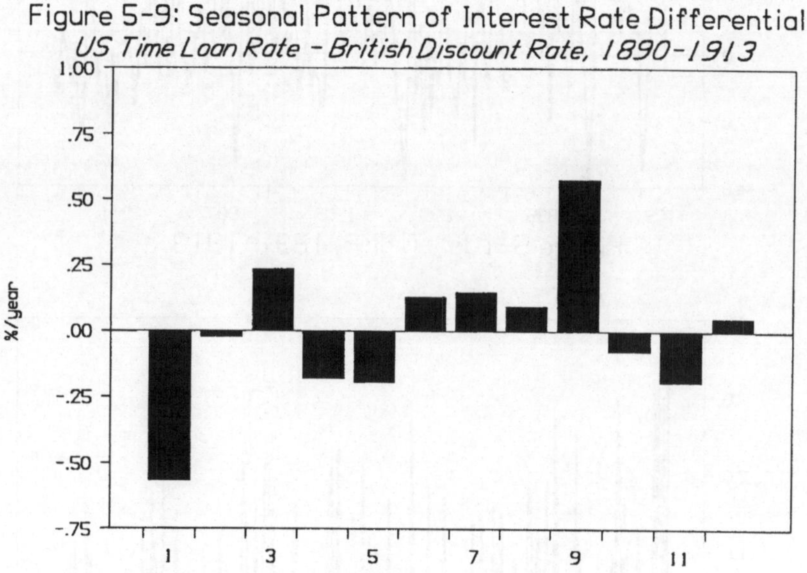
Figure 5-9: Seasonal Pattern of Interest Rate Differential
US Time Loan Rate - British Discount Rate, 1890-1913
1.00
.75
.50
.25
.00
-.25
-.50
-.75
%/year
1
3
5
7
9
11

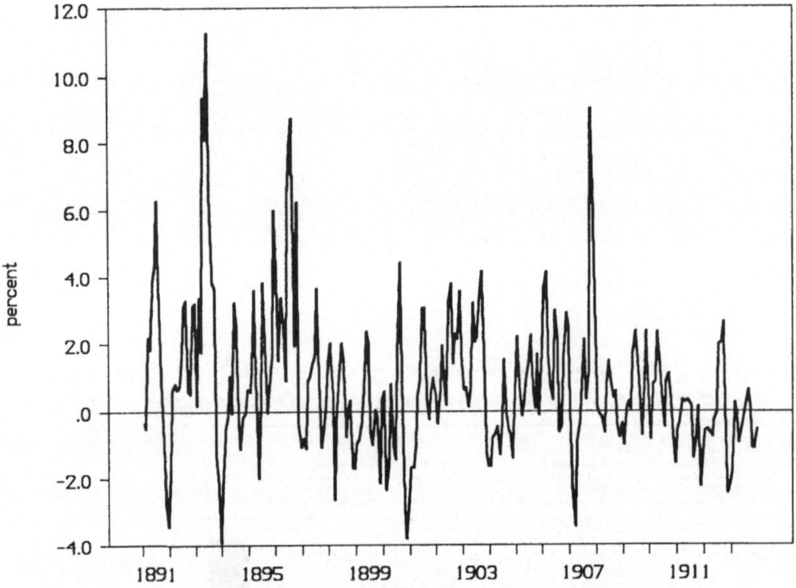

Figure 5-10a: TMIMP, 1891-1913

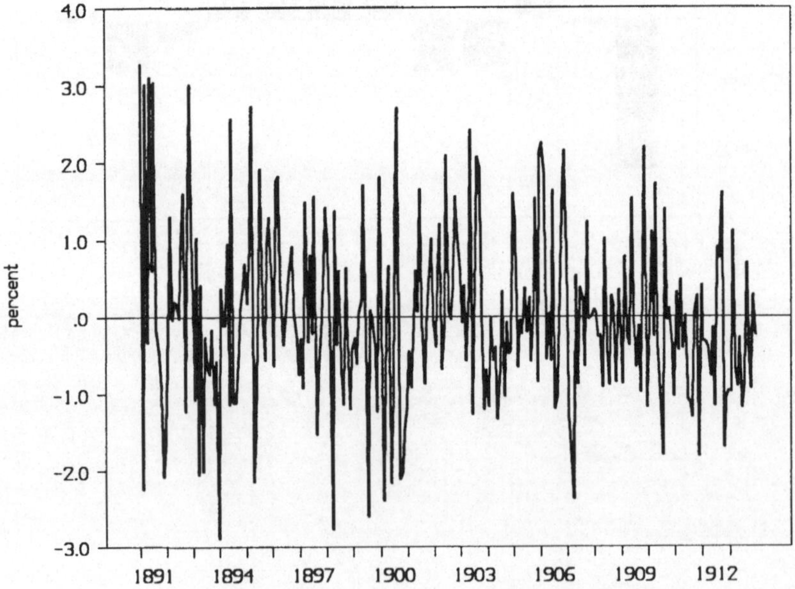

Figure 5-10b: Model Residuals

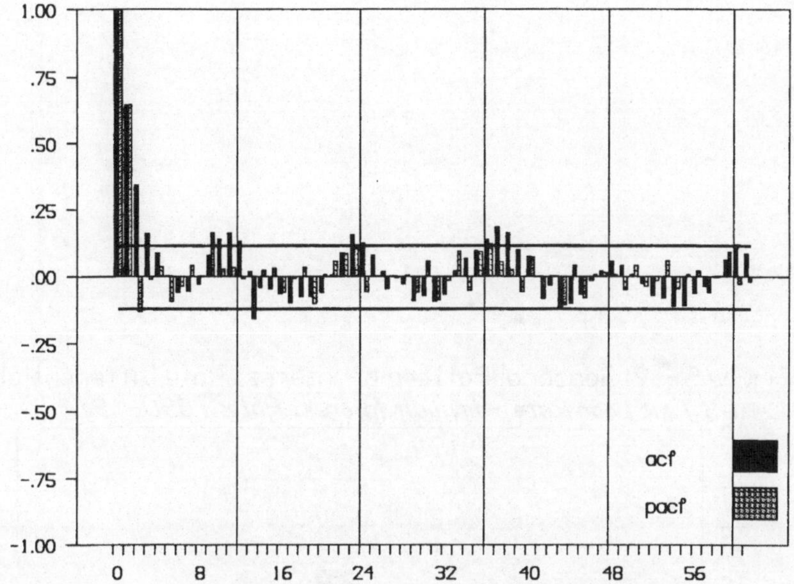

Figure 5-11a: ACF and PACF of TMIMP

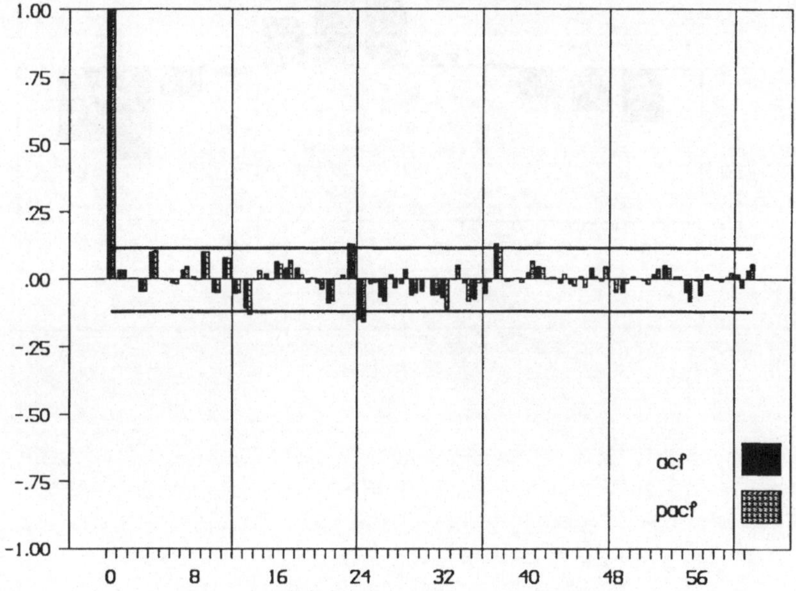

Figure 5-11b: ACF and PACF of Model Residuals

Figure 5-12: Seasonal Pattern of Interest Rate Differential
US Time Loan Rate - Implicit Interest Rate, 1890-1913

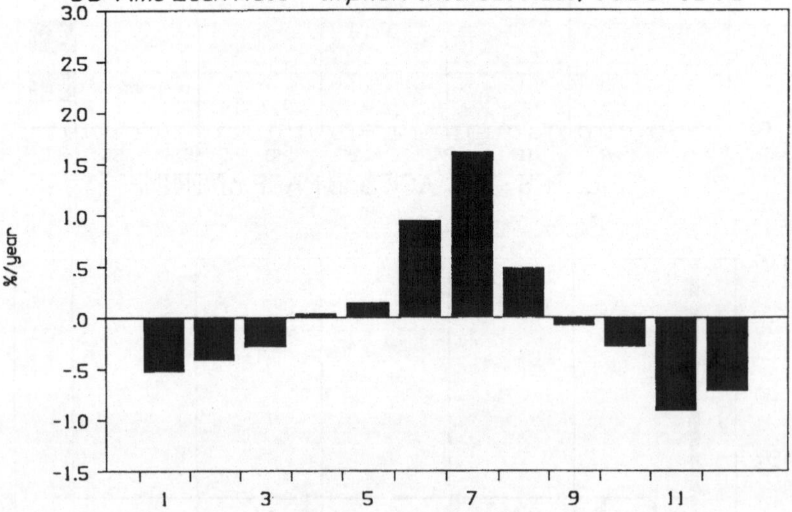

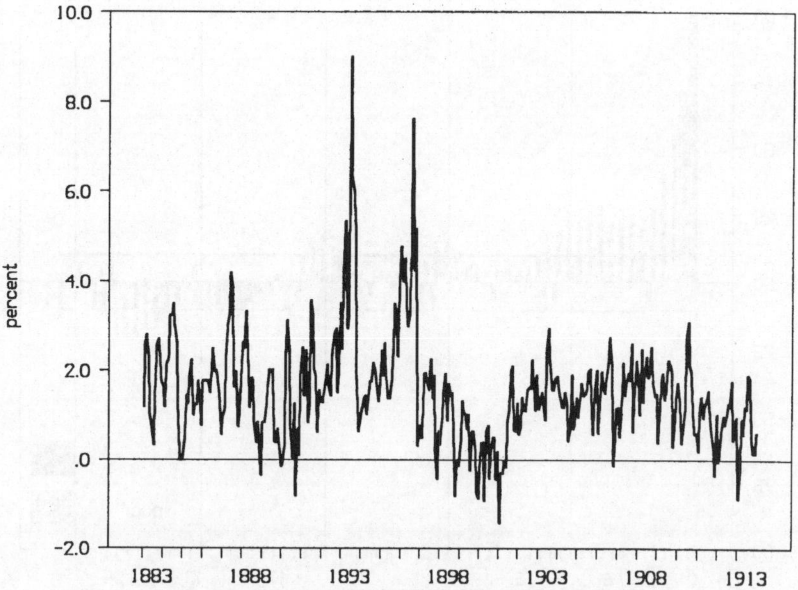

Figure 5-13a: CMNYSTER, 1883-1913

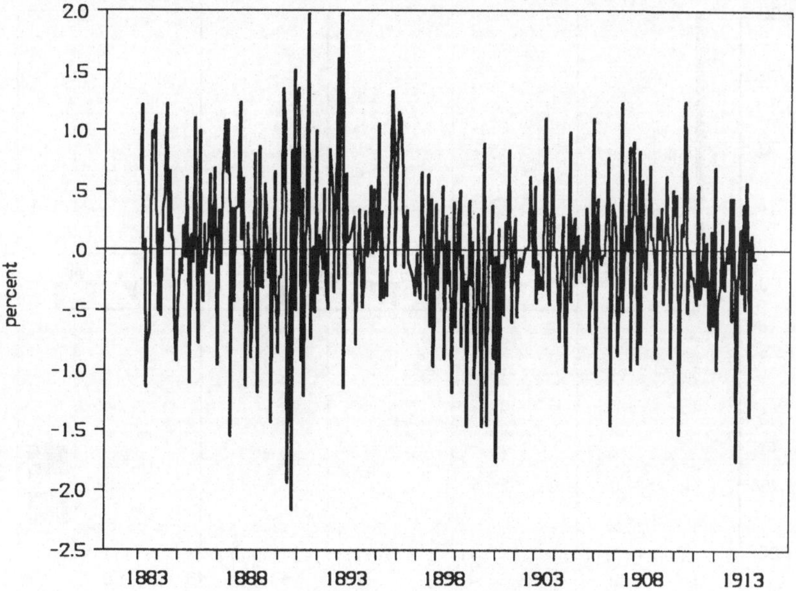

Figure 5-13b: Model Residuals

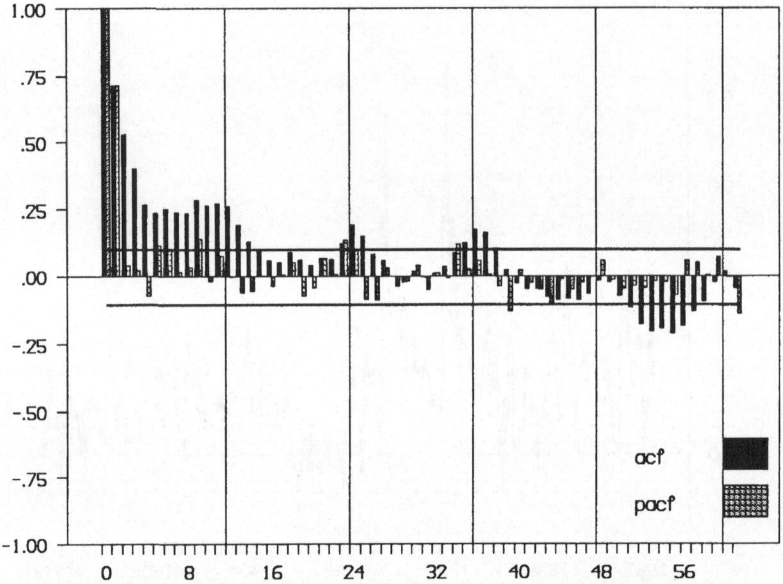

Figure 5-14a: ACF and PACF of CMNYSTER

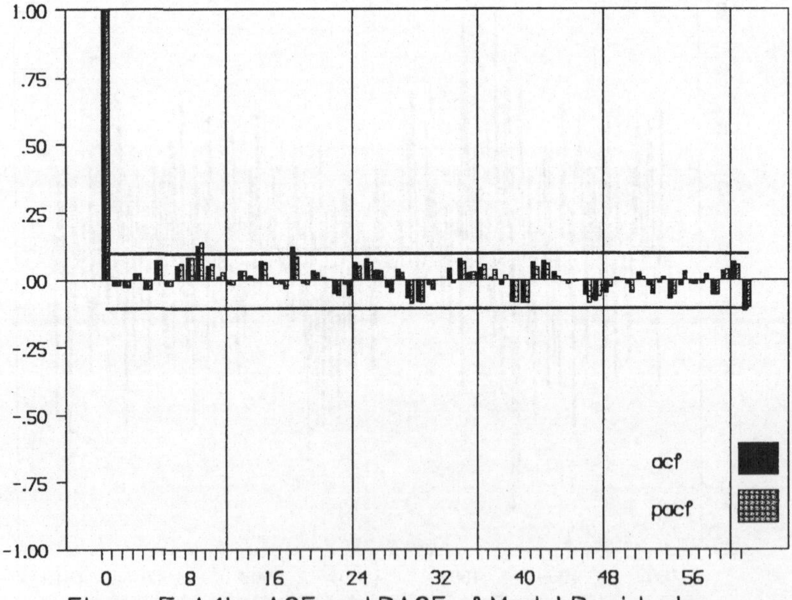

Figure 5-14b: ACF and PACF of Model Residuals

Figure 5-15: Seasonal Pattern of Interest Rate Differential

US Commercial Paper Rate - NY Sterling Bill Discount Rate

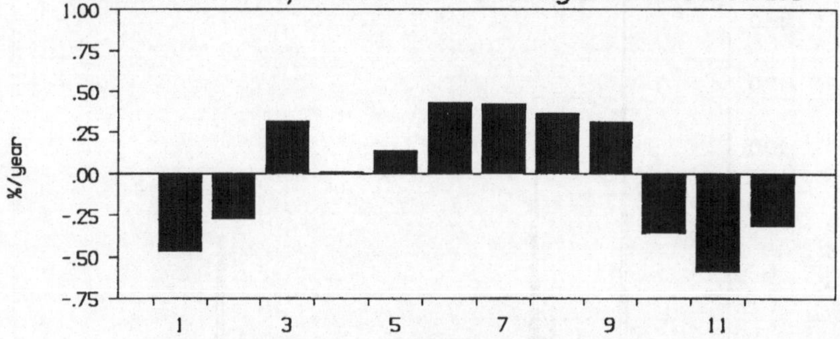

Figure 5-15a: CMNYSTER, 1883-1913

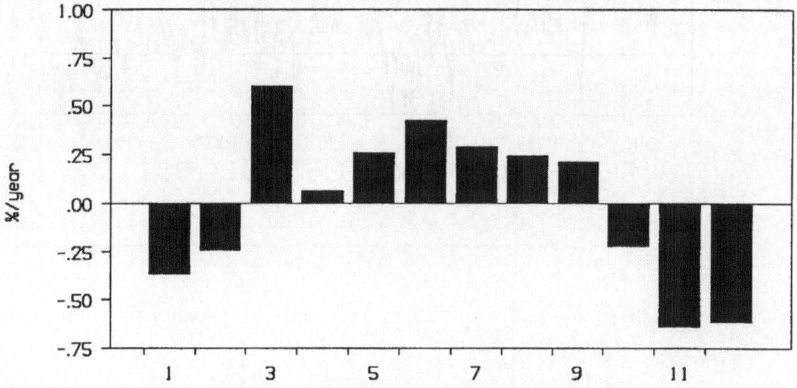

Figure 5-15b: CMNYSTER, 1883-1896

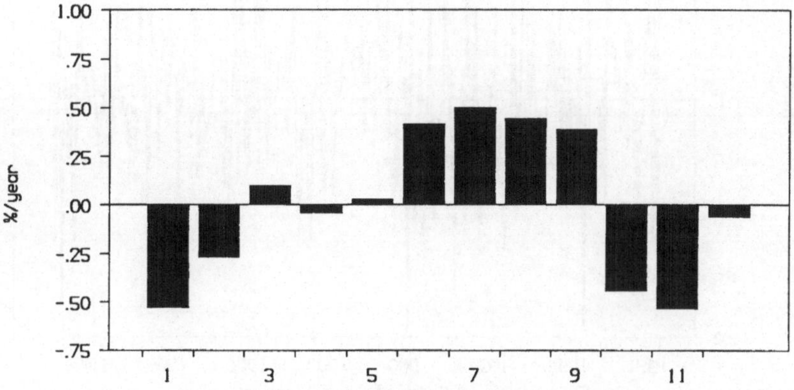

Figure 5-15c: CMNYSTER, 1897-1913

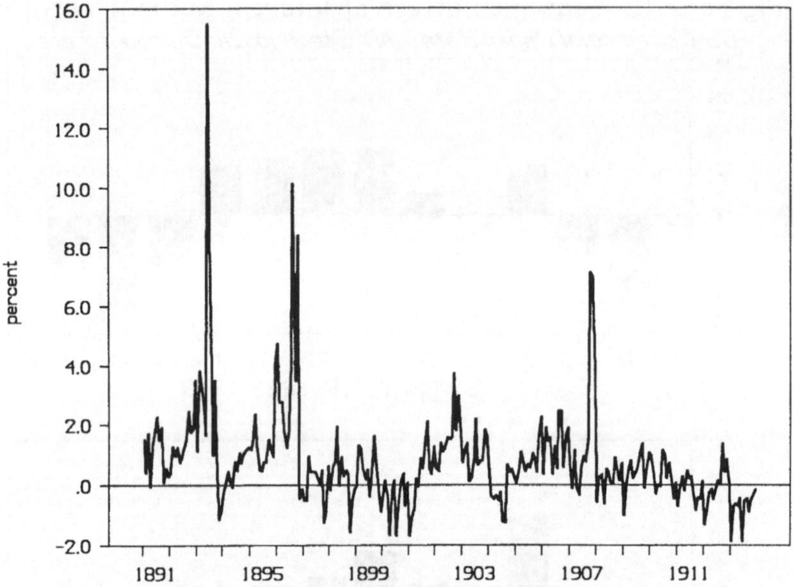

Figure 5-16a: TMNYSTER, 1891-1913

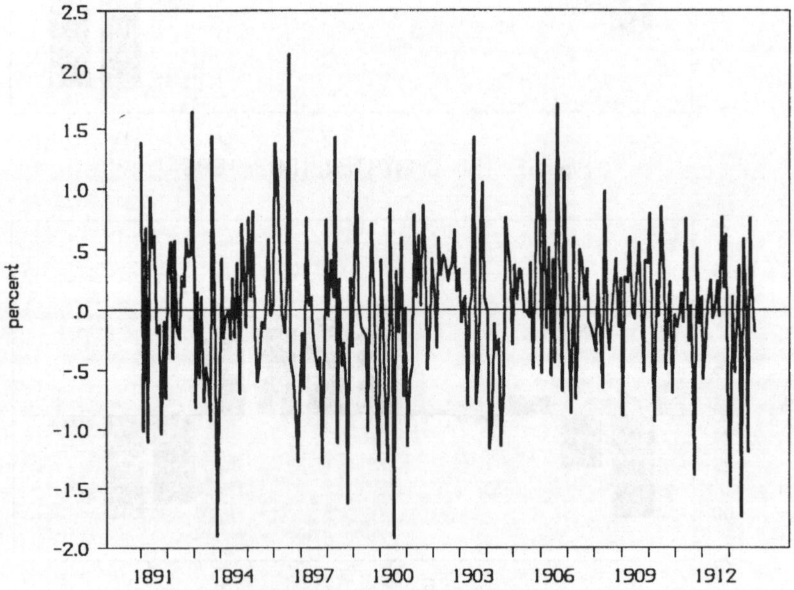

Figure 5-16b: Model Residuals

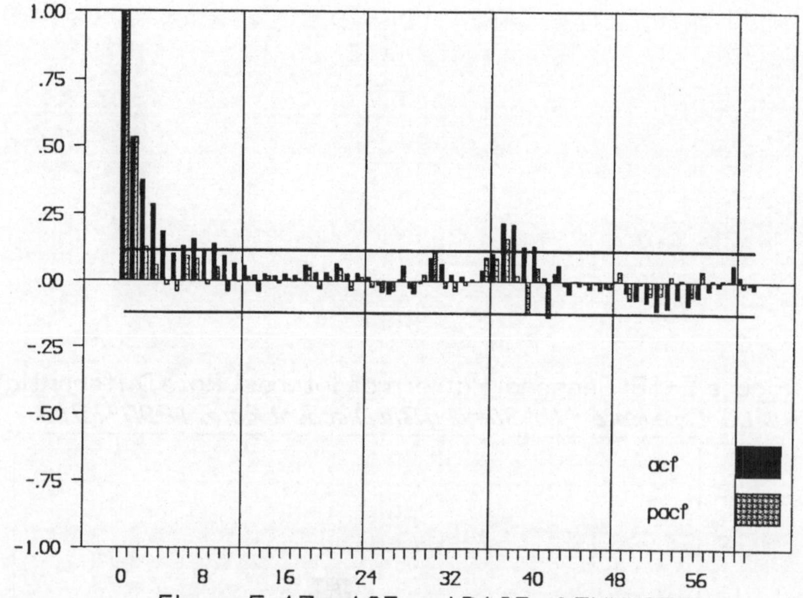

Figure 5-17a: ACF and PACF of TMNYSTER

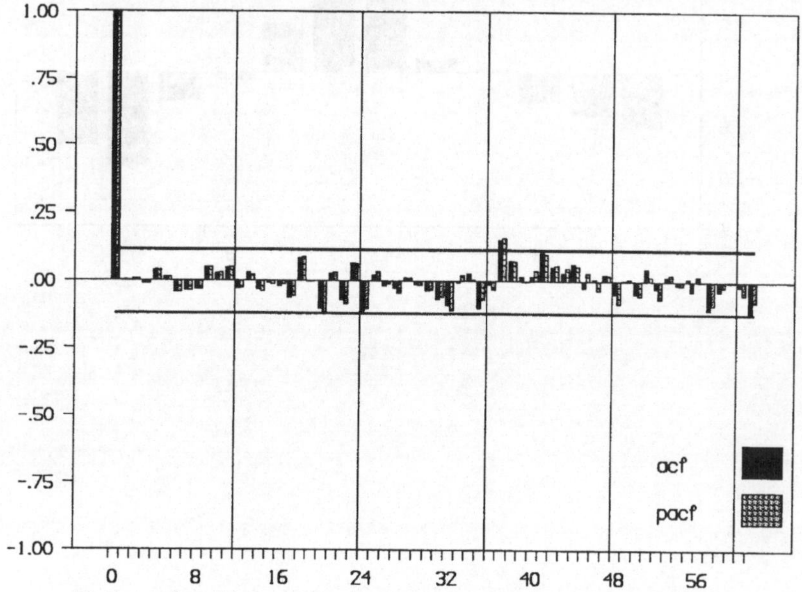

Figure 5-17b: ACF and PACF of Model Residuals

Figure 5-18: Seasonal Pattern of Interest Rate Differential
US Time Rate - NY Sterling Bill Discount Rate, 1890-1913

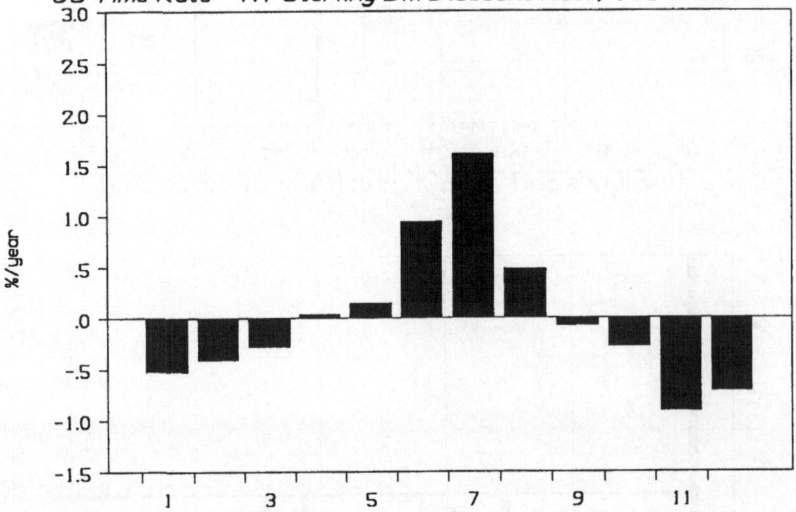

Figure 5-19: Interest Rate Differential Seasonal Patterns

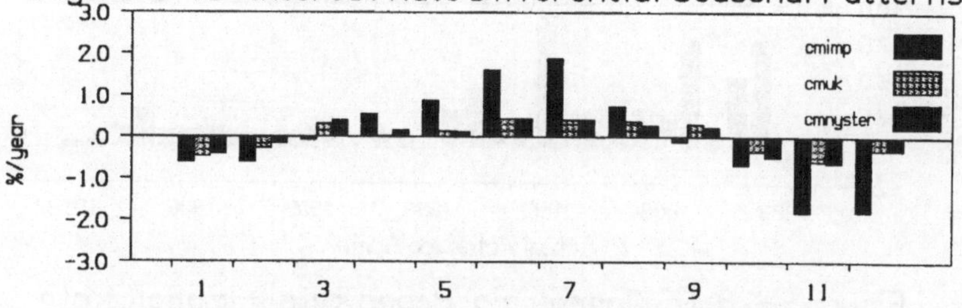

Fig. 5-19a: US Commercial Paper Rate Differentials, 1883-1913

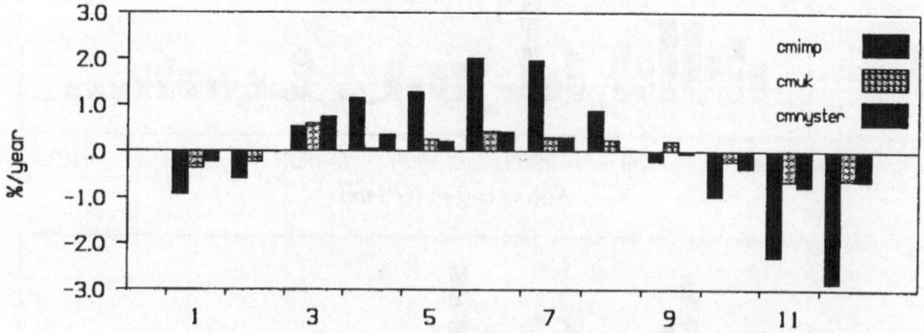

Fig. 5-19b: US Commercial Paper Rate Differentials, 1883-1896

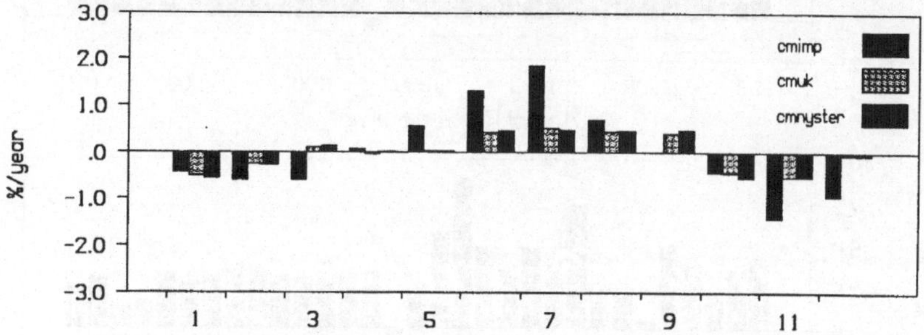

Fig. 5-19c: US Commercial Paper Rate Differentials, 1897-1913

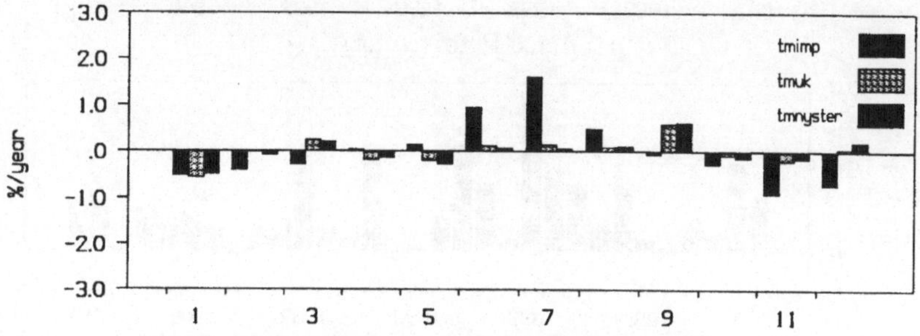

Fig. 5-19d: US Time Loan Rate Differentials, 1891-1913

Figure 5-20: US Commercial Paper Rate - Implicit Rate

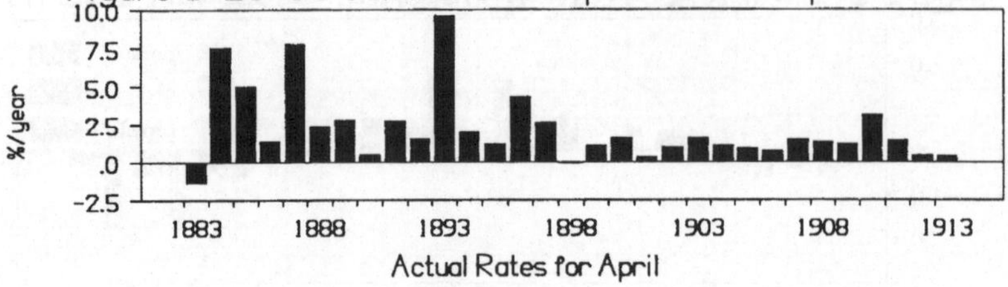

Figure 5-20: US Commercial Paper Rate - Implicit Rate

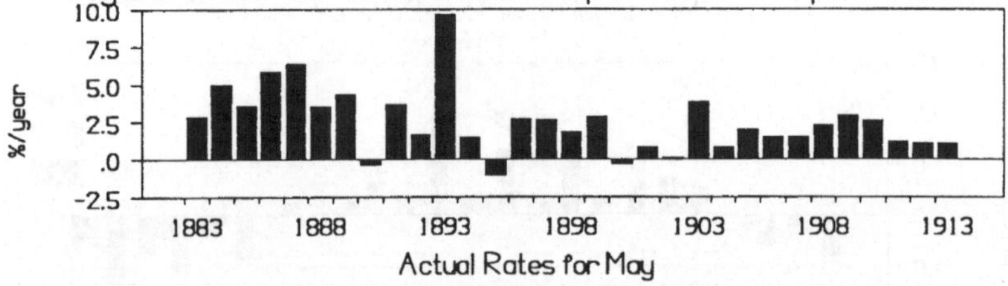

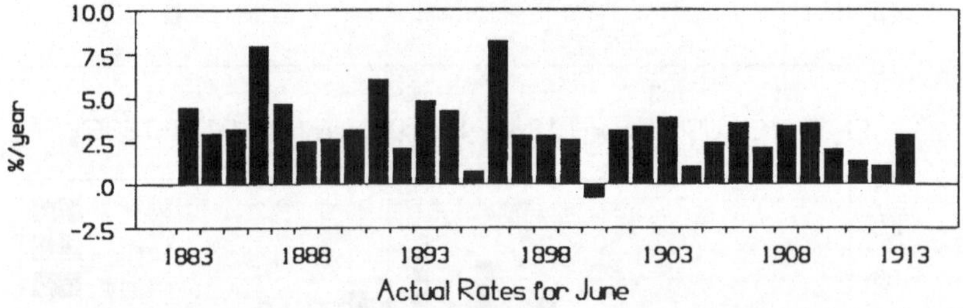

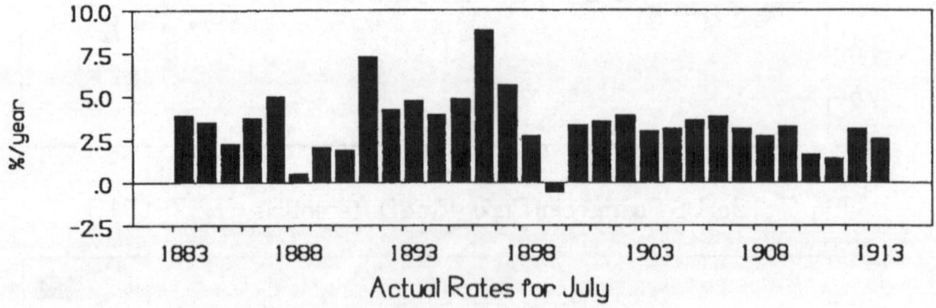

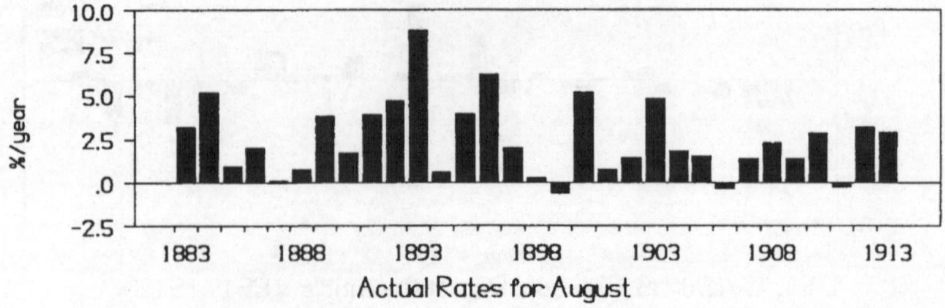

Figure 5-21: US Time Loan Rate - Implicit Interest Rate

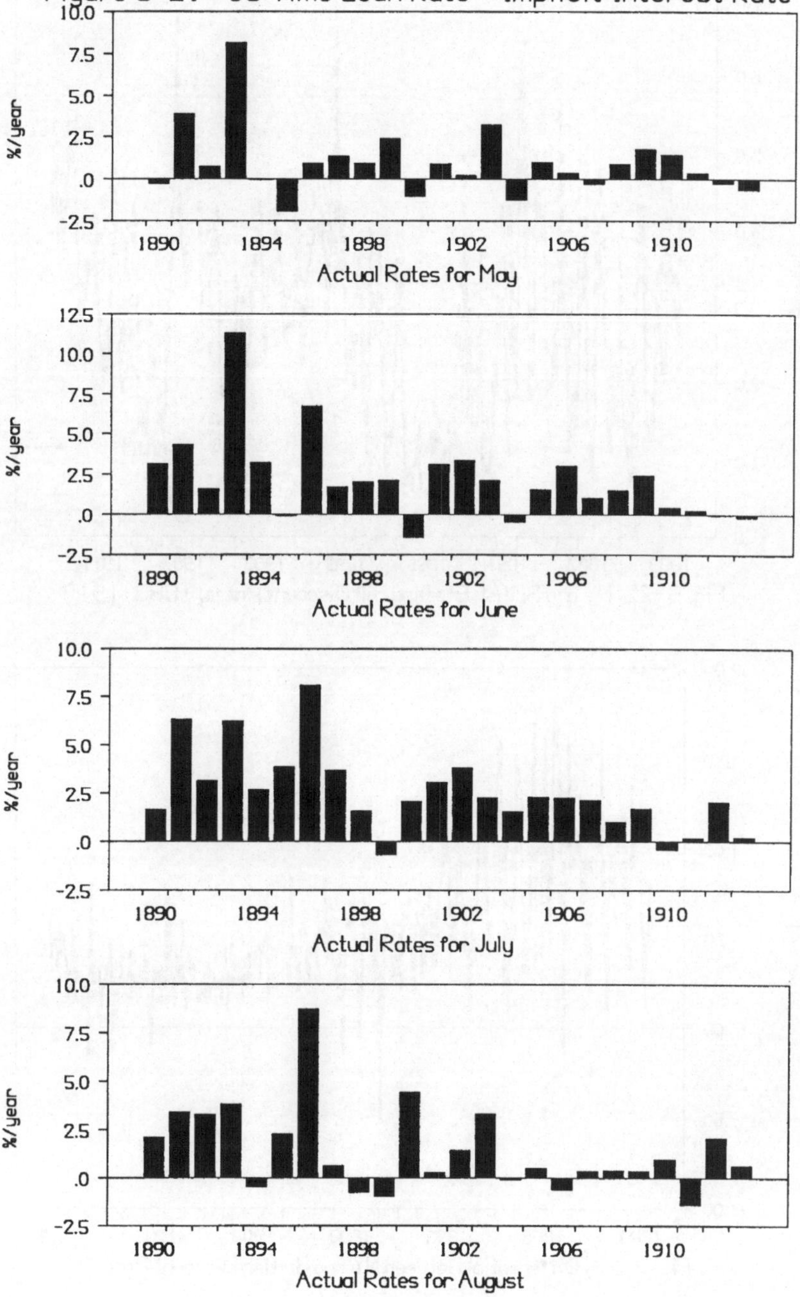

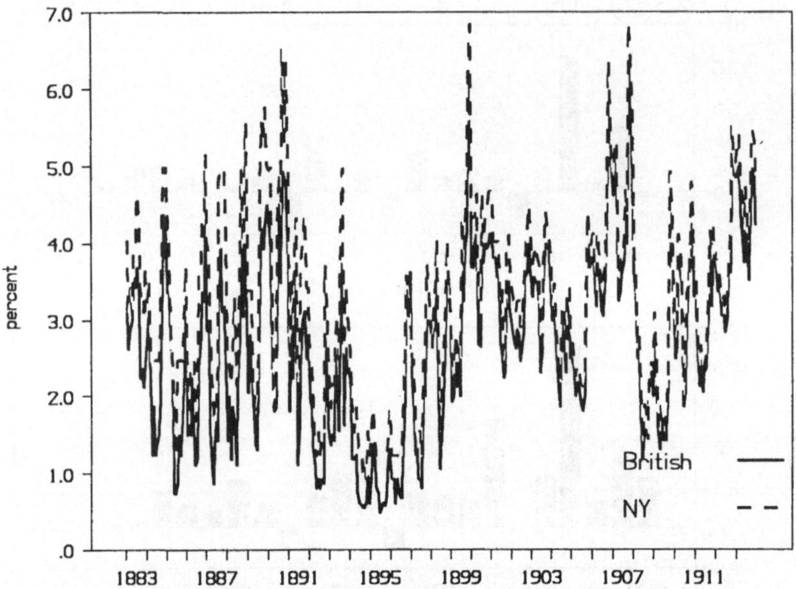

Fig. 5-22: NY and British Sterling Bill Discount Rates, 1883-1913

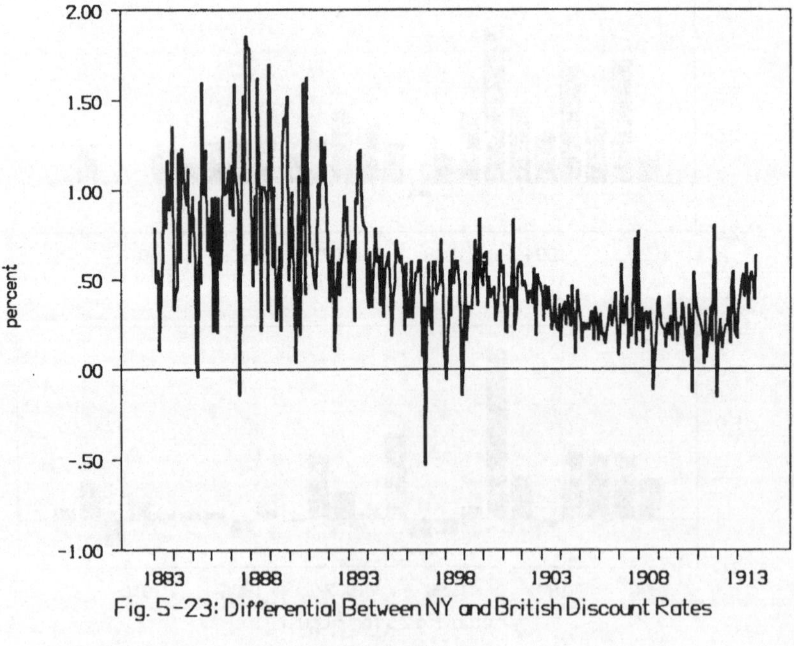

Fig. 5-23: Differential Between NY and British Discount Rates

VI

Conclusion

This empirical investigation of the behavior of short term nominal interest rates in the United States and Britain and the dollar-sterling exchange rate has found significant seasonal fluctuations in both short term nominal interest rates and the dollar-sterling exchange rate. These findings are in accord with the results of other studies of interest rate seasonality during this period, such as Kemmerer (1911), Morgenstern (1959), Goodhart (1969), Miron (1986), Clark (1986), Sharp (1988), and Barsky et al. (1989). They are also in accord with the results of early studies of exchange rate seasonality such as Kemmerer (1911), Cole (1929), and Morgenstern (1959). This study goes further than other recent investigations of interest rate seasonality during this period, and finds significant differences in the pattern of seasonal fluctuations of short term nominal interest rates in the two countries during the period 1883–1913. Seasonal fluctuations of the dollar-sterling exchange rate are found to exacerbate, rather than offset, the seasonal differences in short term nominal interest rates. This result suggests that uncovered interest parity may not have held during this period.

During the pre-World War I gold standard, most short term international capital movements were carried out using sterling bills of exchange. Several contemporary authorities on foreign exchange markets during this period report that predictable seasonal fluctuations in the dollar-sterling exchange rate tended to create profit opportunities for borrowing in London by means of finance bills and investing in U.S. capital markets during the late spring and summer months. Two series of *ex post* returns from borrowing by means of sterling bills of exchange drawn on London and investing in short term U.S. assets were investigated here: the differential between the U.S. 60–90 day commercial paper rate and the *ex post* implicit interest rate on sterling 60 day bills of exchange in New York and the differential between the U.S. 60 day time loan rate and the *ex post* implicit interest rate on sterling 60 day bills of exchange in New York. Significant seasonal fluctuations were found in both series. The months of April through August were identified as profitable months for drawing finance bills on London and investing in the U.S. commercial paper market. The months of May through August were identified as profitable months for drawing finance bills and investing in the U.S. 60 day time loan market. There is some evidence of a weakening in these seasonal fluctuations. A significant shift in seasonal pattern was identified in the case of the differential between the U.S. commercial paper rate and the *ex post* implicit interest rate. The amplitude of seasonal fluctuations of this differential was greater in the early subperiod (1883–1896) than in the later subperiod (1897–1913). Results of a comparison of the out of sample forecast performance of seasonal and nonseasonal univariate time series models of *ex post* returns indicate, however, that seasonal fluctuations remained important through 1913. The results of this empirical investigation are thus consistent with contemporary accounts of opportunities for profit from drawing finance bills in the late spring and summer months.

It is not clear that the apparent systematic profit opportunities identified in the series of *ex post* returns constitute unexploited profit opportunities. The finding of significant seasonal fluctuations in these *ex post* returns does suggest that simple uncovered interest parity did not hold during this period: seasonal fluctuations in exchange rates did not work to offset seasonal differences between short term nominal interest rates in the United States and Britain. However, several potential explanations for these deviations from uncovered interest parity exist: transactions costs, the peso problem, exchange risk premia, risk premia associated with noncomparable assets, and liquidity constraints. Using reasonable estimates of transactions costs, it is possible to show that transactions costs alone can not account for all the seasonal profit opportunities identified in this study. During times of uncertainty concerning whether the United States would remain on the gold standard, agents may have expected a larger depreciation of the dollar that was actually realized. During these periods, the *ex post* returns from borrowing in London using finance bills and investing in U.S. capital markets will systematically overestimate *ex ante* returns. This "peso problem" may account for some of the large positive *ex post* returns in the early part of the period. It can not, however, explain all the seasonal profit opportunities identified in this study because these seasonal profit opportunities persisted up to the outbreak of World War I, long after the uncertainty concerning whether the United States would remain on the gold standard had subsided.

The seasonal patterns of deviations from uncovered interest parity identified here for the pre-World War I period contrast strongly with the pattern of deviations from uncovered interest parity in more recent periods. Cumby (1988) shows that the deviations from uncovered interest parity for many currencies vary considerably and often change signs. Although the existence of exchange risk premia are often cited as an explanation for deviations from uncovered interest parity during more recent historical periods, it has proven difficult to model these time varying risk premia. In order to explain seasonal deviations from uncovered interest parity, a model of the exchange risk premium during the gold standard would have to generate seasonal fluctuations in exchange risk. Investigating the existence and nature of risk premia during the gold standard is beyond the scope of the present study, but stands as a challenge for future research.

The most interesting and potentially the most important explanation for the persistence of seasonal profit opportunities from borrowing by means of finance bills is the existence of liquidity constraints imposed by the London discount market. Escher (1918: 85–98) and Withers (1918:125) both indicate that the London discount market placed limits on the creation of finance bills. Rates charged to financial houses which drew "too many" finance bills would increase. If a risk averse London discount market prevented exchange rate speculators from drawing finance bills at prevailing discount rates, then published rates do not represent market rates at which additional funds could be borrowed. The observed seasonal profit opportunities constitute profit opportunities on "inframarginal" units borrowed from London. In this case, all profit opportunities would be exploited at the margin because rates of discount for bills drawn by arbitrageurs were higher than the published rates. Seasonal profit opportunities on inframarginal units would tend to persist over time.

The pattern of seasonal fluctuations in short term nominal interest rates, the dollar-sterling exchange rate and interest rate differentials between the United States and Britain point out the need for further research in modeling interest rate and exchange rate fluctuations during the gold standard. Models developed in earlier studies of nominal interest rate and exchange rate fluctuations during the pre-World War I gold standard are not able to explain systematic seasonal movements in both short term nominal interest rates and the dollar-sterling exchange rate. Miron (1986) uses a closed economy model to explain short term nominal interest rate seasonality in the United States during this period. Seasonal fluctuations of short term nominal interest rates were attributed to seasonal fluctuations in the demand for money and credit given an inelastic money supply. Barsky et al. (1989) develop a two country model in which the behavior of interest rates depends on whether or not both countries have central banks. If only one country has a central bank, and that central bank has the two objectives of minimizing gold flows and smoothing interest rates, then fluctuations of nominal interest rates can result. If both countries have central banks, then the two central banks can cooperate to successfully attain both objectives: gold flows can be eliminated and the interest rate can be kept at its target level. This model thus attributes nominal short term interest rate seasonality to institutional features of the gold standard era. Britain had a central bank, the Bank of England, throughout the period. The United States did not have a central bank until the establishment of the Federal Reserve in 1914. The Barsky et al. model thus indicates that the establishment of the Federal Reserve played a key role in the disappearance of nominal interest rate seasonality after World War I. The model does fall short, however, of providing a satisfactory explanation of the patterns of nominal interest rate seasonality and exchange rate seasonality during this period. The real interest rate process in their model is assumed to be exogenous. No attempt is made to explain what might cause fluctuations in real rates. The assumption of a fixed exchange rate and the assumption of absolute purchasing power parity mean that inflation rates and nominal interest rates in the two countries are identical. The model can not, therefore, explain either seasonal differences in patterns of nominal interest rate fluctuations in the two countries or seasonal fluctuations of exchange rates.

Officer (1989) argues that movements of the dollar-sterling exchange rate during the gold standard are best modeled using an asset approach. He maintains that speculative pressures should tend to keep the exchange rate at its equilibrium level, which is at the midpoint of the gold point spread. He maintains that exchange rate speculators during this period had neutral expectations: they believed that every value of the exchange rate between the gold points had an equal probability of occurring at any point in time. Accounts in the contemporary literature that seasonal movements of exchange rates within the gold points were expected, together with the finding of significant seasonal movements of exchange rates, call into question Officer's assumption of neutral speculation. Given the persistence of seasonal exchange rate fluctuations, it is not clear that the asset market approach advocated by Officer is the best approach for understanding and predicting exchange rate movements during the pre-World War I gold standard.

In this study, a two country, optimizing, cash-in-advance model was developed in order to derive the path of interest rates and exchange rates in a world where one country experiences seasonal fluctuations in endowment. The model was designed to investigate the implications of different conventions concerning the finance of international trade. During the pre-World War I gold standard, most international trade was financed using sterling bills of exchange. In other historical periods, other conventions have been adopted. The seasonal fluctuations of nominal interest rates and exchange rates during the gold standard are not consistent with the implications of this optimizing cash-in-advance model. In the version of the model where all international trade is financed using foreign currency, both nominal interest rates and the exchange rate are constant over time. In this world of flexible prices and no transactions costs, changes in price levels in the two countries are all that is needed to maintain equilibrium in goods and asset markets. The path of the exchange rate must satisfy both buyer's and seller's goods market arbitrage conditions in this model. The only possible solution is a constant exchange rate path. Another limitation of this cash-in-advance model is that the demand for money is derived solely from the demand for goods. The velocity of circulation is unitary and money demand is independent of the interest rate. The nominal interest rate thus does not adjust to help bring about equilibrium in the money market.

In conclusion, the empirical investigation of short term nominal interest rates and the dollar-sterling exchange rates conducted in this study has identified several characteristics of the time series behavior of those rates which have yet to be satisfactorily explained. These include the finding of significant seasonal fluctuations in short term nominal interest rates and dollar-sterling exchange rates, as well as the finding of significant differences in the seasonal patterns of U.S. and British short term nominal interest rates and the finding that seasonal fluctuations of exchange rates did not tend to offset differences in the seasonal patterns of short term interest rates in the two countries. Seasonality of short term nominal interest rates during the gold standard has received a great deal of attention in recent literature, but no satisfactory model explaining those seasonal fluctuations has been developed. Neither a closed economy model nor a model which assumes that the exchange rate is fixed at mint par can account for the seasonal fluctuations of the dollar-sterling exchange rate and the apparent profit opportunities created by those seasonal exchange rate fluctuations. The finding that seasonal fluctuations of the dollar-sterling exchange rate did not tend to offset differences in the seasonal patterns of short term nominal interest rates suggests that uncovered interest parity did not hold during the gold standard. Explaining these deviations from uncovered interest parity is another area of future research. Transactions costs are not large enough to account for all the apparent profit opportunities. The existence of liquidity constraints imposed by the London discount market may explain the persistence of these apparent profit opportunities over time. However, the existence of a "peso problem" during periods of uncertainty concerning whether the United States would abandon the gold standard and the possible existence of a seasonally varying exchange risk premium deserve further attention in future work.

References

Andrew, A. Piatt. 1910. *Statistics for the United States: 1867–1909. National Monetary Commission*. Senate Document No. 570, 61st Congress, 2nd session. Washingtonn: Government printing office.

Angell, J.W. [1925] 1965. *The Theory of International Prices: History, Criticism and Restatement*. Reprints of Economic Classics, New York: August M. Kelley.

Ashton, T.S. and Sayers, R.S., eds. 1954. *Papers in English Monetary History*. London: Oxford University Press.

Barsky, Robert B. 1987. The Fisher Hypothesis and the Forecastability and Persistence of Inflation. *Journal of Monetary Economics* 19: 3–24.

Barsky, Robert B., Gregory N. Mankiw, Jeffrey A. Miron and David N. Weil. 1988. The Worldwide Change in the Behavior of Interest Rates and Prices in 1914. *European Economic Review* 32: 1123–1154.

Barsky, Robert and Lawrence H. Summers. 1988. Gibson's Paradox and the Gold Standard. *Journal of Political Economy* 96: 528–550.

Beach, W. Edwards. 1935. *British International Gold Movements and Banking Policy, 1881–1913*. Cambridge: Harvard University Press.

Bilson, J.F.O. and R. Marston, eds. 1984. *Exchange Rate Theory and Practice*. Chicago: University of Chicago Press.

Blanchard, Olivier and Stanley Fischer. 1989. *Lectures on Macroeconomics*. Cambridge, Massachusettes: MIT Press.

Bloomfield, Arthur I. 1959. *Monetary Policy under the International Gold Standard: 1880–1914*. New York: Federal Reserve Bank.

——. 1963. *Short-Term Capital Movements Under the Pre-1914 Gold Standard*. Princeton Studies in International Finance No. 11. Princeton: Princeton University Press.

Bordo, Michael D. and Anna J. Schwartz (eds.). 1984. *A Retrospective on the Classical Gold Standrd, 1821–1931*. Chicago: University of Chicago Press.

Box, George E.P. and Jenkins, Gwilym M. 1976. *Time Series Analysis: Forecasting and Control*. San Francisco: Holden-Day.

Brown, Harry Gunnison. 1914. *International Trade and Exchange: A Study of the Mechanism and Advantages of Commerce*. New York: Macmillan.

Bullock, Charles J., John H. Williams, and Rufus S. Tucker. 1919. The Balance of Trade of the United States. *The Review of Economic Statistics* (July): 215–266.

Calomiris, Charles W. and R. Glenn Hubbard. 1987. International Adjustment under the Classical Gold Standard: Evidence for the U.S. and Britain, 1879–1914. Working Paper No. 2206, National Bureau of Economic Research.

Calomiris, Charles W. and R. Glenn Hubbard. 1989. Price Flexibility, Credit Availability and the Economic Fluctuations: Evidence from the United States, 1894–1909. *The Quarterly Journal of Economics* 54: 429–452.

Capie, Forrest and Alan Webber. 1985. *A Monetary History of the United Kingdom, 1970–1982, Volume I: Data, Sources, Methods*. London: George Allen & Unwin.

Clare, George. 1907. *The A B C of the Foreign Exchanges: A Practical Guide*. London: Macmillan.

Clark, Truman. 1982. *The Seasonal Behavior of Interest Rates, 1890–1913*. Ph.D. dissertation, University of Chicago.

———. 1984. Violations of the Gold Points, 1890–1908. *Journal of Political Economy* 92: 791–823.

———. 1986. Interest Rate Seasonals and the Federal Reserve. *Journal of Political Economy* 94: 76–125.

Clinton, Kevin. 1988. Transactions Costs and Covered Interest Arbitrage: Theory and Evidence. *Journal of Political Economy*. 96: 358–370.

Cole, Arthur H. 1929. Seasonal Variation in Sterling Exchange. *Journal of Economics and Business History* 2: 203–218.

The Commercial and Financial Chronicle. W.B. Dana & Company.

Cooper, Richard N. 1982. The Gold Standard: Historical Facts and Future Prospects. *Brookings Papers on Economic Activity* 1: 1–45.

Cross, Ira B. 1923. *Domestic and Foreign Exchange: Theory and Practice*. New York: Macmillan.

Cumby, Robert E. 1988. Is it Risk? Explaining Deviations from Uncovered Interest Parity. *Journal of Monetary Economics* 22: 279–299.

Cumby, Rober E. and Maurice Obstfeld. 1981. A Note on Exchange-Rate Expectations and Nominal Interest Differentials: A Test of the Fisher Hypothesis. *The Journal of Finance* 36: 697–703.

———. 1984. International Interest Rate and Price Level Linkages under Flexible Exchange Rates: A Review of Recent Evidence. Pp. 121–151 in *Exchange Rate Theory and Practice,* edited by J. Bilson and R. Marston. Chicago: University of Chicago Press.

Deardorff, Alan. 1979. One-Way Arbitrage and Its Implications for the Foreign Exchange Markets. *Journal of Political Economy* 87: 351–364.

Dunbar, Charles F., ed. 1922. *The Theory and History of Banking*. Fourth Revised Edition. New York: G.P. Putnam's Sons.

Einzig, Paul. 1962. *The History of Foreign Exchange*. New York: St. Martin's Press.

Escher, Franklin. 1918a. *Elements of Foreign Exchange: A Foreign Exchange Primer*. New York: The Bankers Publishing Company.

———. 1918b. *Foreign Exchange Explained*. New York: The Macmillan Company.

The Financial Review. W.B. Dana & Company.

Fishe, Raymond P. 1989. The Federal Reserve Amendments of 1917: A Tarnishing Change in Monetary Policy. Department of Economics, University of Miami. Photcopy.

Fishe, Raymond P. and Mark Wohar. 1990. Did the Federal Reserve System Really Represent a Regime Change in 1914? *American Economic Review* 80: 968–976.

Frenkel, Jacob. 1981. Flexible Exchange Rates, Prices and the Role of 'News': Lessons from the 1970's. *Journal of Political Economy* 89: 665–705.

Frenkel, Jacob and Richard M. Levich. 1975. Covered Interest Arbitrage: Unexploited Profits? *Journal of Political Economy* 83: 325–338.

———. 1977. Transactions Costs and Interest Arbitrage: Tranquil versus Turbulent Periods. *Journal of Political Economy* 85: 1209–1226.

———. 1977. Covered Interest Arbitrage and Unexploited Profits? Reply. *Journal of Political Economy* 87: 418–422.

Friedman, Milton and Anna Schwartz. 1963. *A Monetary History of the United States: 1867–1960*. Princeton: Princeton University Press.

Furniss, Edgar S. 1922. *Foreign Exchange: The Financing Mechanism of International Commerce*. Cambridge: Harvard University Press.

Goodhart, C.A.E. 1969. *The New York Money Market and the Finance of Trade, 1900–1913*. Cambridge: Harvard University Press.

Gregory, Allan W. 1987. Testing Interest Rate Parity and Rational Expectations for Canada and the United States. *Canadian Journal of Economics* 20: 289–305.

Hepburn, A. Barton. [1924] 1967. *A History of Currency in the United States*. Reprints of Economic Classics, New York: Augustus M. Kelley.

Hylleberg, Svend. 1986. *Seasonality in Regression*. Orlando, Florida: Academic Press.

Ito, Takatoshi. 1987. Use of (Time-Domain) Vector Autoregressions to Test Uncovered Interest Parity. *The Review of Economics and Statistics*: 296–305.

Ito, Takatoshi and Danny Quah. 1989. Hypothesis Testing with Restricted Spectral Density Matrices, with and Application to Uncovered Interest Parity. *International Economic Review* 30: 203–215.

James, John. 1978. *Money and Capital Markets in Postbellum America*. Princeton: Princeton University Press.

Johnson, Joseph French. 1905. *Money and Currency*. Boston: Ginn and Company.

Kemmerer, Edwin W. 1911. *Seasonal Variations in Demands for Currency and Capital*. Publications of the National Monetary Commission, vol. 22. Washington.

Kimbrough, Kent P. 1986. International Linkages, Exchange Rate Regimes, and the International Transmission Process: Perspectives from Optimizing Models. Department of Economics, Duke University. Photcopy.

Krasker, William S. 1980. The 'Peso Problem' in Testing the Efficiency of Forward Exchange Markets. *Journal of Monetary Economics* 6: 269–276.

Kuznets, Simon. 1933. *Seasonal Variations in Industry and Trade*. New York: National Bureau of Economic Research.

Lindert, Peter. 1969. *Key Currencies and Gold: 1900–1913*. Princeton Studies in International Finance No. 24. Princeton: Princeton University Press.

Macaulay, Frederick R. 1938. *Some Theoretical Problems suggested by the Movements of Interest Rates, Bond Yields and Stock Prices in the United States since 1856*. New York: National Bureau of Economic Research.

Margraff, Anthony W. 1903. *International Exchange: Its Terms, Parts, Operations and Scope*. Chicago: Fergus Printing Company.

Mankiw, N. Gregory and Jeffrey A. Miron. 1986. The Changing Behavior of the Term Structure of Interest Rates. *Quarterly Journal of Economics* 51: 211–228.

Mankiw, N. Gregory, Jeffrey A Miron and David N. Weil. 1987. The Adjustment of Expectations to a Change in Regime: A Study of the Founding of the Federal Reserve. *American Economic Review* 77: 358–374.

———. 1990. The Adjustment of Expectations to a Change in Regime: Reply. *American Economic Review* 80: 977–979.

McAvinchey, Ian D. and Ronal MacDonald. 1990. Some Specification Tests of Interest Parity. *Recherches Economiques de Louvain* 56: 61–78.

McCormick, Frank. 1979. Covered Interest Arbitrage: Unexploited Profits? Comment. *Journal of Political Economy* 87: 411–417.

Miron, Jeffrey A. 1984. *The Economics of Seasonal Time Series*. Ph.D. dissertation, Massachusettes Institute of Technology.

———. 1986. Financial Panics, the Seasonality of the Nominal Interest Rate, and the Founding of the Fed. *American Economic Review* 76: 125–140

Morgenstern, Oskar. 1959. *International Financial Transactions and Business Cycles*. Princeton: Princeton University Press.

Myers, Margaret. 1931. *The New York Money Market, vol. 1 Origins and Development*. New York: Columbia University Press.

Nishimura, S. 1971. *The Decline of Inland Bills of Exchange in the London Money Market, 1855–1913*. Cambridge: Cambridge University Press.

Noyes, A.D. 1894. The Banks and the Panic of 1893. *Political Science Quarterly* (March).

———. 1909. *Forty Years of American Finance*. New York: Putnam.

Officer, Lawrence H. 1985. Integration in the American Foreign Exchange Market, 1791–1900. *Journal of Economic History* 45: 557–585.

———. 1986. The Efficiency of the Dollar-Sterling Gold Standard, 1890–1908. *Journal of Political Economy* 94: 1038–1073.

———. 1989. The Remarkable Efficiency of the Dollar-Sterling Gold Standard, 1890–1906. *The Journal of Economic History* 49: 1–41.

Page, S.A.B. 1977. Currency of Invoice in Merchandise Trade, *National Institute Economic Review*: 77–81.

———. 1981. The Choice of Invoicing Currency in Merchandise Trade, *National Institute Economic Review*: 60–72.

Palgrave, R. H. I. 1903. *Bank Rate and the Money Market*. New York.

Perkins, Edwin J. 1975. *Financing Anglo-American Trade: The House of Brown, 1800–1880*. Cambridge: Harvard University Press.

———. 1978. Foreign Interest Rates in American Financial Markets: A Revised Series of Dollar-Sterling Exchange Rates, 1835–1900. *Journal of Economic History* 38: 392–415.

Perron, Pierre. 1986. Trends and Random Walks in Macroeconomic Time Series; Further Evidence from a New Approach. Cahier 3286, Department of Economics, Universite de Montreal.

Pierce, David. 1978. Seasonal Adjustment When Both Deterministic and Stochastic Seasonality are Present. Pp. 242–269 in *Seasonal Analysis of Economic Time Series,* edited by A. Zellner. Washington D.C.: U.S. Department of Commerce, Bureau of the Census.

———. 1980. A Survey of Recent Developments in Seasonal Adjustment. *The American Statistician* 34: 125–134.

Pozo, Susan. 1989. Exchange-Rate Volatility and the Currency Invoicing of International Trade. Pp. 111-124 in *The 1989 Proceedings of the International Trade and Finance Association,* edited by Khosrow Fatemi and Catherine Mann.

Sargent, Thomas J. 1987. *Dynamic Macroeconomic Theory*. Cambridge, Massachusettes: Harvard University Press.

Sayers, R.S. [1936] 1970. *Bank of England Operations: 1890–1914*. Reprint, Westport, Conn.: Greenwood Press, Publishers.
———. 1976. *The Bank of England, 1891–1944*. Cambridge: Cambridge University Press.
Sharp, Keith. 1988. Tests of U.S. Short and Long Interest Rate Seasonality. *Review of Economic Statistics* 120: 177–182.
Simon, Matthew. 1960. The United States Balance of Payments, 1861–1900. Pp. 629–711 in *Trends in the American Economy in the Nineteenth Century*. Studies in Income and Wealth, Volume 24. Princeton: Princeton University Press.
Spalding, W.F. 1919. *Foreign Exchange and Foreign Bills*. London: Sir Isaac Pitman & Sons.
Spiller, Pablo T. and Robert O. Wood. 1988. Arbitrage during the Dollar-Sterling Gold Standard, 1899–1908: an Econometric Approach. *Journal of Political Economy* 96: 882–892.
Sprague, O.M.W. [1910] 1968. *History of Crises under the National Banking System*. Reprint, New York: Augustus M. Kelley.
———. 1915. The Crisis of 1914 in the United States. *American Economic Review* 5: 499–533.
———. 1922. Foreign Exchange. Pp. 103–131 *The Theory and History of Banking,* edited by C.F. Dunbar. Fourth Revised Edition. New York: G.P. Putnam's Sons.
Taylor, Mark P. 1987. Risk Premia and Foreign Exchange: A Multiple Time Series Approach to Testing Uncovered Interest-Rate Parity. *Weltwirtschaftliches Archives* 123: 579–591.
———. 1989. Covered Interest Arbitrage and Market Turbulence. *The Economic Journal* 99: 376–391.
Triffin, Robert. 1964. *The Evolution of the International Monetary System: Historical Reappraisal and Future Perspectives.* Princeton Studies in International Finance No. 12. Princeton: Princeton University Press.
Whale, P. Barrett. [1937] 1954. The Working of the Pre-War Gold Standard. Pp. 151–164, Reprinted in *Papers in English Monetary History,* edited by T.S. Ashton and R.S. Sayers. London: Oxford University Press .
Whitaker, Albert C. 1919. *Foreign Exchange*. New York: D. Appleton and Company.
Williamson, Jeffrey. 1964. *American Growth and the Balance of Payments: 1820–1913*. Chapel Hill: The University of North Carolina Press.
Withers, Hartley. 1918. *Money Changing: An Introduction to Foreign Exchange*. London: John Murray, Albermarle Street, W.I.
Yeager, Leland B. 1976. *International Monetary Relations: Theory, History and Policy*. Second edition. New York: Harper & Row.

Zellner, Arnold, ed. 1978. *Seasonal Analysis of Economic Time Series: Proceedings of the Conference on the Seasonal Analysis of Economic Time Series, Washington D.C., September 9–10, 1976*. Washington D.C.: U.S. Department of the Commerce, Bureau of the Census.

Index